Excel 3 for Windows™ QuickStart

Que® Development Group

Text and graphics developed by
Sharel McVey

Screen reproductions in this book were created using Collage Plus from Inner Media, Inc., Hollis, NH.

Excel 3 for Windows QuickStart is based on Version 3.0 of Microsoft Excel.

Publisher: Lloyd J. Short

Associate Publisher: Karen A. Bluestein

Product Development Manager: Mary Bednarek

Managing Editor: Paul Boger

Book Designer: Scott Cook

Production Team: Jeff Baker, Brad Chinn, Jeanne Clark, Sandy Grieshop, Denny Hager, Bob LaRoche, Ann Owen, Howard Peirce, Tad Ringo, Bruce Steed, Johnna VanHoose

Product Director
Kathie-Jo Arnoff

Production Editor
Pamela Wampler

Editors
Jo Anna Arnott
Karen Grooms

Technical Editor
John W. Zumsteg

*Composed in Garamond and Macmillan
by Que Corporation*

About the Author

Sharel McVey founded San Francisco Computer Services to provide software consulting and training on DOS, Windows, and Macintosh applications. She has instructed courses and provided consulting services to several major organizations in the San Francisco Bay area.

Sharel authored Que's *Excel for Windows Quick Reference* and was the technical editor for *Using Excel 3 for Windows*. She has a B.A. in Economics from San Francisco State University.

Acknowledgments

Working on *Excel 3 for Windows QuickStart* was an exciting challenge. I had the good fortune of associating with a great team at Que Corporation. This project could not have been successfully completed without the expertise of Kathie-Jo Arnoff and Pamela Wampler. My thanks to Kathie-Jo for her dedication to a high-quality product and her professional guidance throughout this project. Thanks to Pamela Wampler for her great effort and superior management of this project while working under continual deadline pressures.

In addition to the people at Que, I would like to thank Ron Person for his encouragement and technical expertise. Ron's background as an Excel consultant and his high standards as an author were of tremendous value in making *Excel 3 for Windows QuickStart* a reality.

Trademark Acknowledgments

Contents at a Glance

Table of Contents

Introduction

Welcome to *Excel 3 for Windows QuickStart* for version 3.0. Whether you are new to Excel or upgrading to version 3.0 from an earlier version of Excel, this QuickStart tutorial is one of the fastest and easiest ways to get started and become productive.

If you are experienced with Windows, you will find familiar many of the concepts used in Excel for Windows. If you are new to Windows, you will discover that Windows is a much easier and more intuitive environment than the traditional character-based environment.

All aspects of Excel 3.0 contain improvements, including enhanced analytical capabilities, greater flexibility with database management, increased charting options, and the capability to automate tasks and customize Excel with macros. Excel 3.0 also includes many new features designed to enhance its presentation capabilities, such as 3-D charts, drawing tools, and styles and patterns. All Excel features focus on ease of use and increased productivity—which is why Excel is considered by many to be the spreadsheet of choice.

Who Should Use This Book?

Excel 3 for Windows QuickStart is a tutorial developed with easy-to-follow, step-by-step instructions. Because *Excel 3 for Windows QuickStart* concisely covers only the most important concepts, your time on the learning curve is greatly reduced.

If you are a new spreadsheet user, *Excel 3 for Windows QuickStart* will empower you to become productive quickly. If you are an experienced computer user who is new to the Windows environment, *Excel 3 for Windows QuickStart* will give you a head start on learning other Windows applications, such as Microsoft Word for Windows, Microsoft PowerPoint, Aldus PageMaker, or any of the many Windows applications you might use.

What Is New in Excel Version 3.0?

The latest version of Excel makes even the most powerful features easily accessible. The following are some of Excel's significant enhancements:

- Presentation capabilities enable you to draw objects and create a chart directly on your worksheet.
- The tool bar gives you graphical access to commands, including automatic summation, text box, formatting icons, styles, drawing tools, the Button tool, Camera tool, Selection tool, and outline controls.
- Outlining hides detail and quickly displays the desired level of detail for summary reports and charts.
- The Solver application can be used for simple or complex goal-seeking analysis.
- Data consolidation enables you to link similarly labeled data in different worksheets into a summary worksheet.
- 3-D charting offers you the option of building 3-D area, line, column, and pie charts.
- The Q+E utility enables you to access databases from other programs.

How This Book Is Organized

Each chapter follows the same format. First, new commands or procedures are described briefly. Next, procedures are presented in numbered steps to guide you through the required mouse actions or keystrokes. In most cases, illustrations show how the screen should appear during and after taking a certain action.

The early chapters provide an understanding of Excel worksheet basics. The rest of the chapters discuss more advanced features, including functions, charting, database management, and macros.

Chapter 1, "An Overview of Excel 3.0," explains the main components of Excel.

Chapter 2, "Getting Started," covers how to start Windows and Excel, and reviews the basics of the screen, menus, keyboard, commands, and on-line Help.

Chapter 3, "Excel Worksheet Basics," teaches the basic skills required for working on a worksheet, including entering, editing, and selecting data; moving around the worksheet; accessing commands; and saving files.

Chapter 4, "Building a Worksheet," explains cell references, working with ranges and sections of a worksheet, and protecting a worksheet from changes.

Chapter 5, "Modifying a Worksheet," teaches you how to insert and delete cells, columns, and rows; find, clear, move, and copy cells contents; and change column width and row height.

Chapter 6, "Formatting a Worksheet," shows you how to use Excel's various formatting commands to enhance the appearance of your worksheets. This chapter also introduces the tool bar and shows you how to work with objects on your worksheets.

Chapter 7, "Using Functions," introduces Excel's built-in functions and explains the types of functions used for a variety of calculations.

Chapter 8, "Printing a Worksheet," covers all aspects of printing, including the print area, multiple areas, titles, page setup, orientation, and print preview.

Chapter 9, "Working with Multiple Documents," explains how to work more efficiently with multiple files by creating workspace files, linking files, and consolidating data. This chapter also covers how to save to and import from other file formats.

Chapter 10, "Charting," teaches you the basics of creating a chart, changing a chart type, enhancing a chart, editing a data series, creating a picture chart, and printing a chart.

Chapter 11, "Managing Data," introduces the components of a database. This chapter also reviews how to create, edit, and sort a database and find and extract a record that meets defined criteria.

Chapter 12, "Using Macros," gives you an overview of the types of macros available. This chapter also teaches you to record, edit, run, and debug a macro, as well as assign a macro to an object.

The book concludes with Appendix A, "Installing Excel 3.0 for Windows," Appendix B, "Summary of Excel 3.0 for Windows Commands," and a comprehensive index.

Where To Find More Help

Once you have learned the Excel basics covered in the Excel QuickStart, you may want to explore some of the more advanced features in Excel 3.0. These features include add-ins, outlining, advanced charting, function macros, creating custom dialog boxes with the Dialog Editor, using Solver for goal-seeking or "what-if" analysis, and using Q+E for accessing external databases.

Que Corporation has a complete line of Excel books designed to meet the needs of all computer users. Other Excel books include *Using Excel 3 for Windows* and *Excel for Windows Quick Reference*. For more information about Que products, contact Que Corporation at 1-800-428-5331 (outside Indiana). In Indiana, call 1-317-573-2500.

You can use Excel's on-line Help feature, which is explained in Chapter 2, "Getting Started," to answer some of your questions.

Conventions Used in This Book

As with all Windows applications, you can use the mouse, the keyboard, or shortcut keys for most operations. Throughout the chapters, mouse and keyboard techniques are provided.

In some cases, you may need to use key combinations. In this book, a key combination is joined by a comma or a plus sign (+):

Combination	Keystroke
Alt, letter	Press the Alt key, release it, and then press the underlined letter key.
Alt+letter	Hold down the Alt key, press the letter key, and then release both keys.

When a key combination appears in a numbered list of steps, keyboard character icons are used:

Combination	Keystroke
Alt, R	Press the Alt key, release it, and then press the R key.
Ctrl F6	Hold down the Ctrl key, press the F6 function key, and then release both keys.

When you use the mouse to operate Excel, you can perform four kinds of actions:

Action	Technique
Click	Place the mouse pointer on the item you want to select and click the left mouse button.
Double-click	Place the mouse pointer on the item you want to select and click the left mouse button twice in rapid succession.
Drag	Place the mouse pointer on the item you want to select and hold down the left mouse button as you move the mouse.
Shift+Click	Hold down the shift key as you click on the item you want to select.

This book uses the following special typefaces:

Typeface	Meaning
Italic type	This font is used for words or phrases defined for the first time, and for optional items in functions.
Boldface type	This font is used for user input—what you type, such as commands and functions.
Special font	This font is used to represent system and screen messages and on-screen results of functions.

Figures Used in This Book

As you follow the procedures in this book, the figures show you how your screen should look. Your screen may not always match the figures exactly. Sometimes the screens in the figures have been condensed in Windows so that you can fully see the part of the screen the book discusses.

When a screen is condensed, the menu bar at the top of the screen wraps around like this.

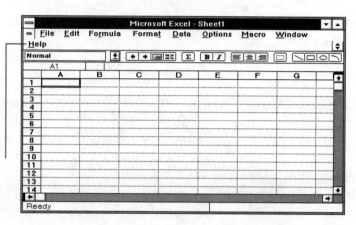

Instead, your screen will probably look like this.

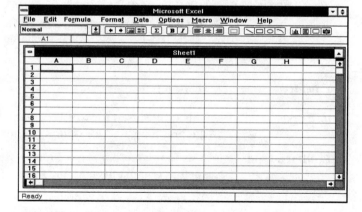

System Requirements for Running Excel 3.0

To provide optimum performance for Excel, your computer and software should meet or exceed the following requirements:

Hardware Requirements

- IBM or compatible computer with a hard disk and an 80286, 80386, or 80486 processor
- 640K or more of conventional memory
- EGA or VGA graphics card, or graphics cards with proprietary Windows drivers
- 1.2M or 1.44M floppy-disk drive

Software Requirements

- Windows version 3.0 running in standard or enhanced mode when using DOS
- MS-DOS 3.1 or higher

An Overview of Excel 3.0

Microsoft Excel 3.0 is a powerful spreadsheet application developed for people at all skill levels. Excel is easy and intuitive for beginning users, yet Excel also provides powerful features suited for programmers and high-level users.

This chapter highlights the main components of Excel 3.0, including worksheet capabilities, formulas and functions, formatting, charting, databases, macros, and on-line Help. As you read through this chapter, you can assess the topics that will be of the greatest value to you. The chapters that follow cover each specific topic in greater detail.

The Windows environment

Worksheets

Charts, databases, and macros

Help

Lotus 1-2-3 compatibility

1

Key Terms in This Chapter

Graphical user interface	A computer interface that uses a mouse, windows, icons, and a consistent menu structure to make computing more intuitive.
Icon	A small picture that represents an application, accessory, or file.
Pull-down menu	A title on the menu bar that displays a list of commands when activated by the keyboard or mouse.
Dialog box	A box used in Windows applications to request information and input from the user.
Cell address	Location of a cell based on the intersection of the column and row.
Active cell	The cell that receives data being entered.
Command	An order from the user that tells the computer to carry out an action.
Clipboard	A temporary storage location for selected information that is cut or copied.
Functions	Predefined formulas included in Excel to simplify input of various types of calculations.
Formatting	The process of enhancing the appearance of selected text, data, or objects.
Database	A collection of records organized into categories.
Macro	An application feature that records keystrokes and commands to be played back with a single command or keystroke.

The Windows Environment

The introduction of Windows 3.0 has been acknowledged as one of the most successful developments in the history of the personal computer industry. By simplifying computer applications, Windows has transformed the way people use personal computers. Windows uses the operating system commonly referred to as *DOS*. Instead of interacting with the operating system through the use of DOS commands, however, Windows creates a graphical user interface that employs icons (small pictures), a consistent pull-down menu structure, and dialog boxes to access commands. All of these features make the program more intuitive so that users become productive with less effort.

Microsoft Excel 3.0 operates within the Windows environment. If you are comfortable working in a graphical environment, you will be at ease with the Excel basics. Many of the new features in Excel 3.0 have made spreadsheet computing even more graphical and easier to use.

What Is a Worksheet?

Sometimes referred to as *an electronic spreadsheet*, a worksheet is a grid with labeled columns and rows. Column headings are labeled with letters across the top of the worksheet; row headings are labeled with numbers down the left side of the worksheet. The intersection of a column and a row is called a *cell*. The *cell address* consists of the column letter and row number. B3, for example, is the cell address for the cell located at the intersection of column B and row 3.

In this Excel worksheet, cell B3 is the active cell.

A worksheet contains 256 columns and 16,384 rows, which means more than 4 million cells are available. Information can be recorded in a cell in the form

1

of text, numbers, formulas, or functions for calculating numbers. The *active cell* in a worksheet, defined by a bold border around the cell, is the cell that receives the data you enter. You can activate another cell in the worksheet by clicking on it with the mouse or by using the arrow keys on the keyboard to move to the new active cell.

Menus and Commands

The Excel window has a menu bar that displays nine menus. The File, Edit, Formula, Format, Data, Options, Macro, Window, and Help menus are listed across the menu bar. When selected, each menu on the menu bar displays a list of commands. You can access a menu by using the mouse or the keyboard.

The File menu has been selected from the menu bar at the top of the screen, and the File commands are displayed.

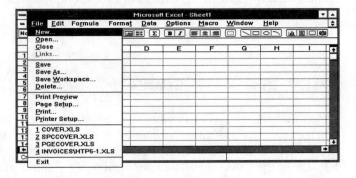

To access a menu with the mouse, point to the menu and click the left mouse button.

To access a menu with the keyboard, press the Alt key to activate the menu bar. Then press the letter of the underlined character in the menu name. If you want to access the File menu, for example, press Alt and then press F, the underlined character in the File menu name.

When a menu is selected, a list of commands drops down. The number of commands listed under a menu depends on the menu option. Excel enables you to display either Short Menus or Full Menus. Short Menus include the primary Excel commands most users want to access. The Short Menus option is sometimes preferred by new users who want to focus on learning basic Excel commands and finding them quickly. Full Menus enables you to see all Excel commands. The Options pull-down menu lists the menu option that you are not using. If you select, for example, the Options menu and see Full Menus at the bottom of the list of commands, you know that you are currently using Short Menus and that not all Excel commands are displayed when you choose a menu. If you want to change to Full Menus, select the command from the Options pull-down menu. Once you choose the Full Menus option, the command changes to Short Menus.

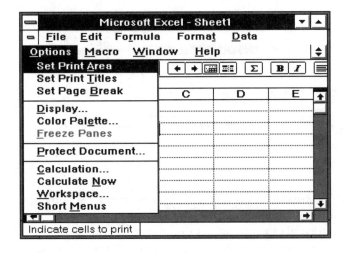

Because the Options menu shows the Short Menus command, the current menu option is Full Menus.

You select commands from the drop-down list that appears when a menu is selected. To select a command, you can use the mouse to point and click on the command, or you can press the underlined character of the command name on the keyboard. If you want to access the Paste Function command with the keyboard, for example, press Alt to activate the menu bar, and then R to access the Formula menu, and then T, the underlined character in the Paste Function command.

If a command appears dimmed or grayed on a pull-down menu, the command is not accessible. If an active worksheet does not contain a link to another worksheet, for example, the Links command under the File menu appears dimmed or grayed.

Dialog Boxes

When you access certain commands in Excel, you see a box that appears in the center of your screen. This is a *dialog box*, which is used in Excel to request input from you or to confirm that you want to proceed with the settings defined in the dialog box. The type of dialog box that appears depends on the command you select. Some commands, such as the Edit Copy command, do not cause a dialog box to appear. Some dialog boxes contain several elements, but other dialog boxes request only a yes or no response from you before

1

proceeding with the command. Chapter 3, "Excel Worksheet Basics," includes a section on dialog boxes. The section explains the different types of dialog boxes, the elements of a dialog box, and how to change settings in a dialog box.

This dialog box
appears when you
select the File
New command.

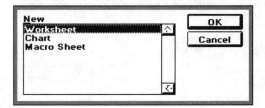

Formulas

The true power of using a worksheet for financial reports, income statements, budget forecasts, and other business applications comes from using formulas. You can enter in a cell a formula that calculates numbers that you have entered in other cells. A formula starts with an equal sign (=) and uses mathematical symbols (to indicate what type of operation will be performed) and cell addresses that identify the location of the data that will be calculated. As you create the formula, it is displayed in an area of the worksheet called the *formula bar*.

The formula
being entered in
cell C1 appears in
the formula bar.

After a formula is entered in a cell, Excel performs the calculation for you.

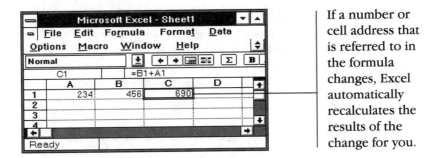

If a number or cell address that is referred to in the formula changes, Excel automatically recalculates the results of the change for you.

The most common type of formula in spreadsheets is a formula that sums a group of numbers. In Excel, entering this formula is quite simple. The Auto-SUM tool on the tool bar enables you to total a group of numbers that are directly adjacent to the active cell.

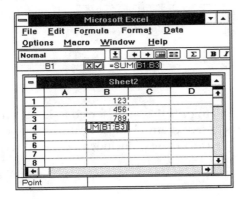

Clicking on the Auto-SUM tool enters the sum function in the active cell with reference to the adjacent cells.

Click on the Auto-SUM tool again. The result of the SUM function appears in the active cell.

In many cases, formulas are entered on a single worksheet with reference to other cells on the same worksheet. Sometimes, however, you will need to refer to numbers or formulas that are located in another worksheet. Suppose, for example, that you are building a worksheet that will summarize annual data based on four other worksheets that summarize quarterly data. You can build a formula on the annual worksheet that refers to formulas in the four quarterly worksheets. The procedure for entering a formula that refers to cells in another worksheet works the same way as entering a formula that refers to cells on the same worksheet.

1

With Excel, you can have multiple worksheets open at the same time. As you build a formula in a cell on one worksheet, you can easily activate another worksheet and continue building the formula. Excel recognizes that the data to be included in the formula is located on another worksheet, and Excel places a reference to the activated worksheet and the selected cells in the formula.

The formula being built in cell A1 refers to another worksheet.

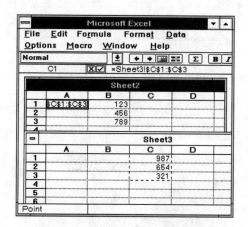

A completed formula creates a link to cells that are referred to in the formula. The result of the formula adjusts to reflect any changes in the linked data. Chapter 9, "Working with Multiple Documents," includes a detailed section on linking files.

What-If Analysis

Entering a formula into a cell enables you to test results using different numbers. If you type a new number, the formula calculates the new result. But Excel also has some sophisticated built-in features that enable you to make adjustments in your worksheet data to produce a desired result. The Formula Goal Seek command that comes with Excel 3.0 affords you the capability of selecting a cell that contains a formula. If you want to find a different result, Excel asks you which cell in the formula to adjust to meet the desired result.

This is the Goal Seek dialog box.

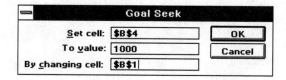

1

If you require tighter control over your data analysis, Excel 3.0 includes another feature called Solver that enables you to define results and specific constraints based on several cells of data, and comes up with the best solution for meeting your desired result.

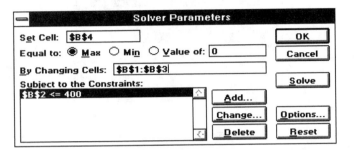

This is the Solver Parameters dialog box.

The Formula Goal Seek and Formula Solver commands are found under the Formula menu. These commands are discussed in greater detail in Chapter 5, "Modifying a Worksheet."

Sharing Information

The clipboard is one of the most powerful features of the Windows environment. The clipboard is the Windows accessory that temporarily stores selected data, charts, or objects that are cut or copied using Cut or Copy commands. The **Edit Cut** command enables you to move selected data from one location to another. The **Edit Copy** command enables you to duplicate selected data and place it in multiple locations. All Windows applications support the clipboard, which enables you to share information among applications and documents. Information created in Excel, for example, can be copied to the clipboard and pasted into Word for Windows or another Windows application.

When you use the clipboard to copy worksheet cells, formulas, charts, and objects, you efficiently can build a worksheet, ensure accuracy, and share information within the same worksheet, with other worksheets, and with other applications. Although you can access the clipboard to see what is on it, you will seldom need to do so. For more information on how to access the clipboard, you may want to refer to your Windows 3.0 documentation or on-line Help.

To copy information to the clipboard, select the information you want to copy and choose the **Edit Copy** command. The copied information appears enclosed by a marquee, or small moving dashes.

1

The selected range of cells, surrounded by a marquee, has been copied to the clipboard and can be pasted in another location.

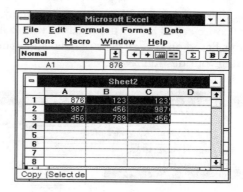

After information is copied or cut to the clipboard, you can place it in another location on the same worksheet, on another worksheet, or in another application that supports the clipboard. The **Edit Paste** command places information that is on the clipboard in the selected location. Information that has been copied to the clipboard stays on the clipboard until you use a cut or copy command again or until you turn off your computer.

The **Edit Copy** command is one method for copying data within a worksheet. The **Edit Copy** command requires two steps: choosing the Copy command, and then choosing the Paste command. If you want to copy data from one cell to other cells that are directly adjacent to the active cell, Excel has a one-step process for copying. The Edit menu includes Fill Right and Fill Down commands. (If you hold down the Shift key when you select the Edit menu, the Fill Right command changes to Fill Left and the Fill Down command changes to Fill Up.) These commands enable you to copy the contents of the active cell in any direction to selected cells that are adjacent to the active cell. If, for example, you want to copy a formula in one cell to cells that are directly to the right of the cell containing the formula, select the cells and choose the **Edit Fill Right** command.

Using the Edit Fill Right command, the contents of the active cell will be copied to the adjacent cells.

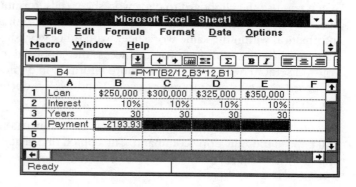

Copying, pasting, and using Fill commands are covered in greater detail in Chapter 5, "Modifying a Worksheet."

Worksheet Functions

You can use common mathematical operators (+, –, /, *) to create simple formulas for calculating data in a worksheet. In many cases, however, using one of Excel's many built-in functions is much more efficient. A function is a prewritten formula that takes a value, performs an operation, and returns a result in the form of a value.

A function simplifies entering a formula. For example, instead of typing a formula, in a matter of seconds you can use Excel's PMT function for such operations as calculating the monthly mortgage payment for a 30-year loan with a fixed interest rate of 10 percent.

This worksheet is using Excel's PMT function to calculate a mortgage payment.

Functions enable you to perform easily various mathematical, statistical, logical, financial, and other business calculations. Chapter 7, "Using Functions," covers Excel functions in greater detail.

Formatting

One of the most exciting improvements in Excel 3.0 is the capability to transform an ordinary worksheet into a more visual presentation. Excel 3.0 introduces the tool bar, which enables you to draw objects, create styles, format text, and produce charts on your worksheet in a minimal amount of time. Other enhanced capabilities provide cell formatting with patterns, borders, and color support, all designed to produce high-quality, professional-looking worksheets.

1

With Excel 3.0, you can now create a document that includes worksheet data, a chart, and objects all on the same page.

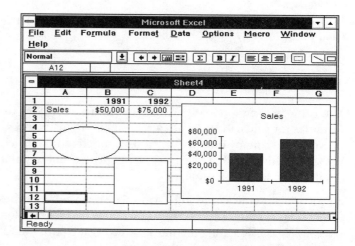

If you want to enhance your worksheet with objects, you can select a drawing tool from the tool bar, then click and drag on the worksheet area to create the selected object.

The Excel tool bar contains four drawing tools for creating objects on a worksheet.

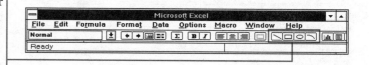

A double-click on an object brings up a dialog box; you then can enhance lines and choose a pattern for the object's area.

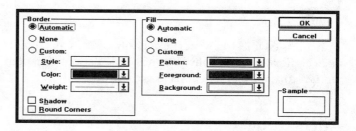

Cell formatting now enables you to put borders, including a double under-line, around a cell or a selected range of cells. You also can format cells with color and patterns to accentuate sections of your worksheet.

You can format numbers as well, using dollar signs, commas, or decimals; or you can format numbers so that negative numbers appear in parentheses. You also can format date and time numbers, using the Format Number command, and you can create custom number formats.

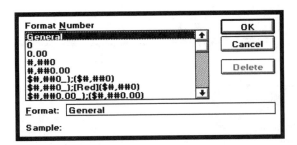

The Format Number dialog box enables you to format numbers, including currency, decimals, percentages, and date and time numbers.

Formatting a worksheet also includes adjusting the column width and row height. If your column width is not wide enough to display all of a cell's contents, you can use Excel's Best Fit feature. This feature enables you to adjust the column width instantly to the widest cell in the column. You can execute the command using the mouse or keyboard. See the section in Chapter 5 for procedures on changing column width and row height.

What Is a Chart?

Charts are probably the most impressive way to represent data. If data is displayed in the form of a chart, the numbers are expressed in a visual manner that is likely to make an impact on the viewer. The visual nature of a chart enables immediate interpretation of worksheet data.

To create a chart in Excel, you simply select the data you want to chart and press a single key. Charts are linked to the selected worksheet data. If you make a change in the data, the chart automatically updates to reflect that change. After you create a chart, you are able to choose from eleven different chart types, including seven 2-dimensional and four 3-dimensional types.

Each of the eleven chart types has a selection of predefined chart formats. This selection is a gallery of pre-defined column chart formats.

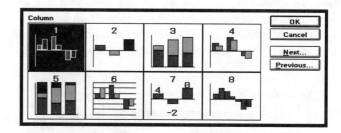

Double-click on the chart format you want. The selected data appears instantly in the selected chart format.

The commands for chart formatting enable you to add a legend, text, arrows, or gridlines, or to format individual data points and axes. Chapter 10, "Charting," covers creating, formatting, and editing a chart.

What Is a Database?

You also can use an Excel worksheet to create a database. To create a database, you define field names or categories in the first row of the database and enter data in each row below in the form of a record.

After a database has been created, Excel database commands enable you to sort records in a particular order, find records that match certain criteria, and extract records from a database to be analyzed or used in reports.

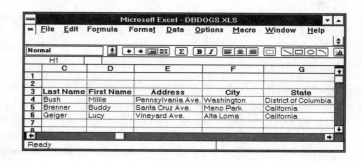

You can enter a database record in the worksheet cells or in a database form.

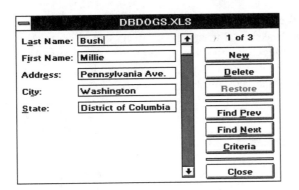

When you use the Data Form view, you enter data as though you were entering it on a form.

The field names in the first row of the database determine the named sections on the form. The buttons on the right side of the **Data Form** box enable you to execute various database commands.

Chapter 11, "Managing Data," covers the multiple components of a database, including what a database is, how to build a database, and using database commands.

What Are Macros?

A *macro* records commonly used keystrokes and commands, saving you time on repetitive tasks. Instead of using several keystrokes, for example, you can simply select a macro to perform a task. The macro recording is documented in the form of macro function names on an Excel macro sheet. If you need to make modifications to a macro, you make the changes on the macro sheet. Recorded keystrokes and commands can be executed with a single keystroke or from the Macro menu.

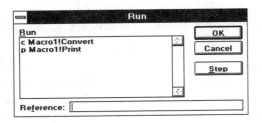

The **Macro Run** command displays a list of macros from which you can choose.

1

A new feature in Excel 3.0 enables you to assign a macro to an object on a worksheet. When a macro is assigned to an object, users can execute the macro by clicking on the object. Chapter 12, "Using Macros," covers macros in greater detail and reviews the procedures for planning, recording, running, debugging, and assigning a macro to an object on a worksheet.

How To Get On-Line Help

Excel contains comprehensive on-line assistance to help users at all levels with every aspect of the program. The Help menu is the last menu on the menu bar. The menu includes commands for accessing the Help Index, Keyboard procedures, Lotus 1-2-3 Help, Multiplan Help, and on-line Tutorials to help new users get started with Excel.

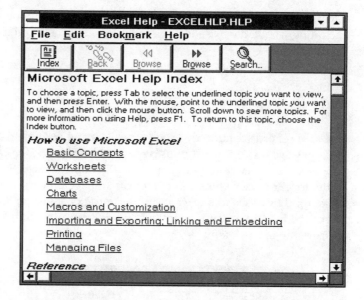

The F1 function key brings up a Help window at any time.

If you have selected a command or if a dialog box is displayed on your screen, you can press F1 to bring up a Help window. The window provides assistance on the selected command or dialog box. If you have not selected a command or if a dialog box is not on-screen, pressing F1 displays the Help index.

On-line Help enables you to browse forward or backward to other related topics or to backtrack to previous Help screens. The Search button enables you to search for a specific Help topic and shows you the selected Help topic and related topics.

Lotus 1-2-3 Compatibility

If you are experienced with Lotus 1-2-3 spreadsheets, Excel has built-in features that take advantage of some of your Lotus 1-2-3 skills. Many of Excel's function keys are the same as those for Lotus 1-2-3. To name a few examples, F2 is used for Edit in Excel, F5 is Excel's Goto key, and F9 is used for manual calculation. If you want Excel to act even more like Lotus 1-2-3, you can modify Excel settings so that the movement keys in Excel work more like the movement keys in Lotus 1-2-3.

```
Workspace                    ┌──────────┐
                             │    OK    │
  ☐ Fixed Decimal            └──────────┘
    Places: [2]              ┌──────────┐
                             │  Cancel  │
┌─Display──────────────────  └──────────┘
│ ☐ R1C1          ☒ Scroll Bars
│ ☒ Status Bar    ☒ Formula Bar
│ ☒ Tool Bar      ☐ Note Indicator

  Alternate Menu or Help Key: [/]
    ● Microsoft Excel Menus
    ○ Lotus 1-2-3 Help

  ☒ Alternate Navigation Keys
  ☐ Ignore Remote Requests
  ☒ Move Selection after Enter
```

Excel's Options Workspace command displays the dialog box from which you can select the Alternate Navigation Keys check box to change the movement keys in Excel.

Excel's Lotus 1-2-3 Help feature enables you to use Lotus 1-2-3 procedures to execute Excel commands. You can set the Lotus 1-2-3 Help feature to show an instruction box that explains how to complete the equivalent command in Excel, or you can set the feature to demonstrate how to complete the equivalent command in Excel. For specific details on how to use Excel's Lotus 1-2-3 Help feature, refer to the section "Lotus 1-2-3 Help" in Chapter 2.

Excel is capable of accessing Lotus 1-2-3 files. You also can save Excel files as Lotus 1-2-3 files if you need to create a document you can use in either application. If you want to open a Lotus 1-2-3 file onto a blank Excel spreadsheet, choose the File Open command and use the same procedures you use to open an Excel file. If you want to save an Excel file as a Lotus 1-2-3 file, choose the File Save As command and select the Options button.

1

The Options dialog box provides a list of file formats including WKS, WK1, and WK3, which are extensions used to define a Lotus 1-2-3 file format.

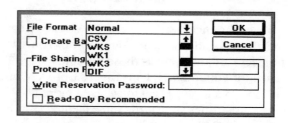

Refer to the sections in Chapter 9, "Saving Files to Other File Formats" and "Importing a File from Another File Format," for detailed instructions on these commands.

Summary

This discussion of Excel 3.0 acquainted you with some of the features in Excel and gave you an overview of the benefits of using a spreadsheet application for calculating, analyzing, charting, and presenting data. This chapter also covered the main components of working with Excel and some basic worksheet techniques. Finally, this chapter included information about windows, worksheets, formulas, functions, formatting, charting, database management, macros, and on-line Help. The specific topics are covered in greater depth in the chapters that follow.

In this chapter, you were introduced to the following key information about Excel 3.0:

- Windows is the graphical environment in which Excel operates.
- Icons and pull-down menus are primary components of the Windows graphical environment.
- A worksheet is a large grid that contains more than 4 million cells for storing data, formulas, and functions.
- A cell is the intersection of a column and a row.
- A cell address defines the location of a cell based on the intersection of the column and row.
- The active cell has a bold border around it and receives the data you enter.
- A command is listed below a menu and carries out a specific action.

1

- A dialog box requests input and confirms command settings.
- Formulas are entered in cells, starting with the equal sign (=) and continuing with mathematical operators and cell addresses of data to be calculated.
- The Auto-SUM tool on the tool bar provides a quick way to enter the SUM function and total cells adjacent to the active cell.
- You can create formulas that refer to data located on another worksheet.
- A function is a predefined formula used to perform simple and advanced calculations.
- You can use the tool bar and multiple formatting commands to enhance your worksheet.
- Excel has eleven chart types, including seven 2-D chart types and four 3-D chart types.
- You can use Excel database commands to sort, analyze, find, and extract information from a database.
- You can view or enter database information using the **Data Form** view.
- A macro records commonly used keystrokes and commands.
- On-line Help provides assistance on a selected topic.
- Excel is compatible with the Lotus 1-2-3 spreadsheet program and includes features that enable you to open Lotus 1-2-3 files in Excel and save Excel files in a Lotus 1-2-3 format.

Now that you are familiar with some of the features and capabilities of Excel 3.0, you are ready to start learning how to use the program. Chapter 2 will tell you how to start Windows and Excel. The chapter also will present mouse and keyboard techniques and introduce you to the components of the Excel screen. You will learn how to use on-line Help and tutorials. If you are familiar with Lotus 1-2-3 commands, review the section that covers using Lotus 1-2-3 Help.

Getting Started

2

If you are new to Windows, this chapter will help you understand the parts of the Excel window and some of the basic terminology. You will learn how to start Excel, understand the screen, use on-line Help for assistance, and exit Excel.

If you are experienced with other Windows applications, you will be familiar with some of this introductory material. You may want to get acquainted with Excel's on-line Help features and move on to Chapter 3.

2

Key Terms in This Chapter

Enhanced keyboard	A keyboard that contains separate movement keys, a numeric keypad, and 12 function keys.
Application window	The outer window identified by the application's name in the title bar.
Document window	The window inside the application window that contains the document.
Tool bar	An area of the screen that contains a series of icons that you use to access commands and other features.
Formula bar	The area of the screen where you actually enter and edit data.
Control menu	The drop-down menu located in the upper left corner of a window and represented by a horizontal bar. Used for moving, sizing, closing, and other commands.
Context-sensitive Help	The on-line Help provided about a chosen command.

Starting Windows

Windows is a graphic computer environment that uses icons and pull-down menus to make computing easy and intuitive. Starting Windows is an easy, one-step procedure. Simply type **win** at the DOS prompt and press Enter.

After Windows is loaded, the Windows Program Manager appears. The Program Manager is a window that contains several folder icons or windows called *program groups*. A program group stores icons that are used to start an application or Windows accessory. Each program group is labeled. One of the program groups may be labeled *Excel 3.0*.

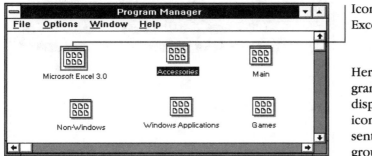

Icon that starts Excel

Here, the Program Manager displays folder icons that represent program groups.

The Excel icon may also be stored in another program group called *Windows Applications*. After you have found the program group containing the Excel 3.0 icon, you are ready to start Excel.

Starting Excel

You can start the Excel program from within the Windows environment or from the DOS prompt. Within Windows, you can use the mouse or keyboard to start Excel. The sections that follow explain how to start Excel within Windows using the mouse or keyboard, or how to start Excel from the DOS prompt.

Starting Excel with the Mouse

To start Excel with the mouse, follow these steps:

1. Select the program group containing the Excel 3.0 icon by double-clicking on the program group, or select the program group and choose the Restore command.

2. Point to the Excel 3.0 icon and double-click the left mouse button. An hourglass picture appears on your screen, indicating that you must wait a few seconds for the program to load. When the program is loaded, the hourglass disappears.

2

After Excel is loaded, the application window and document window labeled Sheet1 appear on the screen.

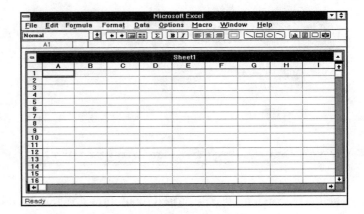

Starting Excel with the Keyboard

To start Excel with the keyboard, follow these steps:

1. Press Ctrl Tab⇅ to select the program group that contains the Excel 3.0 icon.

2. Press ⏎Enter to open the program group window.

3. Use the arrow keys to select the Excel 3.0 icon.

4. Press ⏎Enter to start Excel. An hourglass picture appears on your screen, indicating that you must wait a few seconds for the program to load. When the program is loaded, the hourglass disappears. The Excel application window with a blank worksheet window titled Sheet1 appears on the screen.

Starting Excel from DOS

To start Excel from DOS, follow these steps:

1. At the DOS prompt, change to the directory containing the EXCEL.EXE file. If the EXCEL.EXE file is located in the EXCEL3 subdirectory, for example, type **cd windows\excel3** at the DOS prompt and press ⏎Enter

2. Type **excel** at the prompt and press ⏎Enter. Both Windows and the Excel program are loaded. An hourglass picture appears on the screen, indicating that you must wait a few seconds for the program to load. When the program is loaded, the hourglass disappears. The Excel application window with a blank worksheet window titled Sheet1 appears on the screen.

32

Learning the Keyboard

Most of the interaction required in Windows and Windows applications is supported by the keyboard or mouse. The mouse simplifies working in a graphical environment. Menus and commands are accessed by pointing and clicking with the mouse. Objects and windows can be sized and moved by dragging with the mouse, and documents and programs can be loaded by double-clicking on icons.

Sometimes you might want to activate menus and commands from the keyboard. To work from the keyboard, you need to be familiar with its structure. Most keyboards consist of four main parts: the alphanumeric keys, the direction keys, the numeric keypad, and the function keys.

The original IBM Personal Computer AT keyboard

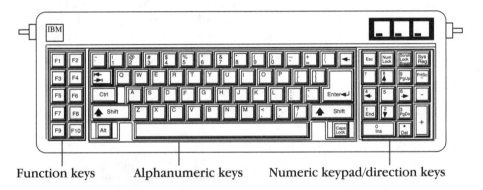

Function keys   Alphanumeric keys   Numeric keypad/direction keys

The enhanced keyboard

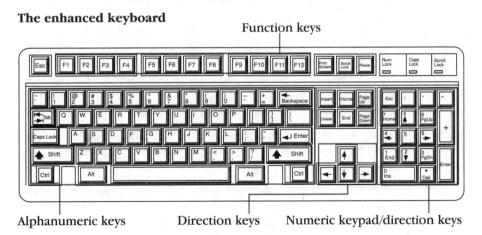

Function keys

Alphanumeric keys   Direction keys   Numeric keypad/direction keys

33

2

Alphanumeric Keys

The alphanumeric keys make up the main portion of the keyboard. These keys are usually used for entering data or text. When you want to choose a menu using the alphanumeric keys, you must first press the Alt key to activate the main menu bar. After you have activated the main menu, press the underlined letter of the menu you want to access. The menu's list of commands drops down.

Numeric Keypad and Direction Keys

On some keyboards, the numeric keypad and direction keys are assigned to the same keys. When Num Lock is turned on, the numeric keypad is active and you can use these keys like a calculator. When Num Lock is turned off, the direction keys are in control and you can use them to move around a document or spreadsheet. Direction keys are identified on the keyboard by the up, down, left, and right arrows. On enhanced keyboards, the direction keys and numeric keypad are separate. Num Lock can be turned on at all times so that you can use the numeric keypad for data entry and calculations. The separate direction, or movement, keys are not affected by Num Lock on enhanced keyboards.

Function Keys

The function keys on the keyboard are grouped together and are used as shortcut keys for certain application commands. Some commands require a function key only; other commands require a function key in conjunction with the Shift, Alt, or Ctrl key. All standard keyboards have at least 10 function keys labeled F1 through F10. Enhanced keyboards have 12 function keys. For the commands assigned to the F11 and F12 function keys, Alt+F1 or Alt+F2 can be used for the commands respectively. The F11 function key, for example, is the shortcut key in Excel for creating a chart. On keyboards with 10 function keys only, the shortcut keys for creating a chart are Alt+F1.

If you prefer to use keyboard commands, see table 2.1. You can memorize the function keys and key combinations assigned to various Excel commands and actions. These speed keys save you time.

Table 2.1
Function Keys

Commands	Actions
F1	Help
⇧Shift F1	Context-sensitive Help
F2	Edit mode (activates formula bar)
⇧Shift F2	Formula Note
Ctrl F2	Window Show Info
F3	Formula Paste Name
⇧Shift F3	Formula Paste Function
Ctrl F3	Formula Define Name
Ctrl ⇧Shift F3	Formula Create Names
F4	Formula Reference
Ctrl F4	Control Close (document window)
Alt F4	Control Close (application window)
F5	Formula Goto
⇧Shift F5	Formula Find (cell contents)
Ctrl F5	Control Restore (document window)
F6	Next pane
⇧Shift F6	Previous pane
Ctrl F6	Next window
Ctrl ⇧Shift F6	Previous document window
F7	Formula Find (next occurrence)
⇧Shift F7	Formula Find (previous occurrence)
Ctrl F7	Control Move (document window)
F8	Extend mode (on/off)
⇧Shift F8	Add mode (on/off)
Ctrl F8	Control Size (document window)

2

continues

35

2

Table 2.1 *(continued)*

Commands	Actions
[F9]	**Options Calculate Now**
[⇧Shift][F9]	**Options Calculate Document**
[F10]	Activate menu bar
[Ctrl][F10]	**Control Maximize (document window)**
[F11]	**File New (chart)**
[⇧Shift][F11]	**File New (worksheet)**
[Ctrl][F11]	**File New (macro sheet)**
[F12]	**File Save As**
[⇧Shift][F12]	**File Save**
[Ctrl][F12]	**File Open**
[Ctrl][⇧Shift][F12]	**File Print**

Using the Mouse

The mouse is an optional external device attached to your computer and used for selecting menus and commands, editing and selecting text and objects, and moving and resizing windows. If you are new to the mouse, it may seem awkward at first. After you have experimented with the mouse, you probably will find that it is easier and more intuitive to use than the keyboard for moving around in a graphical environment.

To operate the mouse, place your right hand on top of it. Position your index finger over the left mouse button, which is the only button you press to perform basic mouse techniques. The three techniques for operating the mouse are explained in table 2.2.

If you are left-handed and are having trouble using the mouse, you may want to swap the left and right mouse buttons, which will enable you to operate the mouse with your left hand. To swap the left and right mouse buttons, go to the Control Panel and follow these steps:

1. Select the application Control menu or press [Alt]+**space bar**
2. Select **R**un or press [U]

3. Select the Control Panel option button or press [Alt][P]

Table 2.2
Mouse Operating Techniques

Technique	Description
Point and click	Position the mouse pointer on the item you want to select. Press the left mouse button once.
Click and drag	Press the left mouse button and hold it down as you gradually drag the mouse on a flat surface.
Double-click	Press the left mouse button twice in rapid succession.

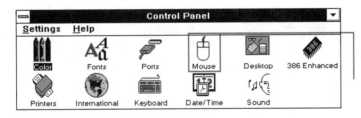

The Control Panel window contains a Mouse icon.

4. Choose **OK** or press [↵Enter]
5. Double-click on the Mouse icon in the Control Panel window, or press the direction keys to select the Mouse icon and press [↵Enter]

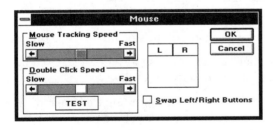

The Mouse window appears on the screen.

6. Select the **S**wap Left/Right Buttons check box to display an X in the box, or press [Alt][S]
7. Choose **OK** or press [↵Enter] The Mouse window closes.
8. Double-click on the Control menu bar in the Control Panel window, or press [Alt][F4] to close the Control Panel window.

As you gradually move the mouse on a flat surface, the mouse pointer moves on the screen. Depending on where you position the pointer on the screen, the pointer may change to another shape. The various mouse shapes are detailed in table 2.3.

Table 2.3
Mouse Shapes

Shape	Description
Mouse pointer	An arrow that appears when the mouse is positioned in a menu bar, scroll bar, or other area where an item can be selected.
I-beam	Appears when positioned in the formula bar. Used for changing the cursor location and selecting text.
Cell pointer	A cross-shaped marker that appears over cells in the worksheet area. Used to select cells.
Cross bar	Appears when positioned between row or column headings. Used to change the row height or column width.
Double-sided arrow	Appears when positioned on a window's border. Used to resize the window.
Split screen arrow	Appears when positioned over the split bar directly above the vertical scroll arrow and to the left of the horizontal scroll arrow. Used to split the worksheet area into divided sections.
Magnifying glass	Appears in Print Preview mode. Used to zoom in for a closer view of a section of the document to be printed.
Help finger	Appears when positioned over a Help topic. Used to move directly to the selected topic.
Hourglass	Appears whenever Excel is executing a command; indicates that you must wait until the hourglass disappears to continue the next action.

Understanding the Screen

The parts of the Excel screen include the application window, document window, Control menus, title bar, window position icons, menu bar, tool bar, formula bar, scroll bar, worksheet area, and status line.

2

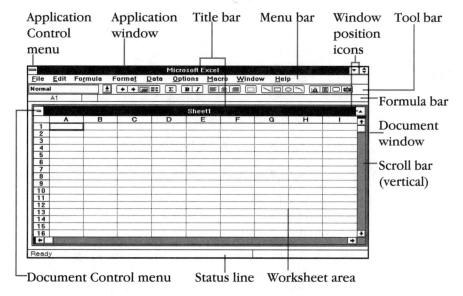

Application Control menu   Application window   Title bar   Menu bar   Window position icons   Tool bar

Formula bar
Document window
Scroll bar (vertical)

Document Control menu   Status line   Worksheet area

A brief description of each screen component is outlined in table 2.4. Some of the parts are described in more detail in the sections after the table.

Table 2.4
The Excel Screen

Component	*Description*
Application window	The outer window in which Excel runs.
Document window	The inner window that contains the document.
Application Control menu	Represented by a horizontal bar in the upper left corner of the application window. Used to move, size, and close the application window.
Document Control menu	Represented by a small horizontal bar in the upper left corner of the document window. Used to move, size, and close the document window.

continues

2

Table 2.4 *(continued)*

Component	Description
Title bar	Top middle portion of the window that lists the application or document name.
Minimize icon	Represented by the downward-pointing triangular icon. Reduces the application window to a small picture on the desktop.
Maximize icon	Represented by the upward-pointing triangular icon. Expands the application window to fit the entire screen. Expands the document window to fill the application window.
Restore icon	Represented by the double triangular icons. Restores window to the middle position between minimized and maximized positions.
Menu bar	Located directly below the title bar. Each menu item contains a list of commands that drops down when the menu is activated.
Tool bar	Located between the menu bar and the formula bar. Contains tools represented by icons for graphical access to commands and drawing capabilities.
Formula bar	Located above the document window. Displays cell contents and can be activated to edit cell contents.
Scroll bars	Located along the right side and bottom of the document window. Used to move the screen display horizontally or vertically. Contains arrows and a box that moves along the bar as the arrows are activated.
Worksheet area	Enclosed by numbered row and lettered column headings. Worksheet cells are outlined by the intersection of a row and column.
Status line	Located at the bottom of the window. Displays a prompt line to tell you what a command will do or what to do next to complete the execution of the command.

The Application Window

The *application window* is the outer window, with Microsoft Excel in the title bar. This window contains the menu bar, formula bar, tool bar, and any open document windows. The application window does not contain scroll bars. To minimize, maximize, or restore the application window, use the Control menu in the upper left corner or the window-position triangular icons in the upper right corner of the window. The application window is the only window you can minimize. When the window is minimized, it appears as an icon on the screen.

Here, the application window is minimized, appearing as an icon.

You can restore the application to its previous position by double-clicking on the icon.

The Document Window

The *document window* is the inner window that operates within the application window. The title bar of the document window contains the name of the document. If a new document has not been saved, Excel assigns a default name to the document window. Excel assigns *Sheet1*, for example, to an unnamed worksheet, *Chart1* to an unnamed chart, and *Macro1* to an unnamed macro sheet.

You can manipulate the document window in two ways. You can maximize the document window to fill the application window.

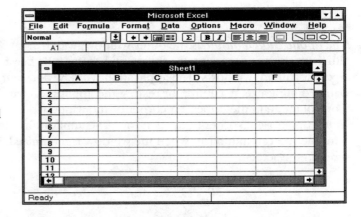

Or, you can restore the document window so that you can move and size it within the application window.

Unlike the application window, a document window cannot be minimized.

If a document window is maximized, the title of the document window appears in the title bar of the application window.

Here, the document window is maximized within the application window.

If a document window is maximized and you want to restore the window to its previous size, click on the double triangular icon in the upper right corner of the document window. Or, press Alt+- (hyphen) to activate the document Control menu and choose the **Restore** command.

Control Menus

The application window and the document window contain separate Control menus, each represented by a horizontal bar in the upper left corner of the window. The application Control menu bar is larger than the document Control menu bar. The Control menus share some of the same commands, such as **R**estore, **M**ove, **S**ize, Ma**x**imize, and **C**lose. Each Control menu also contains commands that are unique to its respective window. The application Control menu, for example, has a command for minimizing the window; the document Control menu does not. The application window can be minimized; the document window cannot. The document Control menu has a command for splitting the document window; the application Control menu does not. Only a worksheet or macro sheet can be split into panes. The keyboard command to access the application Control menu is Alt+space bar. The keyboard command to access the document Control menu is Alt+- (hyphen).

Window Positions

An application window can assume one of three positions: minimized, maximized, or restored. A document window can assume the restored position or the maximized position. The maximized position enlarges the application window to fill the entire screen. A document window can be maximized to fill the application window. To maximize a window, click the upward-pointing triangular icon in the upper right corner of the window. Or, activate the window's Control menu and choose the Ma**x**imize command. When a window is maximized, the maximize triangle is replaced by a double triangular icon that restores the window. The restored position is the middle position between minimized and maximized. When a window is in the restored position, it has a border around the window; the border enables you to resize the window. When a window is in the restored position, you also can move the window.

Only the application window can be minimized. To minimize the application window, click on the downward-pointing triangular icon in the upper right corner of the window. Or, press Alt+space bar to activate the Control menu and choose the Mi**n**imize command. When an application window is minimized, it reduces to an icon on the desktop. When an application is minimized, it is still running, even though you cannot see the application on your screen. You can display the minimized window in its previous position by double-clicking on the icon. In some cases, when you are not able to see your desktop, you are not able to see the icon representing the minimized window.

2

If you cannot see the icon on your desktop, you can activate the minimized window by using the Windows Task List. To display the Task List, press Ctrl+Esc.

A box called the
Task List appears
on the screen,
displaying all
active applica-
tions.

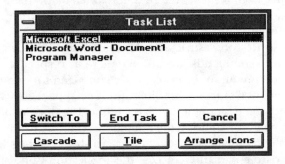

Select the application from the Task List and choose the **S**witch To command, or double-click on the application you want to activate. The Task List box disappears from the screen when you activate an application.

Moving and Resizing a Window

If a window is in the restored position, the window has a border around its outer edge. When the mouse pointer is positioned over the window border, the pointer changes to a two-sided arrow. You can resize the window by clicking and dragging the window border with the two-sided arrow. To resize a window using keyboard commands, activate the window's Control menu and select the **S**ize command. Use the arrow movement keys to reduce or enlarge the window's size. Press Enter when the window reaches the desired size.

A window must be in the restored position before you can move it on the screen. To move a window with the mouse, click in the window's title bar and drag the window to the desired location. To move a window using keyboard commands, activate the window's Control menu and select the **M**ove com-mand. Use the arrow keys to move the window to the desired location and press Enter.

Tool Bar

The tool bar is a new feature in Excel 3.0. The tool bar provides easy access to common formatting commands, automatic summation, outlining features, and tools for drawing objects on a worksheet.

This is the tool bar.

2

Table 2.5 describes what each tool does. Chapter 6, "Formatting a Worksheet," discusses the tool bar in greater detail.

Table 2.5
The Tool Bar

Tool	Purpose
Style box	Defines and applies styles.
Outlining buttons	Promote and demote rows and columns to create an outline.
Select visible cells buttons	Selects visible cells on a worksheet so that visible cells only are affected by changes.
Auto-SUM button	Inserts SUM function and sum numbers directly above or directly to the left of the active cell.
Bold and Italic buttons	Apply bold or italic formatting to the selection.
Text Alignment buttons	Left-, center-, or right-align the selection.
Selection tool	Selects all graphic objects enclosed by the selection border.
Drawing tools	Draw lines, rectangles, circles, arcs, and other objects on a worksheet.
Chart tool	Creates a chart on a worksheet based on selected data.
Text tool	Creates a text box for entering text that will wrap to the size of the text box.
Button tool	Creates a button that can be linked to a macro and activated when the button is clicked.
Camera tool	Creates a picture of selected cell with underlying data linked to the picture.

2

Formula Bar

The formula bar is located directly above the column headings in a worksheet. The formula bar becomes active when you enter data into a cell. When the formula bar is active, a box with an X and a box with a check mark appear to the left of the area that displays the data you are entering into the active cell in the worksheet.

The formula bar is active as data is entered.

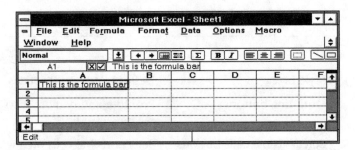

If you want to accept the entry, point and click on the box with the check mark or press Enter. If you do not want to accept the entry, point and click on the box with the X in it or press the Esc key.

If you want to activate the formula bar after data has been entered into a cell, click in the formula bar with the mouse or press the F2 function key. A blinking bar appears in the formula bar when the formula bar is activated, indicating the cursor's point of insertion. You can move the cursor in the formula bar with the arrow keys. Edit text using normal editing procedures.

Scroll Bars

The document window contains horizontal and vertical scroll bars that enable you to display other parts of a worksheet. The scroll bars represent the graphical equivalent of using the up-, down-, left-, and right-arrow keys on the keyboard. Each scroll bar is made up of three parts: the scroll arrows, the scroll box, and the scroll bar. As you click on the up or down vertical scroll arrows, the scroll box moves up or down the scroll bar. You can move to the top or bottom of your document by dragging the scroll box to the top or bottom of the scroll bar.

Worksheet Area

The worksheet area comprises most of the document window. The area is enclosed at the top by lettered column headings and on the left by numbered rows. The intersection of a column and a row defines a cell. A cell address is determined by the column and row intersection. Cell B6, for example, refers to the cell in column B, row 6.

Using On-Line Help

Excel comes with a complete on-line Help system designed to assist users with commands and other Excel topics. This section is intended to provide you with an overview of how to use the Help index, look for a specific topic, browse and backtrack to previous Help screens, and use Lotus 1-2-3 Help.

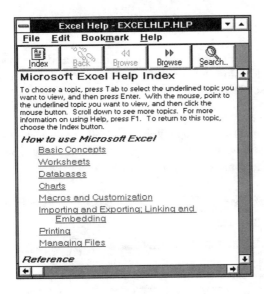

The on-line Help system is organized with an index that lists two main categories: *How to Use Microsoft Excel* and *Reference*.

Each category has several topics listed below the category heading. If you want assistance, for example, with learning how to create a chart in Excel, you can find the Help topic "Charts" under the category *How to use Microsoft Excel*. If you want to see a list of worksheet functions, you can find this topic under the *Reference* category.

2

The Help Index

To access the Help index using the mouse, follow these steps:

1. Choose the Help menu and select Index.

2. Use the scroll bar to scroll through the Help window. Position the mouse over the topic you want. Click once when the mouse pointer changes to a pointing finger.

To access the Help index using the keyboard, follow these steps:

1. Press Alt, H, I or press F1.

2. Use the arrows keys, PgUp, or PgDn to scroll through the Help window. Use Tab⇥ and ⇧Shift Tab⇥ to move forward or backward, respectively, among Help topics. Highlight the topic you want and press ↵Enter.

Searching for a Topic

The on-line Help system has a built-in list of Excel commands and key words. You can access a specific topic using the Search feature. To search for a topic using the mouse, follow these steps:

1. Choose the Help menu and select Index.

2. Choose the Search button. Use the scroll bar to scroll through the list. Because the list is alphabetically sensitive, you can save time by typing the first few letters of the topic you want.

A dialog box displays an alphabetical list of topics.

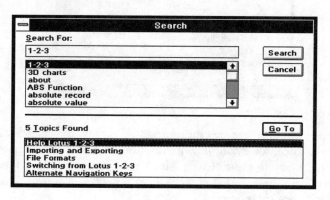

3. Double-click on the topic you want. That topic and any related topics appear in the Topic(s) Found box.

4. Use the scroll bar in the Topic(s) Found box to scroll through the list. Select the specific topic you want and double-click, or select the topic and choose the Goto button.

To search for a specific topic using the keyboard, follow these steps:

1. Press Alt, H, I or press F1 to access the Help index.

2. Press Alt S to activate the Search feature. A dialog box displays an alphabetical list of topics.

3. Type the topic you want. As you type, the closest topic in the list is selected. If you have not typed an exact topic, you probably will see a close match in the list. After the topic you want is selected, press ⏎Enter. That topic and any related topics appear in the Topic(s) Found box.

4. Use the arrow keys to scroll through the list displayed in the Topic(s) Found list. Select the specific topic you want and press Alt G, or press ⏎Enter to go to the selected topic.

Browsing and Backtracking

When a Help window is displayed, you will notice five buttons below the menu bar of the Help window. The five buttons include Index, Back, Browse (backward), Browse (forward), and Search.

Here, you see the five Help buttons.

The Index button displays the Help index with the Help categories listed. The Search button enables you to search for help on a specific topic or key word. The Browse buttons are used to browse forward or backward to related Help topics. The Back button enables you to go back to previous Help screens. To use the mouse to choose a Help button, point to the button and click the left mouse button once. To use the keyboard to choose a Help button, press Alt and the underlined letter in the button. Press Alt+O, for example, if you want to choose the Browse forward button.

Many Help topics contain related topics that are grouped together in a series. The Browse buttons enable you to move forward or backward to the next or preceding topic in the series. The Browse forward button enables you to move

2

to the next topic in the series. The Browse forward button appears dimmed when you reach the last topic in the series. The Browse backward button enables you to move backward. The Browse backward button appears dimmed when you reach the first topic in the series.

The Back button displays the last topic you viewed. The button continues backtracking in the order you viewed each topic until it reaches the Help index.

Context-Sensitive Help

Another way to access Help on a specific command is to use context-sensitive Help. To activate context-sensitive Help, press Shift+F1. A question mark appears next to the mouse pointer. Select the command you want help with. The Help window appears with the Help topic displayed on the chosen command.

Using Lotus 1-2-3 Help

Many experienced spreadsheet users are familiar with Lotus 1-2-3 concepts and commands. Excel's Lotus 1-2-3 on-line Help feature is intended for 1-2-3 users who are new to Excel. To start Help for 1-2-3 users, follow these steps:

1. Choose the Help menu and select Lotus 1-2-3 Help, or press (Alt), (H), (L).

You can use the Lotus 1-2-3 Help dialog box to set Lotus 1-2-3 Help to display either instructions or a demonstration of equivalent Excel commands.

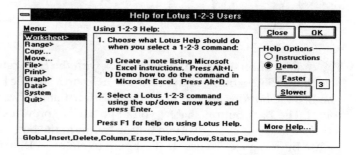

2. Select the Instructions option, or press (Alt)(I); or select the Demo option, or press (Alt)(D).
3. Select a Lotus command from the list, using the mouse or arrow keys or by pressing the first letter of the command.

50

Instructions Option

If you select the Instructions option in the Lotus 1-2-3 Help dialog box, you can choose a Lotus command from the dialog box. Excel closes the Help window and displays an instruction box explaining how to complete the equivalent command in Excel. Press Esc to clear the instruction box and proceed with the Excel command.

Demonstration Option

If you select the Demo option in the Lotus 1-2-3 Help dialog box, Excel executes the 1-2-3 command you choose and provides a demonstration of the Excel procedure for completing the equivalent command. If the command requires input, the demonstration halts until you enter the input, then the command proceeds with the remainder of the command. The Help window closes when the demonstration is completed.

In Lotus 1-2-3, the / (slash) key activates the main menu of commands. Excel 3.0 enables you to assign the / (slash) key to automatically access the Lotus 1-2-3 Help window. To activate this option, follow these steps:

1. Select the Options menu and select Workspace, or press (Alt), (O), (W).
2. Select the Lotus 1-2-3 Help option button, or press (Alt)(L).
3. Choose OK or press (↵Enter).

Working with On-Line Tutorials

Excel 3.0 includes six interactive tutorial lessons to help new users learn the skills necessary to take full advantage of Excel's extensive features. The tutorial topics include Introduction, Worksheets, Charts, Databases, Macros, and Help. At the beginning of each lesson, you see a display of the topics covered in the tutorial and the approximate amount of time required to complete the lesson. The tutorial guides you through the lesson with on-screen instructions and requests for input. You can exit the tutorial at any point in the lesson using the Control menu. To access the on-line tutorial lessons, follow these steps:

1. Select the Help menu and select Tutorial, or press (Alt), (H), (T). Excel prompts you to save any open documents.
2. Select from the six pictorial options the lesson you want to complete. The screen prompts you for input from this point on.

3. Choose Exit or press ⟨X⟩ if you are at the main menu and want to quit the tutorial. If you are in a lesson, press ⟨Ctrl⟩⟨F1⟩ to access the Control menu. From the Control menu, select the Exit button or press ⟨X⟩.

2

Exiting Excel

At the beginning of this chapter, you learned how to start Excel. This section of the chapter shows you how to exit, or quit, the Excel program. The following four ways to exit Excel are available:

• Choose the **F**ile menu and select E**x**it, or press Alt, F, X.

• Press Alt+space bar, C to close Excel from the application Control menu.

• Double-click the application Control menu bar.

• Press Alt+F4.

If you forgot to save any open documents, Excel prompts you with a reminder dialog box.

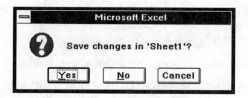

After the Excel program is closed, you return to the Program Manager in the Windows environment. The procedure to exit Windows works the same as the procedure to exit Excel. Use any one of the four methods for exiting Windows. When you exit windows, a dialog box asks you to confirm that you want to exit Windows.

Summary

In this chapter, you learned some of the fundamental techniques for starting and using Windows and Excel. Topics included keyboard features and function keys, mouse techniques, window components, and using Excel's on-line Help feature.

In this chapter, you were introduced to the following key information about Excel:

■ You can start Excel by double-clicking on the Excel icon.

■ Your keyboard consists of 10 to 12 function keys you can use alone or in conjunction with the Shift, Alt, or Ctrl keys to access Excel commands.

■ You can swap the left and right mouse buttons using the Mouse icon in the Control Panel.

■ The document window operates within the application window.

■ The Control menu is represented by a horizontal bar in the upper left corner of both the application and document windows.

■ The application window can assume one of three positions: minimized, maximized, or restored. The document window can assume the maximized or restored position.

■ You can move or resize a window when it is in the restored position.

■ The tool bar provides easy access to drawing tools, formatting and text tools, an Auto-SUM tool, and other powerful features.

■ The formula bar displays the data you enter in a cell.

■ On-line Help enables you to look for a specific Help topic and displays the selected topic in the Help window.

■ Shift+F1 displays a question mark next to the mouse pointer and activates context-sensitive Help, enabling you to get assistance on a chosen command.

■ Lotus 1-2-3 Help assists users who are already familiar with that program by providing instructions or a demonstration of how to execute a Lotus 1-2-3 command using Excel procedures.

If you are comfortable with these Excel fundamentals, you are ready to move on to the next chapter. In Chapter 3, "Excel Worksheet Basics," you will learn how to create a worksheet; enter data, formulas, and functions; and access commands from the menu bar.

Excel
Worksheet
Basics

In Chapter 2, you learned the components of the Excel screen and some fundamental skills for getting started. Now you are ready to learn the basics for working in a graphical environment and for accomplishing a variety of common tasks in Excel.

In this chapter, you learn how to move around in a worksheet; create a worksheet; enter data, formulas, and functions; and use worksheet commands. In addition to learning these skills, you will become familiar with commands to open and close a file, and to name, save, and delete a file.

3

Key Terms in This Chapter

Cell pointer   A cross-shaped marker that appears on the screen. You use the cell pointer to select an active cell with the mouse.

Cursor   A blinking bar in the formula bar, indicating the point of insertion.

Edit mode   A mode in which the formula bar is activated and you can change active cell contents using normal editing procedures.

Range   A defined cell or group of cells that can be acted upon with Excel commands.

Extension   The last three characters of a file name, which follow the period. These characters identify the type of file or file format.

Moving around in a Worksheet

When you start Excel, a blank document appears in the document window on your screen. The document is titled Sheet1. This is the name Excel automatically assigns to the document until you save the document and give it the name you want.

The worksheet is the main document used in Excel for storing and manipulating data.

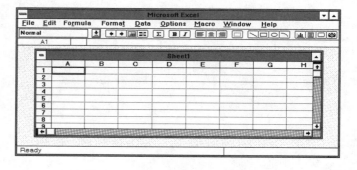

A worksheet is made up of 256 columns and 16,384 rows. The columns are lettered across the top of the document window, beginning with A through Z and continuing with AA through AZ, then BA through BZ, and so on through column IV. The rows are numbered from 1 to 16,384 down the left side of the document window. The worksheet consists of more than 4 million cells defined by the intersection of columns and rows. The cell is the basic unit in the worksheet for storing data in the form of text, numbers, and formulas.

On a blank worksheet, the cell at the intersection of column A and row 1 is outlined with a border that is darker than the other cells' borders. The darker border indicates that cell A1 is the active cell. If you start typing, the data appears in the active cell. If you want to enter data in another cell, you must make the cell active by moving to that cell, using either the mouse or the keyboard.

Mouse Movements

A mouse enables you to accomplish tasks easily in Excel. If you are using a mouse in a worksheet, you can make a cell active by positioning the cell pointer on the cell and clicking the left mouse button once.

Keyboard Movements

Using the keyboard, you can press the arrow keys, PgUp or PgDn, or key combinations to move to another cell and make that cell active. The keys that you use to move to new locations are listed in table 3.1.

Table 3.1
Moving among Cells with the Keyboard

Keys	*Description*
← → ↑ ↓	Moves one cell to the left, right, up, or down, respectively. The new cell becomes the active cell.
Ctrl + ← → ↑ ↓	Moves to the next cell of data separated by a blank cell.
Home	Moves to column A of the active row.
Ctrl Home	Moves to cell A1, the Home cell. The Home cell becomes the active cell.

continues

3

Table 3.1 *(continued)*

Keys	Description
End	Moves to the far right column containing data.
Ctrl End	Moves to the last cell used in the worksheet. The cell becomes the active cell.
PgUp	Moves up one screen.
PgDn	Moves down one screen.
Ctrl PgUp	Moves one screen width to the left.
Ctrl PgDn	Moves one screen width to the right.

You also can use the F5 function key to move to a specific cell.

When you press F5, the Goto dialog box appears on-screen.

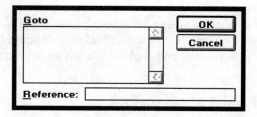

When the Goto dialog box appears, type in the **Reference** text box the address of the cell that you want to become active, and then press Enter. If, for example, you want to move to the cell in column D, row 5, enter **D5**, and then press Enter or select the OK button in the Goto dialog box. Cell D5 becomes the active cell.

In addition to pressing the F5 key, you also can access the Goto command from the Formula menu. Choose the Formula menu and select the Goto command; or press Alt, R, G to display the Goto dialog box.

Alternate Navigation Keys

If you are experienced with Lotus 1-2-3, you can use 1-2-3 procedures to move around in Excel. Excel enables you to change to navigation keys that imitate the movement procedures in 1-2-3. To change to the alternate navigation keys, follow these steps:

1. Choose the Options menu and select the Workspace command; or press $\boxed{\text{Alt}}\boxed{\text{O}}\boxed{\text{W}}$

The Options Workspace dialog box appears.

2. Select the Alternate Navigation Keys check box so that it displays an X; or press $\boxed{\text{Alt}}\boxed{\text{K}}$.

   (To turn off the alternate navigation keys, select the check box again; or press $\boxed{\text{Alt}}\boxed{\text{K}}$.)

3. Choose OK or press $\boxed{\leftarrow\text{Enter}}$

Scrolling

To view another section of the worksheet without moving the active cell, use the horizontal or vertical scroll bars. In Chapter 2, you learned the parts of the scroll bar and how it works. Using the mouse, click on the up or down scroll arrows; the screen scrolls line by line. You see the scroll box move up or down the scroll bar as you click on the scroll arrows. You also can scroll the screen by dragging the scroll box up and down the scroll bar. If you click on the scroll bar above the scroll box, the screen scrolls up one page. If you click on the scroll bar below the scroll box, the screen scrolls down one page.

3

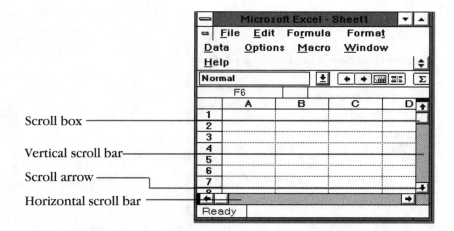

Scroll box

Vertical scroll bar

Scroll arrow

Horizontal scroll bar

If you want to view another worksheet section that is not visible, use the vertical and horizontal scroll bars to reposition the screen. If you see a cell that you want to activate, position the cell pointer over the cell and click to make it the active cell.

If you want to scroll through a worksheet using the keyboard, press the Scroll Lock key on your keyboard, and then use the arrow keys to scroll to the section of the worksheet you want to view. Scrolling moves the *screen*—it does not move the active cell.

Entering Data

After you have activated the cell in which you want to enter data, you can type text, numbers, formulas, or functions in the cell. As you enter data, the data appears in the active cell and in the area above the worksheet called the *formula bar*. The formula bar displays the cursor (a blinking bar), which represents the insertion point.

Rejects entry

Two small boxes also appear in the formula bar to the left of the insertion point.

Accepts entry

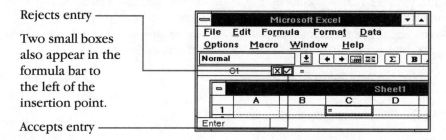

The left box displays an X; the right box displays a check mark. These boxes enable you to accept or reject the data you have entered. The data you enter appears in the formula bar to the right of the two boxes. To accept your entry in the active cell, click on the check mark box or press Enter. To reject your entry, click on the X box or press the Esc key.

To edit your entry, first use the left- and right-arrow keys to move the cursor in the formula bar. Then press the Backspace or Delete key to delete characters to the left or right of the cursor, respectively.

3

Entering Formulas

One of the most valuable features of a worksheet is its ability to calculate numbers based automatically on a predefined formula. Formulas can add numbers that you type into cells. Formulas also can refer to other cells that contain numbers in a worksheet. Excel recognizes a formula in a cell if the entry starts with an equal sign (=) or a plus sign (+).

To enter a formula, first type an equal sign. Next, type the formula. If, for example, three numbers have been entered into cells A1, A2, and A3, and you want to add the total of the three numbers in cell A4, you can type **=A1+A2+A3** in cell A4. The active cell and the formula bar display the formula as you enter it.

Because the entry in cell A4 starts with an equal sign, Excel recognizes the entry as a formula. After the formula is complete and you press Enter, cell A4 displays the result of the formula. If, however, cell A4 is the active cell, the formula bar always displays the actual formula =A1+A2+A3. The active cell displays the result of the formula after it is entered. The formula bar displays the formula as it is entered in the active cell.

You can, unfortunately, make errors when entering cell addresses. If your typing skills are less than adequate or you want to be more precise about entering the exact cell address when you enter a formula, you may choose to build a formula by selecting cells rather than typing the cell address. You can use the mouse or the keyboard to select cells to build a formula.

Suppose that you want to build a formula in cell C4 that subtracts the total in cell B4 from the total in cell A4. To build the formula with the mouse, follow these steps:

1. Type = (equal sign) in cell C4 to start the formula.
2. Click on cell A4 to add the cell address to the formula.
3. Type – (minus sign).

4. Click on cell B4 to add the cell address to the formula.

5. Select the check box in the formula bar or press ⏎Enter to complete the entry.

The result of the formula is displayed in cell C4. The formula in cell C4 is displayed in the formula bar.

3

If you want to build a formula by selecting cells with the keyboard, follow these steps:

1. Type = (equal sign) in cell C4 to start the formula.

2. Press ← twice to select cell A4, and then press ⏎Enter. Cell A4 is added to the formula.

3. Type – (minus sign).

4. Press ← once to select cell B4, and then press ⏎Enter. Cell B4 is added to the formula.

5. Select the check box in the formula bar or press ⏎Enter to complete the entry.

The completed formula is entered in cell C4 with the results displayed in the cell and the formula displayed in the formula bar.

Using Mathematical Operators

While building a worksheet, you often enter numbers into cells. Excel recognizes numbers as data that can be calculated. At some point, you probably will want to perform a calculation that uses numbers entered into cells. The following are the mathematical operators used in basic calculations:

+   Addition

–   Subtraction

*   Multiplication

/	Division
%	Percentages
^	Exponentiation

Remember that errors often occur when mathematical operators are not in the order of precedence, or the order in which calculations take place. The order of precedence for mathematical operations in a formula is as follows:

3

^	Exponentiation
*, /	Multiplication, division
+, –	Addition, subtraction

Exponentiation occurs before multiplication or division in a formula, and multiplication and division occur before addition or subtraction. If a formula includes mathematical operators that are at the same level, the calculations are evaluated from left to right. If, for example, a formula includes addition and subtraction, and the addition appears in the formula first, the addition is evaluated before the subtraction.

Parentheses can be used to enclose mathematical operations that are part of a long formula. Operations enclosed in parentheses are evaluated first, and use an order or precedence if multiple mathematical operators are used within the parentheses.

The following examples show various formulas using multiple mathematical operators and the result of the formulas. Assume that cell A3 contains the number 2, cell B3 contains the number 4, and cell C3 contains the number 5.

Formula	Evaluation	Result
+C3–B3/A3	5–(4/2)	3
(C3–B3)*A3	(5–4)*2	2
+C3*B3–B3 ^ A3	(5*4)–(4 ^ 2)	4
+C3*A3+(B3*C3)/C3	(5*2)+(4*5)/5	14

Using Built-In Functions

If you are working with only a few cells, building a formula by typing the formula and selecting cells may not seem too difficult. In many cases, however, your formula will involve several cells or groups of cells. Typing formulas

3

and selecting cells may prove cumbersome and inaccurate. Excel's built-in functions enable you easily to create a formula that involves several cells or groups of cells.

A function is a predefined formula that consists of the equal sign (=), the function name, and the argument or cells that will be used for carrying out the calculation. The SUM function, for example, adds the numbers in selected cells. The selected cells make up the argument portion of the function. The result of the function is returned in the active cell.

This formula uses the SUM function to total the entries in cells B1, B2, and B3.

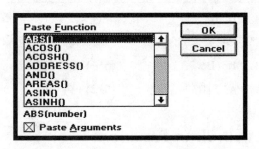

To enter a function into the active cell, you can type an equal sign (=), followed by the function name (**SUM**), followed by an open parenthesis. Then you can enter the cell or range of cells you want the function to use, followed by a close parenthesis. Or, you can use the Formula Paste Function command to insert automatically the elements required for using a function.

Choosing the Formula Paste Function command displays this dialog box.

The Paste Function dialog box displays an alphabetical list of Excel's built-in functions. If you want to access the SUM function, press the S key. Excel selects the first function beginning with the letter S. Scroll the list until the SUM function is visible for selection.

While the Paste Function dialog box is displayed, you have the option of choosing Paste **Arguments**. An argument is the data you supply that is necessary for the function to perform the calculation. An argument can be a single cell reference, a group of cells, or a number. Some functions require a single argument while others require multiple arguments. Function arguments are enclosed in parentheses, and each argument is separated by a comma.

If you are not sure which arguments are required for a particular function, select the Paste Arguments option. This option displays temporary placeholders in the formula bar to remind you of the data needed to complete the function. To include temporary placeholders, select the Paste **Arguments** check box, or press Alt+A to display an X in the check box. Choose OK or press Enter to clear the dialog box and enter the function into the active cell. The function also appears in the formula bar, and the formula bar is activated. If Paste **Arguments** was turned on in the dialog box, the first argument placeholder is selected. If Paste **Arguments** was turned off, the insertion point appears between the parentheses.

The argument placeholders must be replaced by a cell address or data that the function will act upon. With the argument placeholder selected, use the mouse to select the cell(s) that will replace the placeholder, or use the keyboard to enter the cell address(es). If the function contains multiple arguments, each placeholder must be selected and replaced with a cell reference or data.

To select an argument placeholder using the mouse, position the I-beam in the formula bar over the placeholder and double-click.

To select an argument placeholder using the keyboard, position the cursor at the beginning of the placeholder name, hold down the Shift key, and press the right-arrow key until the placeholder is selected. Do not select the comma separating argument placeholders.

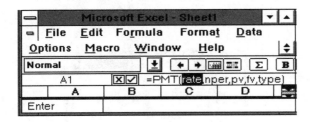

Here are multiple argument placeholders for the PMT command.

65

3

Here, the SUM function is entered using the Formula Paste Function command with Paste Arguments turned off.

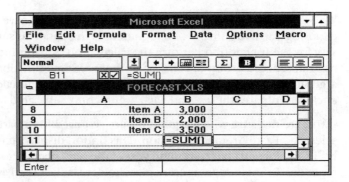

To enter a single group of cells to be summed, use the mouse to drag over the cells containing the data you want to sum. You also can enter the cell addresses from the keyboard. If, for example, you want to sum the numbers in cells B1, B2, and B3, enter **B1:B3** or **B1,B2,B3** between the parentheses in the formula bar.

A group of cells is selected with the cell address appearing in the formula bar.

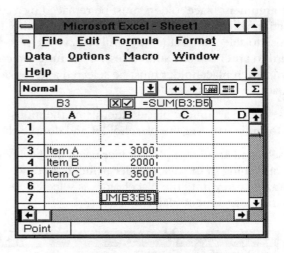

If you have an error in the formula, this dialog box appears.

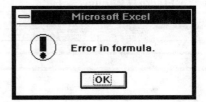

You can press F1 to find out more about the error. A Help window that explains possible reasons for the error appears. To clear the error message, choose OK or press Enter or Esc. Excel selects the part of the function that is causing the error. Edit the function in the formula bar, and select the check mark box or press Enter when the formula is complete.

Excel comes with a large number of built-in worksheet functions, including mathematical, database, financial, and statistical categories. Other categories include date, time, information, logical, lookup, matrix, statistical, text, and trigonometric functions. Functions are covered in detail in Chapter 7.

Performing What-If Analysis

Previous sections of this chapter acquainted you with the value of building formulas in a worksheet. If you have a list of numbers that you want to total, you can build a formula to calculate the sum automatically.

	A	B
		JAN
1		
2	Sales	$10,000
3		
4	Expenses	
5	Item A	3000
6	Item B	3000
7	Item C	2500
8		
9	Total Expenses	8500
10		
11	Net Income	$1,500
12		

Microsoft Excel - INCOME.X
File Edit Formula Format Data Options Macro Window Help
Normal
B11   =B2-B9

This worksheet has a formula in the active cell that adds the group of numbers in the range above the active cell.

The formula refers to cells containing values. If the values in the referenced cells change, the cell containing the formula will adjust to reflect the change. Formulas allow you to conduct what-if analysis. You can change a number and immediately see the results of the change.

Excel 3.0 includes two additional features that let you conduct another type of what-if analysis. Suppose that you have decided what you want the result of a formula to be. Excel has a Goal Seek command and an add-in program, Solver, that enable you to adjust numbers to meet a desired result.

The Goal Seek command enables you to change a single value to meet a desired result. The Solver add-in is much more extensive and enables you to modify a range of numbers to meet a maximum, minimum, or specified value. Solver also enables you to include parameters and constraints when finding a solution.

3 Using Goal Seek

If you have a result you want to achieve, the Goal Seek command enables you to specify the desired result and adjust a single cell to meet the result. To use the Goal Seek command, follow these steps:

1. Select a cell containing a formula.

2. Choose the Formula menu and select the Goal Seek command.

This window appears. The active cell appears in the Set cell text box.

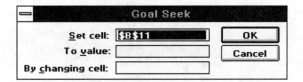

3. Select the To value text box or press [Tab⇄]. Enter the desired result in the To value text box.

4. Select the By changing cell text box or press [Tab⇄]. Select the single cell you want to change to meet the desired result. Use the mouse to select the cell, or enter the cell address using the keyboard. (You can move the Goal Seek window if it is covering the cell you want to select.) The cell you select must be a cell that is referenced in the active cell formula.

5. Choose **OK** or press [↵Enter].

The Goal Seek Status window appears showing the target value (the desired result) and the current value.

The **Pause** button in the Status window enables you to halt the seeking process temporarily. The **Pause** button changes to Continue when selected. After you pause the seeking process, you can choose the **Step** button to proceed through the calculation one step at a time.

6. Choose **OK** or press ⏎Enter if you want to accept the results of the Goal Seek and replace the value of the cell selected for changing. Choose **Cancel** or press Esc to clear the Goal Seek Status window. The cell value remains unchanged.

7. If you inadvertently choose **OK** or press ⏎Enter to accept the Goal Seek results, choose the **Edit Undo Goal Seek** command to restore the original numbers.

Using Solver

Unlike the Goal Seek command just described, Solver enables you to specify a maximum, minimum, or set value. Solver also enables you to work with a range of numbers and formulas, and to specify parameters and constraints to use when solving for the best solution. To use Solver, follow these steps:

1. Choose the **Formula Solver** command. The first time you access this command, Excel takes a few seconds to load the add-in program.

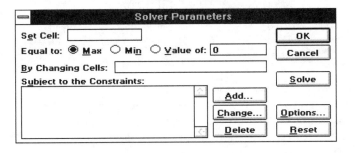

The Solver Parameters window appears.

2. Use the mouse to select the cell containing the formula you want to adjust, or enter the cell address in the **Set Cell** text box. Choose the **Max**, **Min**, or **Value of** option button. If you choose the **Value of** option, enter a value into the text box to the right.

3. Use the mouse to select the **By Changing Cells** text box or press Tab↔. Select the cells that can be used to reach the desired result, or enter the range address. (You can move the Solver Parameters window if it is covering cells you want to select.)

4. If you want to establish constraints that must be taken into consideration when solving for the desired solution, choose the Add button to define the constraint(s).

The Add Constraint window appears.

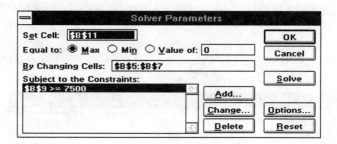

In the Cell Reference text box, select or enter the cell whose value you want to constrain. Use the drop-down list next to the Cell Reference text box to specify the relationship between the cell reference and the constraint. The options include less than or equal to (<=), equal to (=), or greater than or equal to (>=). Choose the option from the list and enter the constraint into the Constraint text box.

This specification constrains cell B9 to be greater than or equal to (>=) 7500.

5. Choose OK or press ↵Enter when you have added all constraints. The window disappears, and you return to the Solver Parameters window. The defined constraints are listed. You can change or delete constraints, using the buttons to the right of the Constraints list.

6. After all parameters have been set, choose the Solve button. Solver takes a few seconds to perform the calculation based on the defined parameters and constraints.

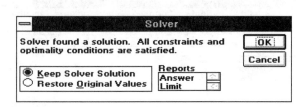

When Excel finds the ideal solution, this dialog box appears. You have the option of accepting Solver results or keeping the original figures.

3

7. To accept the results, select the **K**eep Solver Solution option. To keep the original results, select the Restore **O**riginal Values option.

Suppose that you want to see a report that summarizes the changes made to the original data to achieve the desired solution. Excel can create two types of reports: the Answer report and the Limit report. The Answer report lists the Set Cell defined in the Solver Parameters window and the adjustable cells, with their original and final values. The Answer report also details constraint information. The Limit report lists the Set Cell defined in the Solver Parameters window and the adjustable cells with their values, lower and upper limits, and target results.

If you want to generate a report that summarizes the results of the solution process, select in the Reports box the type of report you want. You can select both reports by holding down the Shift key as you make your selections. Excel produces reports on a separate worksheet.

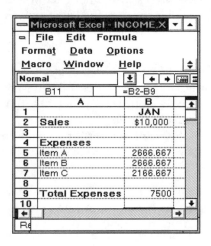

This worksheet shows the changes made based on the Solver parameters and constraints.

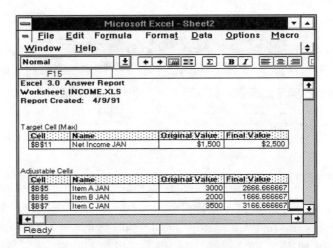

This Answer report shows the parameters and constraints information.

The Solver add-in is a very powerful program that comes with Excel. If you want to explore some of the more advanced features of Solver, you might consider purchasing Que's *Using Excel 3 for Windows*, Special Edition, by Ron Person. The book explains Solver in greater detail.

Editing Data

Making changes to a cell's contents is often required when building a worksheet. If you want to replace a cell's contents with other data, you do not need to delete the data first. Select the cell that contains the data you want to replace and enter the new data. Data entered into a cell replaces any data that currently exists in the cell.

Often you will want to change part of the data entered in a cell, or you will need to make a correction in a formula. In either case, you will want to edit the cell's contents rather than replace the entire cell's contents. To edit a cell's contents, you must activate the formula bar to display the cursor. The cursor is a vertical blinking bar that indicates the point of insertion in the formula bar. Select the cell that contains the data you want to edit, using the cell pointer or the keyboard arrow keys.

To activate the formula bar using a mouse, move the mouse pointer to the formula bar. The mouse pointer changes to an I-beam when positioned in the formula bar. Click the left mouse button; the cursor appears in the formula bar, indicating that you are in Edit mode.

To activate the formula bar from the keyboard, press the F2 function key. The cursor appears in the formula bar, indicating that you are in Edit mode.

You can use normal editing procedures to change the selected cell's contents. If you need to move the cursor to another location in the formula bar, press the left- or right-arrow key to move the cursor one character at a time. Pressing Ctrl with the left- or right-arrow key moves the cursor forward or backward to the next or previous segment separated by spaces. If you want to relocate the cursor in the formula bar using the mouse, move the mouse I-beam to the position in the formula bar where you want the cursor to appear and click the left mouse button once.

If you want to delete a character to the left of the cursor, press the Backspace key. To delete a character to the right of the cursor, press the Delete key. To insert text, numbers, or other data, place the cursor where you want the information to appear, and then type the data. If you select a cell after entering Edit mode, the selected cell address is added to the formula bar. If you edit the cell incorrectly and want to cancel the changes you made, select the X box in the formula bar or press Esc. The cell's contents remains the same as it was before you made any changes.

Selecting Cells and Ranges

To select a single cell, you simply activate the cell using the movement keys described in the preceding section. You also can select several cells at once. A group of cells is called a *range*. You can select a range using the keyboard or mouse.

To select a range using the mouse, follow these steps:

1. Click on the cell at the corner of the range you want to select.
2. Drag the mouse over the range.
3. When you reach the end of the selection range, release the mouse button.

To select a range with the keyboard, follow these steps:

1. Move to a cell at a corner of the range you want to select.
2. Hold down ⇧Shift and press the arrow keys to select the range.

A range is se-
lected. The first
cell of the selec-
tion is the active
cell and is out-
lined with a white
background.

3

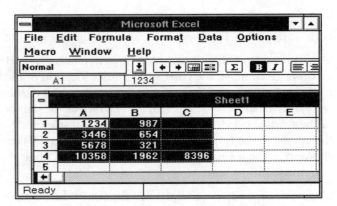

You easily can select cells that are grouped together with the mouse or the keyboard. Excel also enables you to select more than one range of cells at a time with the same ease as selecting a single range of cells. The mouse is the easiest method for selecting multiple ranges.

To select multiple ranges using the mouse, follow these steps:

1. Click and drag the mouse over the first range you want to select.

2. Hold down Ctrl and continue selecting other ranges.

To select multiple ranges using the keyboard, follow these steps:

1. Press ⇧Shift and an arrow key to select the first range.

2. Press ⇧Shift F8. The indicator ADD appears in the status bar at the bottom of the screen, meaning that you are in Add mode.

3. Move to a cell at a corner of the next range you want to select.

4. Press ⇧Shift and an arrow key to select the range. ADD disappears from the status bar. If you want to add another range, press ⇧Shift F8 to go back to Add mode and repeat steps 3 and 4.

Here, two
nonadjoining
ranges are
selected at the
same time.

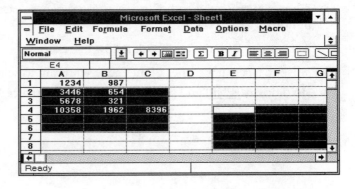

If you want to select the entire worksheet, click on the rectangle directly above the row numbers and to the left of the column headings; or press Ctrl+Shift+space bar.

Using Worksheet Commands

Every Windows application has a menu bar directly below the application title bar. Excel's menu bar has nine menus, starting with the File menu on the left and ending with the Help menu on the right. Each menu stores a group of commands. When you select one of these commands, Excel carries out a specific task. To see a list of the commands for each menu, you must select the menu.

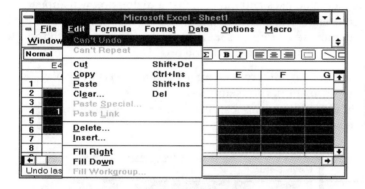

This list of Edit commands is found under the Edit menu.

To select a menu and a command with the mouse, follow these steps:

1. Point to the menu and click the left mouse button once. A list of the commands drops down from the menu.

2. From this list, point to the command you want Excel to execute and click the left mouse button once.

To select a menu from the keyboard, follow these steps:

1. Press [Alt] to activate the menu bar.

2. Press the letter that is underlined in the menu name. (If you want to choose the File menu, for example, press [F].) A list of commands drops down from the menu.

3. To select a command from the menu, press the letter that is underlined in the command name.

3

You also can activate the menu bar from the keyboard with the / (slash) key, and you can use the left- and right-arrow keys to select a menu. If you select a menu with the arrow keys, you must press the down-arrow key to see the list of commands.

Certain Excel commands require a specific action before you can use the command. If, for example, you do not cut or copy something, the Paste command is not available and is dimmed or grayed on the list of commands. If an object is not selected, the commands that are relevant only to selected objects are dimmed and unavailable.

Using Dialog Boxes

Many Excel commands are followed by three dots (...) next to the command name. These dots are called ellipses and indicate that a dialog box will appear on the screen if the command is selected. A dialog box requests additional information, such as command settings; or it enables you to proceed with the command, using the settings defined in the dialog box.

A dialog box can consist of many different elements that are used to display lists, enter text, select information, turn settings on or off, or cancel the command. The type of elements that appear in a dialog box depends on the type of command selected.

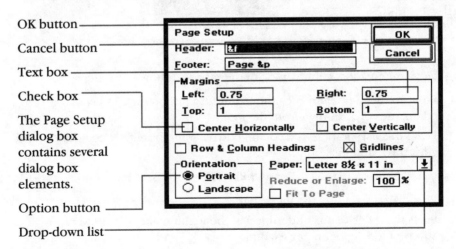

OK button

Cancel button

Text box

Check box

The Page Setup dialog box contains several dialog box elements.

Option button

Drop-down list

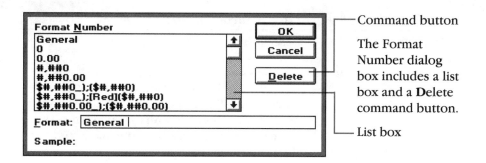

Table 3.2 describes the elements shown in the dialog boxes.

Table 3.2
Dialog Box Elements

Element	Description
Text box	A rectangular box used to display and enter information.
Check box	A square box used to turn an option on or off. An X in the box indicates that the option is turned on.
Option button	A circle to the left of an option. The circle is filled if the option is selected. You can select only one option in a group of options.
Drop-down list	A list of options that drops down from a rectangular box. To view the list, you activate the down arrow to the right of the box.
List box	A square area that displays the available choices. If all choices cannot be viewed in the square, a vertical scroll bar appears on the right side of the box, enabling you to view other choices in the list.
Command button	A rectangular icon, with a label describing the button's function, which is used to carry out a specific command. If a button has ellipses (...) next to the label, another dialog box appears when the button is selected.

continues

3

Table 3.2 *(continued)*

Element	Description
OK and Cancel buttons	Buttons used in most dialog boxes as a way to continue or discontinue the selected command. The OK button accepts the dialog box settings and proceeds with the command. The Cancel button cancels the command and closes the dialog box.

Moving within a Dialog Box

When a dialog box is displayed, you may want to change one or more of the settings. You must select the section of the dialog box that controls the setting you want to change. You can access sections of the dialog box using the mouse or keyboard.

To activate a section of the dialog box with the mouse, point to the section with the mouse pointer and click the left mouse button once to select an option, turn a check box on or off, or select a button. To activate a text box, position the mouse pointer over the text box until the mouse pointer changes to an I-beam. Click in the text box, and a cursor appears for data entry. To replace text in a text box, select the text by dragging the I-beam over the text, and then type the new text.

To activate a section of the dialog box with the keyboard, press the Alt key and the underlined letter of the option you want to choose. To move from one section of the dialog box to the next section, press Tab. Press Shift+Tab to move to the previous section. Press Enter to confirm the dialog box settings and proceed with the command. Press Esc to cancel the command and close the dialog box.

To choose from a drop-down list with the mouse, point to the down arrow at the right of the text box and press the left mouse button once. A list of available choices appears in a list. If the list requires scrolling, a vertical scroll bar appears to the right of the list. Point to the option you want and click the left mouse button once. The drop-down list disappears after you make your selection.

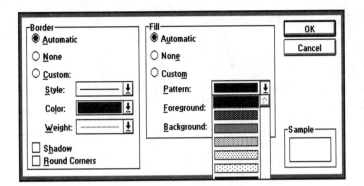

The drop-down list is displayed when you click on the down arrow.

3

To choose from a drop-down list with the keyboard, first activate the list by pressing Alt with the underlined letter of the option. If you want to activate the Patterns drop-down list in the Patterns dialog box, for example, press Alt+P. Then press Alt with the down-arrow key to display the list. Use the up- and down-arrow keys to scroll through the list. Press Enter to complete your selection, and the list disappears.

Using the Edit Undo Command

Excel has a built-in safety net that allows you to reverse many commands or actions. The Edit Undo command will undo the last command selected or the last action performed. If you want to undo a command or action, choose the Edit menu and select the Undo command; or press Alt+Backspace. Excel retains only the last action or command. Therefore, you must select the Undo command immediately after the command or action.

The Undo command is not available for all commands. If, for example, you choose the File Delete command and delete a file from disk, the Edit menu shows Can't Undo as a dimmed command. Although the Undo command can reverse many actions, you must still use certain commands with caution.

If you want to reverse the Undo command, choose the Edit menu and select the Redo command; or press Alt+Backspace.

Saving and Naming a File

When you are working with a computer file, the data you enter or edit actually is stored in a temporary memory zone called *RAM* (random-access memory). If a power outage or computer failure occurs while you are working, the temporary memory is wiped out, taking with it the data you entered or edited. To avoid losing your work, you must save it frequently.

When you save a file, the file is put in a permanent storage area. Your internal hard drive is the part of your computer that permanently stores information. A floppy disk also will permanently store your data. To place a file into a permanent storage area, you must give a command to save the file and provide the file with a name if you are saving the file for the first time. The file name enables you to identify and find your file in the permanent storage area.

The File Save Command

To save a file in Excel, choose the File menu and select the **Save** command.

The File Save
dialog box
appears on-screen
when you are
saving a file for
the first time.

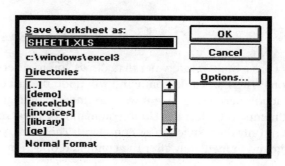

Type a name that will help you identify the document in the future. A file name is limited to a total of eight characters. These characters can include letters and numbers, but cannot include spaces. If you want to use a space in a file name, use the underline (_) or hyphen (–) to separate characters.

Excel automatically assigns an extension after the file name. If you are saving a worksheet, the extension is XLS; a macro sheet will have the extension XLM; a chart will have the extension XLC. If you are saving multiple files as a workspace, Excel assigns the extension XLW.

The File Save As Command

After you have named a file and you later choose the **File Save** command to save changes you have made, the File Save dialog box will *not* appear. The File Save command overwrites the named file with the changes you have made.

Sometimes you will want to keep different versions of a file. In situations when you need to refer to a previous version of a document, you actually will want to have two copies of the document: one incorporating the changes and one without the changes. The File Save **As** command enables you to keep the original document and assign another file name to save the changed document. The File Save As dialog box looks like the File Save dialog box that appears when you are saving an unnamed document for the first time.

You can use the File Save **As** command to save an Excel file to another file format, including the Lotus 1-2-3 file format. This procedure is covered in greater detail in Chapter 9, "Working with Multiple Documents."

Opening and Closing a File

When you first start Excel, the program begins with a blank worksheet called Sheet1. When you want to work on a document that already exists, you close Sheet1, the blank worksheet, and then open the other worksheet. To open a file that already exists, choose the **File** menu and select the **Open** command.

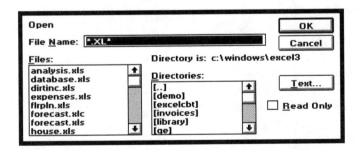

When you choose the File Open command, the File Open dialog box appears.

Excel always remembers the last four files you have worked on. These files are listed at the bottom of the File menu. To open one of these files, select the file name from the File menu.

3

The File Name Text Box

The File Name text box is selected when the File Open dialog box is displayed. You can open a file by typing the file name in the text box and choosing OK or pressing Enter. The *.XL* in the File Name text box indicates that all files in the current directory ending with the extension XL plus any other character will appear in the Files list box. The asterisk (*) is a wild card that is used to represent any other characters that may appear in the requested order.

The Files List Box

The Files list box provides an alphabetical list of all Excel files in the current directory. The current drive and directory are displayed above the Directories list box on the "Directory is:" line. To select a file from the list using the mouse, position the mouse pointer on the file name and double-click the left mouse button. (Use the scroll bar if necessary to view choices that are not visible in the list box.)

To select a file from the list box using the keyboard, press Alt+F to activate the Files list box; then press the down-arrow key to scroll the list. This list is alphabetically sensitive. After a file in the list is selected, you can press any letter on your keyboard, and Excel will select the first file beginning with that letter. Press Enter when you have selected the file you want to open.

The Directories List Box

The Directories list box provides a list of all available directories and drives. This list box enables you to locate a file in another directory or drive. If you want to change to another directory or drive using the mouse, position the mouse pointer on the selection you want to make and double-click the left mouse button. (Use the scroll bar if necessary to view choices that are not visible in the list box.)

If you want to change to another directory or drive using the keyboard, press Alt+D to activate the Directories list box; then press the down-arrow key to scroll the list. Press Enter when you have selected the directory or drive you want to switch to. The current drive and directory are displayed above the Directories list box on the "Directory is:" line.

The first choice in the Directories list box is an entry that displays two periods enclosed in brackets ([..]). This choice enables you to change to the directory above the current directory. If the current drive and directory is C:\WINDOWS\EXCEL, for example, and you select the directory represented by [..] in the list box, the current directory will change to C:\WINDOWS.

Closing a File

When you have finished working on a document, you will want to close the file. Choose the **File** menu and select the **Close** command, or press Ctrl+F4.

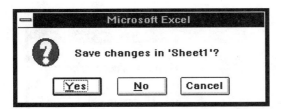

If you did not save the file, Excel prompts you to save the changes before closing the document.

To close the document and save the changes, choose **Yes** or press Enter. To close the document and ignore the changes, choose **No** or press N. To close the dialog box and keep the document open, choose **Cancel** or press Esc. If you saved all your changes before selecting the **File Close** command, you do not need to save again. The document window closes without prompting you to save changes.

If you have multiple files open at the same time, you can close all the files at once. Press and hold down the Shift key and choose the **File** menu; the **Close** command on the menu changes to **Close All**. Select **Close All**. All open files close. If you did not save a file, a dialog box appears prompting you to save the changes.

Deleting a File

Over time, you can accumulate many files. These files take up space on your hard drive. You can delete these files from within Excel by choosing the **File** menu and selecting the **Delete** command. A dialog box similar to the File Open dialog box appears.

3

Select the file you
want to delete
from the Files list
box and choose
OK or press
⏎Enter

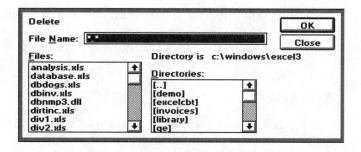

An alert box asks
you to confirm
the deletion of a
file from disk.

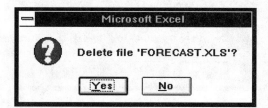

Remember that you are deleting the file from a disk that is a permanent
storage location. If you do not have a backup copy of this file on a floppy disk,
you will not be able to access the file again once it is deleted. You cannot use
the Edit Undo command to undo a file deletion. If a file has been deleted, the
Cancel button will *not* cancel the file deletion. Selecting the Cancel button in
the dialog box only closes the dialog box. Although file deletion is a conve-
nient feature, you must use this command with care.

Summary

In this chapter, you were introduced to many concepts crucial for using Excel,
including moving around in a worksheet; entering and editing data, formulas,
and functions; and using worksheet commands and dialog boxes to select
cells and multiple ranges. Additionally, you were introduced to procedures for
opening, saving, naming, closing, and deleting files.

In this chapter, you were introduced to the following key information about
Excel:

■ With the mouse, the cell pointer is used to move among cells. Using
the keyboard, the arrow keys and other keys are used to move among
cells.

- The F5 function key is the Goto key that enables you to enter a cell address and move to that location.

- Data can be entered in a cell in the form of text, numbers, formulas, or functions. A number is recognized as a value.

- A formula is entered by starting with the equal sign (=).

- A formula can refer to a cell that contains a number you will use in a calculation.

- A formula is displayed in the formula bar. The result of the formula is displayed in the cell.

- The F2 function key activates the formula bar and enables you to edit a cell's contents.

- Functions are predefined formulas that you can enter into a cell, using the Formula Paste Function command.

- The Goal Seek command enables you to change a formula's value to meet a desired result. You change one cell to meet the result.

- Excel comes with an add-in program called Solver, which enables you to perform what-if analysis and adjust numbers to meet a specific result.

- Solver will solve for a minimum, maximum, or specified value, and enables you to set parameters and constraints for performing what-if analysis.

- Solver enables you to generate two types of reports that summarize changes made to original data to achieve the desired solution.

- A range is a defined cell or group of cells that can be acted upon with Excel commands.

- Multiple groups of cells can be selected at the same time. Press and hold the Ctrl key as you select nonadjoining ranges with the mouse.

- Shift+F8 enables you to add another nonadjoining range to a selection.

- The Alt key activates the menu bar. A list of commands appears when a menu is selected. A command carries out an action.

- A dialog box enables Excel to request input and enables you to select options and continue or discontinue the selected command.

- The Edit Undo command reverses the last command or action performed.

- The File Save command saves the document or document changes in a permanent storage area.

3

3

- The File Save As command enables you to save a named document with a new name so that you can keep previous versions of the document.

- The File Open command displays a list of all Excel files in the current directory.

- Excel remembers the last four files opened and lists them at the end of the File menu.

- The File Delete command enables you to delete a file from a disk. You must use this command with caution because you cannot reverse or undo a file deletion.

If you are comfortable with the information in this chapter, you are ready to start building a worksheet. In Chapter 4, you will learn about topics including cell references, working with ranges, and protecting documents.

Building a Worksheet

Chapter 3 covered a variety of topics, including moving around a worksheet, entering data, and accessing commands. In this chapter, you will learn how to build a worksheet more efficiently.

Previous chapters mainly discussed cells and cell addresses. In this chapter, you will learn how to name a cell or a range of cells. Naming cells or ranges can save you considerable time when you organize and access data on a worksheet. Referring to a cell or a range by a name rather than an address simplifies working with a worksheet.

Other topics covered in this chapter include splitting the screen into panes, freezing panes to prevent scrolling, and opening new windows for viewing flexibility. Finally, you will learn how to protect a document from unwanted changes.

Working with ranges

Splitting the screen

Freezing a pane

Creating a window

Protecting a document

Key Terms in This Chapter

Named cell	A cell assigned a name using the Formula Define Name command.
Panes	Sections of the screen created by splitting the screen.
Freezing a pane	The process of keeping data within a pane stationary.
New window	A feature that enables you to view additional windows that display the active document.
Document protection	A feature that prevents users from making changes to a document.

Working with Ranges

By definition, a *range* is a group of selected cells. While building a worksheet, you save time by applying a command to a group of cells all at once rather than applying a command to each individual cell. If, for example, you want to format the cell contents of several cells, first select all cells whose contents you want to format first, and then apply the formatting command. Any command or action you can apply to a cell can usually be applied to a range. Excel Format commands, such as Number, Alignment, Fonts, and Patterns, are commonly applied to a range. You also can use ranges in functions and with the Goto command.

The selected range is formatted to display currency.

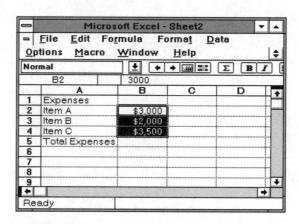

A range can be any size. You can select a range using the mouse or keyboard. To select a range with the mouse, hold down the left mouse button and drag the cell pointer over the cells you want to select. To select a range with the keyboard, hold down the Shift key and use the arrow keys to select the cells. Refer to Chapter 3's section "Selecting Cells and Ranges" to review the procedures for selecting multiple, nonadjacent ranges.

A function can refer to a range. If, for example, you are using the SUM function to add a group of numbers, you can select the range to be summed. When a group of cells is selected, the formula bar displays the cell address of the first cell in the range followed by a colon, and the cell address of the last cell in the range.

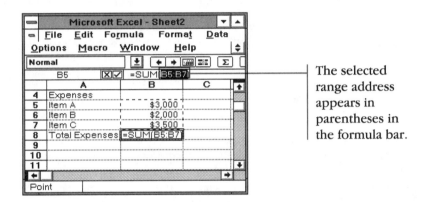

The selected range address appears in parentheses in the formula bar.

Later in this chapter, you will learn how to name a range. A named range enables you to refer to a cell or section of your worksheet by a name rather than a cell address. The section titled "Naming Cells and Ranges" explains this procedure. After a range is named, you can select the range quickly, using the Goto command.

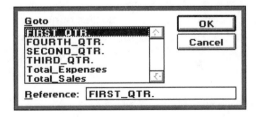

The Goto dialog box lists ranges that have been named.

89

Moving within a Range

After a range is selected, you can use certain keystrokes to move the active cell within the range only. Table 4.1 lists keys and key combinations for moving to the next cell within a selected range of cells.

Table 4.1
Moving among Cells within a Selected Range

Key(s)	Action
↵Enter	Moves one cell down or to the top of the next column.
⇧Shift ↵Enter	Moves one cell up or to the bottom of the preceding column.
Tab⇥	Moves one cell to the right or to the start of the next row.
⇧Shift Tab⇥	Moves one cell to the left or to the end of the preceding row.

Selecting a range of blank cells can make data entry easier. If you enter data in the active cell and press Enter, the data is entered and you move one cell down. If the range consists of a single row, you move one cell to the right. You can move only to cells within the selected range. When you reach the last cell in the range and press Enter, you move to the cell at the beginning of the range.

Naming Cells and Ranges

Naming a cell or range has many advantages. For example, a cell that is named Total_Sales is more descriptive than a cell that is called B2. You can build formulas more accurately when you use names. If you know that you will build a formula to calculate net income based on total sales minus total expenses, you can name each cell accordingly. Then build a formula in the net income cell that shows =Total_Sales-Total_Expenses rather than =B2-B9.

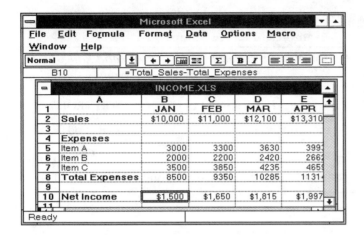

The active cell uses a formula that refers to named cells rather than cell addresses.

4

Cells must be named before they can be referenced in a formula by name. Cell B2 must first be named Total_Sales; cell B9 must be named Total_Expenses. After the cells have been named, the formula =Total_Sales–Total_Expenses can be entered in cell B11. If cell B11 is the active cell, the formula using the named cells appears in the formula bar. If cell B2 or cell B9 is the active cell, the value or cell contents appears in the formula bar.

Here are a few rules for naming a cell or range. Keep these rules in mind when deciding what to name a cell or range:

- Names must start with a letter.
- Names cannot contain spaces. Use an underline (_) or period (.) if you want to separate words.
- Names are not case sensitive. Excel changes names to uppercase.
- Names can include up to 255 characters. However, you will want to keep names somewhat brief and easy to interpret.
- Names cannot look like cell references, such as A$1 or R1C1.
- TRUE and FALSE cannot be used as names.
- If you enter a name that already exists, the new definition replaces the old definition.

Table 4.2 shows examples of invalid range names and valid alternative names.

Table 4.2
Examples of Range Names

Invalid Range Name	Reason Name Is Invalid	Valid Range Name
1STQTR.PROFIT	Cannot begin with a number.	QTR1.PROFIT
PROFIT QTR 1	Cannot contain spaces.	PROFIT_QTR_1
A1$.PROFIT	Cannot resemble a cell reference.	A1.PROFIT
TRUE	TRUE or FALSE cannot be used alone.	TRUE_PROFIT

If you enter a name that is invalid, this dialog box appears.

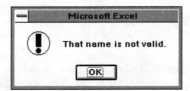

Choose OK or press Enter to clear the dialog box and enter a valid name. If you are not sure why the name is invalid, press F1 while the dialog box is on-screen. A Help window appears. The Help window contains the underlined topic `valid name`. Position the pointing finger on the topic and click the left mouse button once, or press the Tab key to select the underlined topic and press Enter.

The Help window appears, displaying the requirements for valid names.

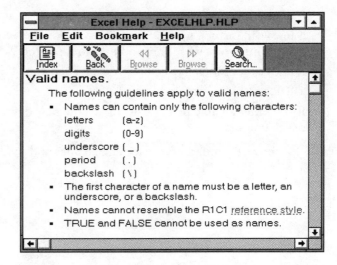

92

To name a cell or range, follow these steps:

1. Select the cell or range you want to name.

2. Choose the Formula Define Name command.

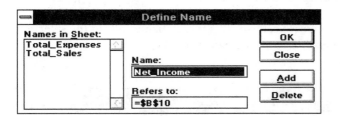

Excel displays the
Define Name
dialog box.

3. Type the name you want in the Name box, or accept the name that
   may appear in the box. (If the name that appears in the box has a
   space in it, the space will convert to an underline.)

4. Choose **OK** or press ⏎Enter.

Selecting a Range

Named ranges provide quick access to sections of your worksheet. In
Chapter 3, you were introduced to the F5 function key as the Goto key.
The Goto command is an ideal way to select a range quickly.

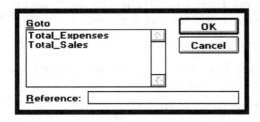

Pressing F5
displays the Goto
dialog box.

The Goto dialog box enables you to enter a cell address or select a named cell
or range from those listed. To select a named range, follow these steps:

1. Press F5, or choose the Edit menu and select the Goto command.

2. Select the name from the Goto list, using the mouse; or press Alt G
   and use the arrow keys to select the name; or type the name in the
   Reference text box.

3. Choose **OK** or press ⏎Enter. The named range is selected.

Creating Names from Existing Text

You may not want to take the time to define names for several cells within a range. For this reason, Excel has a command that enables you to create names using text that already exists in the cells along the edge of the range. You can choose to use text in cells on the top and bottom rows, or left and right columns of a selected range. Excel uses this text to name cells in the selected range. This procedure enables you to create a number of names at the same time.

Suppose, for example, that you select the range shown here.

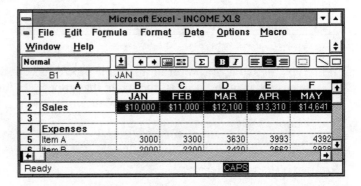

If you choose to create names using the text in the top row, the names Jan, Feb, Mar, Apr, and May will identify the cells below. The name Jan refers to the cell B2. If you create a formula that refers to cell B2, you can type the name rather than the cell address. Using named cells is especially useful when building a formula that references a cell that is not in view.

To create a group of names from existing text, follow these steps:

1. Select the range of cells you want to name, including a top or bottom row or left or right column with the existing text.

2. Choose the Formula Create Names command.

A dialog box with four check boxes appears.

3. Click on the check box that indicates the location of the cells with the text you want to use for names: Top Row, Left Column, Bottom Row,

94

or **R**ight Column. Or, using the keyboard, press the underlined letter to select the check box. You can turn on more than one check box.

4. Choose **OK** or press ↵Enter.

If the text in the cells has a space, Excel automatically replaces the space with an underline (_). For example, Total Sales is named Total_Sales. If the **T**op Row check box is selected, Excel creates names from the top row of the selected range.

Changing or Deleting a Name

The Formula **D**efine Name command enables you to define a name and the range or cell reference the name is applied to. You also can use this command to change a name, modify the cell or range address the name refers to, or delete a name from the list.

To change or delete a name, follow these steps:

1. Choose the Formula **D**efine Name command.

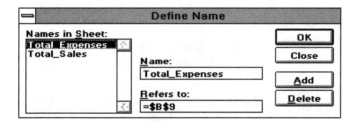

The Formula Define Name dialog box appears.

2. Select the name from the Names in Sheet list.

3. To change the name, enter a new name in the **N**ame text box.

   To change the cell or range address, use the mouse or press Tab⇥ to select the text in the **R**efers to text box. Then, type or select the new address on the worksheet.

   To delete the selected name from the list, choose **D**elete or press Alt D

4. Choose **OK** or press ↵Enter.

If you are thinking about deleting a name, do so with caution. Remember: when you delete a name, the action cannot be reversed. The Cancel button in the dialog box does not cancel a deleted name. You cannot use the Edit Undo command to reverse a deleted name.

95

If a cell contains a formula that refers to a named cell and the name has been deleted, the cell containing the formula will display #name?. To correct a formula that refers to a named cell or range that has been deleted, you must locate the cell or range that the deleted name referred to. If you use names that accurately describe cell contents, finding the correct cell or range should not be too difficult. Select the cell or range and choose the Formula **D**efine Name command. Rename the cell or range with the same name used in the formula, and then choose OK or press Enter.

Applying Names

Excel has a built-in command that enables you to select defined names from a list and apply the names to a selected range. If you select a range that includes formulas referring to named cells, you can apply names to the range. The cell references in the formula are then replaced by the named cells. For example, suppose that cell B11 contains the formula =B2–B9. Cell B2 has been named Total_Sales, and cell B9 has been named Total_Expenses. You could use the Formula **A**pply Names command to apply the names to the formula in cell B11. The formula bar then would display =Total_Sales_Total_Expenses.

Follow these steps to apply names to a range:

1. Select the range you want to apply selected names to. If you select a single cell, Excel assumes that you want to apply names to the entire worksheet.

2. Choose the Fo**r**mula **A**pply Names command.

The Apply Names dialog box appears.

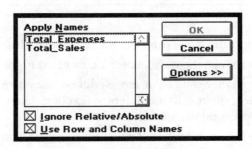

If the selected range contains cells that are named, those names will already be selected in the Apply Names list. You can select or deselect names in the list, using the mouse or the keyboard.

3. With the mouse, hold down ⌂Shift and click to select or deselect a name in the Apply Names list.

With the keyboard, hold down Ctrl and use ↑ or ↓ to move through the list without deselecting names. A light gray outline appears around a name in the list. Press the **space bar** to select or deselect a name in the Apply Names list.

4. Select the **I**gnore Relative/Absolute check box or press Alt I to turn off the option. This option enables you to match absolute names to relative cell references. The default setting is on and enables selected names to replace both absolute and relative cell references.

   The **I**gnore Relative/Absolute check box refers to the type of cell reference used in a formula. A1, for example, is a relative cell reference; $A$1 is an absolute cell reference. A relative cell address adjusts when a formula is copied to another location on the worksheet. If a formula contains an absolute cell address, the formula always refers to the same cell regardless of where the formula is copied to. Chapter 5, "Modifying a Worksheet," discusses cell references in greater detail.

5. Select the **U**se Row and Column Names check box or press Alt U to turn off the option if you want to apply only individual cell names to cell references. The default is on and enables you to rename cell references with range names that are appropriate for the cell's location.

6. Select the **O**ptions button or press Alt O, and more options will appear. The options enable you to omit names in the same row or column, and select the name order.

7. Choose **OK** or press ⏎Enter to accept the dialog box settings and apply the selected names to formulas in the range. If no formulas refer to named cells in the range, a dialog box displays the message No match. Choose **OK** or press Esc to clear the dialog box.

Splitting the Screen

An Excel worksheet contains more than 4 million cells. Only a small fraction of the total number of cells appears on the screen at a time. Scrolling enables you to view other sections of your worksheet, but scrolling does not enable you to view different sections of the worksheet at the same time. You can view different sections of your worksheet at the same time by splitting the screen into panes.

A window can be split into two or four panes. If a window is split horizontally, an additional vertical scroll bar appears on the right side of the window. The additional vertical scroll bar allows the upper and lower panes of the split window to scroll independently.

```
┌──────────────────────────────────────────────────┐
│ ═       Microsoft Excel - Sheet2         ▼  ▲      │
│ ═ │ File  Edit  Formula  Format  Data            │
│    Options  Macro  Window  Help              ♦    │
│ Normal              ▼   ◄ ► ▦ ▦   Σ   B  I        │
│       B2       │ 10000                            │
│          A    │    B     │    C    │  D ▲          │
│  1            │          │         │     ▓         │
│  2  Total Sales │  $10,000 │        │     ▓        │
│  3            │          │         │     ▓         │
│  4  Expenses  │          │         │     ▼         │
│  4  Expenses  │          │         │     ▲         │
│  5  Item A    │  $3,000  │         │     ▓         │
│  6  Item B    │  $2,000  │         │     ▓         │
│  7  Item C    │  $3,500  │         │     ▓         │
│  8            │          │         │     ▼         │
│ ◄ │ │                              │  ► │          │
│ Ready                                             │
└──────────────────────────────────────────────────┘
```

This window is
split horizontally
into two panes.

If a window is split vertically, an additional horizontal scroll bar appears at the
bottom of the window. The additional horizontal scroll bar allows the right
and left panes to scroll independently.

```
┌──────────────────────────────────────────────────┐
│ ═       Microsoft Excel - Sheet2         ▼  ▲      │
│ ═ │ File  Edit  Formula  Format  Data            │
│    Options  Macro  Window  Help              ♦    │
│ Normal              ▼   ◄ ► ▦ ▦   Σ   B  I        │
│       D7                                          │
│       D    │   E   │     B     │    C    │  ▲      │
│  1         │       │           │         │  ▓      │
│  2         │       │  $10,000  │         │  ▓      │
│  3         │       │           │         │  ▓      │
│  4         │       │           │         │  ▓      │
│  5         │       │  $3,000   │         │  ▓      │
│  6         │       │  $2,000   │         │  ▓      │
│  7         │       │  $3,500   │         │  ▼      │
│ ◄ │ │   │ ► │ ◄ │ │      │           │  ►│        │
│ Ready                                             │
└──────────────────────────────────────────────────┘
```

This window is
split vertically
into two panes.

To split the screen using the mouse, follow these steps:

1. Position the mouse pointer on the split bar located directly above the
   up arrow in the vertical scroll bar or directly to the left of the left
   arrow in the horizontal scroll bar. The mouse pointer changes into a
   cross bar when positioned over the split bar. Drag the vertical split bar
   down or the horizontal split bar right. Divider lines appear, indicating
   where the split will occur.

2. Release the mouse button when the split is in the desired location. The screen is split into panes, and each pane has a set of scroll bars.

3. If you want to split the window into four panes, drag both the vertical and horizontal split bars.

To split the screen using the keyboard, follow these steps:

1. Press Alt - (hyphen) to activate the document Control menu.

2. Press T to select the Split command. A four-headed arrow and gray divider lines appear, indicating where the split will occur.

3. Press the arrow keys to move the divider lines.

4. Press ↵Enter when the split is in the desired location.

4

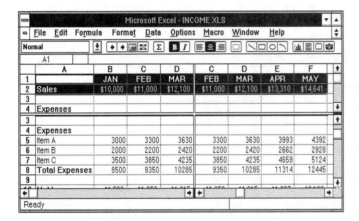

This screen is divided into four panes with two horizontal scrolls and two vertical scrolls.

To return the split screen to a single screen, select the Split command from the document Control menu, or drag the split bars back to their original positions at the edges of the screen.

Freezing a Window Pane

Sometime you might work with a long list of data with titles along the top of the list. As you scroll down toward the end of the list, the titles disappear. Because you cannot see the titles, data entry and interpretation can be difficult, and in some cases impossible.

In the previous section, you learned how to view different sections of a document at the same time by splitting a window into panes. Additional scroll bars enable you to scroll parts of the window independently in a horizontal or vertical direction. However, you may want to prevent one pane from scrolling. This process is referred to as *freezing the pane*. If a pane is frozen, it will not have a scroll bar, and you will not be able to scroll in that pane. The data in the unfrozen pane continues to scroll. This method enables you to scroll through a long list of data and not lose sight of the titles at the top of the list.

4

The screen is split with the top pane frozen. The upper frozen pane remains in place while the lower pane can scroll.

	Microsoft Excel - INCOME.XLS							
File Edit Formula Format Data Options Macro Window Help								
Normal								
D2		12100						
	A	B	C	D	E	F	G	H
1		JAN	FEB	MAR	APR	MAY		
2	Sales	$10,000	$11,000	$12,100	$13,310	$14,641		
3								
4	Expenses							
8	Total Expenses	8500	9350	10285	11314	12445		
9								
10	Net Income	$1,500	$1,650	$1,815	$1,997	$2,196		
11								
12								
13								
14								

Ready

To freeze a pane, follow these steps:

1. Activate the pane that contains the titles or headings you want to remain stationary. Position the cell pointer in the pane you want to activate, and select any cell. Press F6 to move clockwise or ⇧Shift F6 to move counterclockwise to other panes.

2. Choose the Options Freeze Pane command. The scroll bar in the frozen pane disappears, and data displayed in the pane remains stationary.

The **Freeze** command appears in the **Options** menu only when a screen has been split. Once a pane is frozen, the **Freeze** command changes to **Unfreeze**.

To unfreeze a pane, follow these steps:

1. Position the active cell in the frozen pane.

2. Choose the Options Unfreeze command. The scroll bars appear, and you are able to scroll in the pane.

Creating a New Window

The previous section on splitting a screen explained how to view different sections of a worksheet in panes. Panes work well if you display only a small amount of data in the pane. However, you may want to view multiple sections of a document that are too large to be displayed entirely in a pane. When you want to see larger sections of a worksheet, you can create a new window that will enable you to view another section of the document on a separate worksheet. A separate window gives you greater control over the position and size of the window.

To open a new window of the active document, choose the Window New Window command. This command automatically assigns numbers to each window.

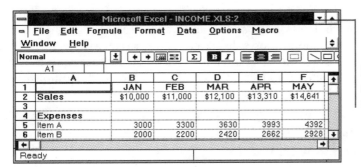

Multiple windows are numbered in the title bar.

In the active window, :1 follows the worksheet title. In the new window, :2 follows the worksheet title. Remember that although you are working with two windows, you are still working with one document. Changes you make in one window are included in the other window. You can open as many new windows as your computer's memory will support.

If one of the document windows is maximized, you will not be able to see the other open windows on the screen. To activate another window, choose the Window menu and select the window name from the list at the bottom of the menu. Press Ctrl+F6 to activate the next window or Ctrl+Shift+F6 to activate the previous window.

To view all open
windows on the
screen at the
same time,
choose the
**Window Arrange
All** command. All
open windows
are tiled on the
screen.

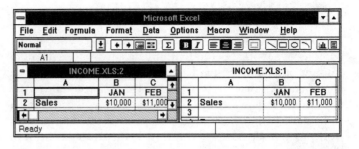

When you are working with multiple windows of a document and choose the
File Close command, all windows of the document close. When you choose
the **File Save** command, Excel saves the changes to the original document
name.

If you arrange several windows on the screen and want to return to that same
display later, you can save the windows displayed on the screen as a
workspace. The **File Save Workspace** command saves the workspace settings
including the window positions and size. Chapter 9, "Working with Multiple
Documents," covers multiple files and how to create a workspace file.

Protecting a Document

Excel has the capability to protect a document from unwanted modification.
You can spend hours building a complex formula that an unfamiliar user can
wipe out with a single key. To prevent accidents like this from happening, you
can turn document protection on or off. If you want a higher level of security,
you can add a password. Users will have to enter this password before they
can turn off the protection.

In Excel, you have the option to protect not only documents from modification, but cells, objects, and windows as well. The protection process generally
requires two steps. First, you specify exactly what you want to protect; then,
you choose the **Options Protect Document** command.

Protecting Cells

To control cell protection, you may want to allow users to change certain cells
even when document protection is turned on. In this case, you will want to
make sure that cell protection for the selected cells is unlocked. You also may

want to hide certain cells that contain proprietary formulas or confidential information. The Format Cell Protection command enables you to turn this option on or off before you protect a document.

Follow these steps to specify cell protection options and use the Options Protect Document command:

1. Select the cells you want to unlock or hide before document protection is turned on.

2. Choose the Format Cell Protection command.

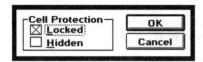

The Cell Protection dialog box appears.

The default settings are Locked turned on and Hidden turned off.

3. If you want, select the check box or press Alt L to turn off the Locked option. Turning off the Locked check box allows users to change the selected cells when document protection is turned on.

4. If you want, select the check box or press Alt H to turn on the Hidden option. Turning on the Hidden check box prevents the selected cell contents from appearing in the formula bar or in the worksheet cell.

5. Choose OK or press ↵Enter.

6. Choose the Options Protect Document command.

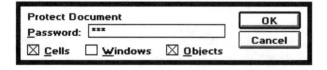

The Protect Document dialog box appears.

7. If you want to add password protection, enter a password in the Password text box. Excel asks you to reenter the password as a confirmation. Be sure you remember the password. Once document protection is turned on, you must enter the password to turn off protection.

The check box options at the bottom of the dialog box control protection of cells, windows, and objects. If the cell protection check box is turned on, none of the cells can be changed, except those cells you selected and unlocked before you turned on document protection. If

103

window protection is turned on, a document window cannot be moved or resized. If object protection is turned on, all graphic objects are prevented from being changed, moved, or resized, except objects that were selected and unlocked prior to turning on document protection.

8. Choose OK or press ⏎Enter to accept the protection settings and turn on document protection.

Turning Off Document Protection

At some point, you will probably have to make a change to a cell that is locked and protected. You will turn off the protection so that you can make changes to the cell.

If document protection is turned on, the Protect Document command on the Options menu changes to Unprotect Document. To turn off document protection, choose the Options Unprotect Document command. If you did not initially use a password to protect the document, the document remains unprotected, and you can resume making changes to the worksheet. If you opted to use password protection, Excel prompts you to enter the correct password to unprotect the document. Enter the password and choose OK or press Enter. If you entered an incorrect password, a dialog box displays the message Incorrect password. Choose OK or press Enter or Esc to clear the dialog box. Select the Options Unprotect Document command again and try to enter the correct password.

Summary

This chapter introduced many fundamental concepts to help you use Excel with greater efficiency. You learned about ranges and how to define a name for a cell or range. You also learned how to create names from existing text, apply names, and change or delete names. Other topics included splitting the screen into panes, freezing a pane, using multiple windows, and protecting a document from unwanted changes.

In this chapter, you were introduced to the following key information about Excel:

■ In the formula bar, a range is referred to by the address of the first cell followed by a colon (:) and the cell address of the last cell in the selection.

■ To make data entry easier, select a range of blank cells. When you enter data in the active cell and press Enter, the data is entered and you move to the next cell.

■ The Formula Define Name command enables you to name a cell or range. A named cell or range is more descriptive than the cell or range address.

■ A name must start with a letter and cannot contain spaces.

■ You can use the Goto command (F5) to select a named range.

■ The Formula Create Names command enables you to create names from existing text in cells at the edge of a selected range.

■ The Formula Apply Names command enables you to select names from a list and apply them to a selected range. If the selected range contains formulas that refer to named cells, the cell addresses are replaced by the selected names.

■ You can use the Formula Define Name dialog box to change a name or the address the name refers to.

■ You can delete a name but should always do so with caution. If a cell contains a formula that refers to a cell or range by name and the name is deleted, the cell will display #NAME?.

■ Splitting the screen enables you to view different sections of a worksheet at the same time.

■ The Freeze Pane command appears on the Options menu when a screen is split into panes. Freezing a pane prevents scrolling and keeps data in the pane stationary.

■ The Window New Window command enables you to view multiple windows of the active document.

■ The Window Arrange All command tiles all open windows on the screen.

■ You can use the Options Protect Document command to protect a document from changes.

■ If you select a range of cells and choose the Format Cell Protection command, you can unlock protection for the selected cells and make changes in those cells even when document protection is turned on.

■ Document protection enables you to protect the document with a password. You must enter the password when you choose to unprotect the document.

Now that you are comfortable with the basic skills for building a worksheet, you are ready to move on to the next chapter. Chapter 5, "Modifying a Worksheet," focuses on making changes to a worksheet, including adding and deleting columns, rows, and cells. You also will learn Excel commands and procedures for copying and moving cell contents. Other topics in Chapter 5 include adjusting column width and row height, finding and replacing cell contents, and converting formulas to values.

4

Modifying a Worksheet

5

The greatest percentage of time spent on worksheets is actually spent making changes to an existing worksheet. Now that you are familiar with some basic worksheet concepts, you are ready to learn the procedures necessary for making changes in a worksheet.

The topics covered in this chapter include moving, copying, and clearing cell contents; inserting and deleting cells, columns, and rows; and changing column width and row height. You also will learn how to make multiple changes throughout a worksheet, and you will learn how to convert formulas to values.

Moving cell contents

Copying cell contents

Clearing and deleting cells

Inserting cells

Working with columns and rows

Converting formulas to values

Key Terms in This Chapter

Clipboard	A temporary storage area for data you have cut or copied.
Marquee	Dashes outlining the area you have cut or copied to the clipboard.
Fill commands	Commands that copy data in the active cell to surrounding cells.
Relative cell reference	A cell address in a formula that adjusts to its new location when copied or moved.
Absolute cell reference	A cell address in a formula that remains the same when copied or moved.
Mixed cell reference	A cell address in which one part is relative and the other part is absolute.
Best Fit	A command that automatically adjusts the column width to the widest cell in the column.

Moving Cell Contents

When a worksheet is created, it is seldom perfect. At some point, a worksheet will require modifications. You may have inserted data in several cells, for example, and then decide that the data should be located elsewhere in the worksheet. Rather than delete the data that you have entered and reenter it in a new location, you can move the data to the new location.

Excel uses the clipboard to temporarily store information you want to move to another location. The **Edit Cut** command enables you to place selected data on the clipboard. Using the **Edit Paste** command, you can paste information you have placed on the clipboard to another location. The clipboard is explained in greater detail in the next section. To place information on the clipboard, follow these steps:

1. Select the data you want to move. Use normal selection procedures.
2. Choose the **Edit Cut** command; or press [Alt], [E], [T] or [⇧Shift][Del].

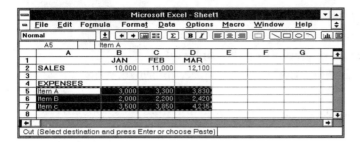

A *marquee* outlines the data that has been placed on the clipboard.

The status line at the bottom of your screen prompts you for the next step.

3. Activate the first cell where you want the data to appear and press ⏎Enter; or choose the Edit Paste command; or press Alt, E, P, or ⇧Shift Ins. The selected data disappears from its original location and appears in the new location.

   Select a single cell to paste data rather than a range. If you select more than one cell for pasting, the range you select must be equal to the range that is on the clipboard.

If the ranges are different sizes, a message dialog box appears.

4. Choose OK or press ⏎Enter or Esc to clear the dialog box.

Understanding the Clipboard

Excel and all other Windows applications use a clipboard to move and copy data. The clipboard is actually a section of your computer's memory that holds information temporarily so that you can move or copy the information. Because the clipboard is memory, information you place on the clipboard is cleared when the computer is turned off.

You can place information on the clipboard and relocate the information to other sections of the current document. You also can relocate information to other documents as well as other applications. The following reminders may help you understand how the clipboard works:

109

- Your computer has only one clipboard for temporary storage.
- You can place only one item on the clipboard at a time.
- You can place text or graphics on the clipboard.
- The **Edit Copy** and **Edit Cut** commands place information on the clipboard.
- The **Edit Paste** command extracts information from the clipboard.

Viewing the Clipboard

5

When you choose the **Edit Cut** or **Edit Copy** command to place selected data on the clipboard, you never actually see the clipboard. In most cases, you immediately paste the data you have cut or copied. If you do want to view the contents of the clipboard, you can access the clipboard from within Excel. These steps explain how to access the clipboard:

1. Select the application Control menu and choose the **Run** command, or press ⌷Alt⌷+**space bar** and press ⌷U⌷.

The Run Applica-
tion dialog box
appears.

2. Select the **Clipboard** option or press ⌷Alt⌷⌷C⌷.

A clipboard
window appears
on the screen; the
window displays
the information
you have placed
on the clipboard.

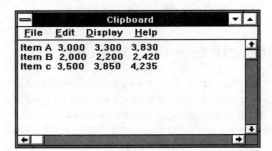

3. Choose the **File Exit** command in the Clipboard window; or press ⌷Alt⌷, ⌷F⌷, ⌷X⌷; or press ⌷Alt⌷⌷F4⌷ or double-click on the Clipboard Control menu bar to close the Clipboard window.

110

You can save the information on the clipboard as a clipboard file. To save the information, choose the **File Save As** command. Enter a name for the file and choose OK or press Enter. Excel will save the information as a clipboard file and assign the extension CLP. You later can retrieve the clipboard file, using the **File Open** command when the clipboard is activated.

Copying Cell Contents

Copying cell contents to the clipboard is similar to moving cell contents. Instead of choosing the **Edit Cut** command, however, you choose the **Edit Copy** command. When you paste the copied information, a copy will appear in the new location, and the original selection remains in its location. To copy information to the clipboard, follow these steps:

1. Select the data you want to copy. Use normal selection procedures.

2. Choose the **Edit Copy** command; or press [Alt], [E], [C], or [Ctrl][Ins]. A marquee outlines the data you have copied to the clipboard. The status line at the bottom of your screen prompts you for the next step.

3. Activate the cell(s) where you want the data to appear and press [↵Enter]; or choose the **Edit Paste** command; or press [Alt], [E], [P], or [⇧Shift][Ins]. A copy of the selected data appears in the new location; the original data remains in the original location.

When you paste data into a cell, any existing data is replaced by the data you paste. If you inadvertently paste over a formula or other important cell contents, choose the **Edit Undo Paste** command immediately after pasting. Excel restores the original data if the paste is undone.

When you copy information to the clipboard, you can paste the information repeatedly by using the **Edit Paste** command. The **Edit Paste** command is available as long as the marquee outlines the copied data. If you paste the copied data by pressing Enter, the marquee that outlines the copied data disappears and the **Edit Paste** command appears dimmed or grayed, indicating that the command is not available. The marquee also disappears if you press the Esc key or if you begin to enter data into a cell.

Copying Formulas to Multiple Cells

If you copy the contents of a single cell, you can select multiple cells and paste the copied data from the single cell into several cells. If you copy more than a single cell, the paste area you select must equal the area of the copied data.

111

If you copy an area of five cells, for example, and you select an area of four cells for pasting, a dialog box displays the message Copy and paste areas are different shapes.

Choose OK or press ↵Enter or Esc to clear the dialog box.

To avoid the problem of unequal copy and paste areas, select a single cell for pasting. When a single cell is selected for pasting, the **Edit Paste** command automatically pastes into an area equal to the copied area. When you select a single cell for pasting, however, you might inadvertently paste over existing data. If you paste over existing data, use the **Edit Undo Paste** command immediately after pasting to reverse the action.

In Excel, you easily can copy a formula from a single cell to multiple cells. In many worksheets, data is organized in a consistent format with formulas built to calculate the data. You may, for example, have several columns of data with a formula in the last row that adds the numbers in each column.

The formula bar displays a formula in cell B11 that subtracts the value in cell B9 from the value in cell B2.

	A	B	C	D	E	F
1		JAN	FEB	MAR		
2	SALES	10,000	11,000	12,100		
3						
4	EXPENSES					
5	Item A	3,000	3,300	3,830		
6	Item B	2,000	2,200	2,420		
7	Item c	3,500	3,850	4,235		
8						
9	Total Expenses	8,500	9,350	10,485		
10						
11	Net Income	1,500				

B11 =B2-B9

112

While summing a range of numbers is not too difficult, some formulas can get very long and complicated. Imagine if you had to enter a long, complex formula repeatedly. Data entry could become very time-consuming and frustrating. Instead, you can use the Edit Copy command to copy a formula to other cells and save a considerable amount of time. In the worksheet example, the user can copy the formula in cell B11 to the other cells, rather than type the formula in each cell. To copy a single cell and paste the formula in several cells, follow these steps:

1. Select the single cell that contains the formula you want to copy.

2. Choose the Edit Copy command; or press ⌐Alt⌐, ⌐E⌐, ⌐C⌐; or press ⌐Ctrl⌐⌐Ins⌐.

3. Select the cells you want to contain the formula.

4. Choose the Edit Paste command; or press ⌐Alt⌐, ⌐E⌐, ⌐P⌐; or press ⌐⇧Shift⌐⌐Ins⌐.

Using Fill Commands

In the previous section, you learned to copy a cell's contents to the clipboard and paste the contents in multiple cells. If you are copying a formula or cell contents to cells that are adjacent to the active cell, you can use Excel's Fill commands for copying. This technique may save you time. Fill commands actually copy the contents of the active cell, or the cell on the outside edge of the selected area, to selected cells that are to the right or below (or to the left or above) the active cell. The Edit menu contains the Fill Right and Fill Down commands. If you hold down the Shift key prior to selecting the Edit menu, the Fill Right and Fill Down commands change to Fill Left (**h**) and Fill Up (**w**), respectively. To fill selected cells with the contents of the active cell, follow these steps:

1. Select the cell that contains the contents you want to copy and the cells to the right, below, left, or above the active cell. (The cell containing the contents to be copied to the other cells must be on the outer edge of the selection.)

The **Edit Fill Right** command copies the formula in the active cell to the selected cells to the right of the active cell.

```
┌─────────────────────────────────────────────────────┐
│ ═         Microsoft Excel - Sheet1          ▼  ▲     │
│ ═  File  Edit  Formula  Format  Data  Options        │
│   Macro  Window   Help                           ↕   │
│ ┌──────────┬─────────────────────────────────────┐  │
│ │ Normal   │  ↓  ← → ▦▦  Σ  B I  ≡ ≣ │           │
│ ├──────────┴─────────────────────────────────────┤  │
│ │    B11        =B2-B9                             │  │
│ │         A         B       C       D         ↑   │  │
│ │  1              JAN     FEB     MAR              │  │
│ │  2  SALES       10,000  11,000  12,100          │  │
│ │  3                                              │  │
│ │  4  EXPENSES                                    │  │
│ │  5  Item A       3,000   3,300   3,830          │  │
│ │  6  Item B       2,000   2,200   2,420          │  │
│ │  7  Item C       3,500   3,850   4,235          │  │
│ │  8                                              │  │
│ │  9  Total Expenses 8,500 9,350  10,485          │  │
│ │ 10                                              │  │
│ │ 11  Net Income   1,500  ██████████████          │  │
│ │ 12                                              │  │
│ │ 13                                         ↓    │  │
│ │ ←                                          →    │  │
│ ├─────────────────────────────────────────────────┤ │
│ │ Ready                                           │  │
│ └─────────────────────────────────────────────────┘ │
```

2. Choose the **Edit** menu. Select the **Fill Right** command if you selected cells to the right of the active cell. Select the **Fill Down** command if you selected cells below the active cell. If you selected cells that are to the left or above the active cell, hold down ⇧Shift when you choose the **Edit** menu. Select the **Fill Left** (**h**) command if you selected cells to the left of the active cell. Select the **Fill Up** (**w**) command if you selected cells above the active cell.

The selected cells are filled with the contents of the active cell.

```
┌─────────────────────────────────────────────────────┐
│ ═         Microsoft Excel - Sheet1          ▼  ▲     │
│ ═  File  Edit  Formula  Format  Data  Options        │
│   Macro  Window   Help                           ↕   │
│ ┌──────────┬─────────────────────────────────────┐  │
│ │ Normal   │  ↓  ← → ▦▦  Σ  B I  ≡ ≣ │           │
│ ├──────────┴─────────────────────────────────────┤  │
│ │    B11        =B2-B9                             │  │
│ │         A         B       C       D         ↑   │  │
│ │  1              JAN     FEB     MAR              │  │
│ │  2  SALES       10,000  11,000  12,100          │  │
│ │  3                                              │  │
│ │  4  EXPENSES                                    │  │
│ │  5  Item A       3,000   3,300   3,830          │  │
│ │  6  Item B       2,000   2,200   2,420          │  │
│ │  7  Item C       3,500   3,850   4,235          │  │
│ │  8                                              │  │
│ │  9  Total Expenses 8,500 9,350  10,485          │  │
│ │ 10                                              │  │
│ │ 11  Net Income   1,500   1,650   1,615          │  │
│ │ 12                                              │  │
│ │ 13                                         ↓    │  │
│ │ ←                                          →    │  │
│ ├─────────────────────────────────────────────────┤ │
│ │ Ready                                           │  │
│ └─────────────────────────────────────────────────┘ │
```

5

114

If the selected cells contained data, the data is cleared and replaced with the contents of the active cell. If you inadvertently replaced existing data, choose the Edit menu and select the Undo Fill command immediately after you do the fill to reverse the action.

Absolute and Relative Cell References

The procedures described earlier explain how to copy a formula to other cells. Please note, however, that when Excel pastes a formula, Excel takes the cell address in the copied formula and makes the cell address relative to the location of the pasted formula. If, for example, a formula in cell B11 displays =B2-B9 and this formula is copied and pasted to cells C11 through F11, the formula in cell C11 displays =C2-C9, cell D11 displays =D2-D9, and so on.

5

The copied formula adjusts to its pasted location.

Cell addresses that automatically adjust to a pasted location are referred to as *relative cell references*. As formulas are entered, Excel assumes you want cell addresses to have relative references. In some cases, however, you will not want to have relative cell references. For example, you may have a formula that refers to a single value in another cell, and regardless of where the formula is pasted, you will want to refer to the value in that particular cell. If you want a cell address to remain the same wherever the copied formula is pasted, you will want to change the cell address from a relative reference to an *absolute cell reference*.

An absolute cell reference is indicated by a dollar sign ($) in front of the column letter and a dollar sign in front of the row number of the cell address. $B$2 is an absolute cell reference. To make a cell reference absolute, enter a dollar sign ($) to the left of the column letter and a dollar sign ($) to the left of the row number of the cell address in the formula bar.

If the formula in cell B11 displays =$B$2-B9 and this formula is copied to other cells, the formula adjusts B9 relative to the pasted location. However, regardless of where the formula is pasted, the first part of the formula always refers to the value in cell B2.

5

The formula copied to cell C11 contains an absolute cell reference that always refers to the value in cell B2.

Using the F4 Function Key

You can change a cell reference by entering a dollar sign ($) in the formula bar, or you can use the F4 function key to change cell references. To change a cell reference using the F4 function key, select the cell address in the formula bar. (If you are not in Edit mode, press F2; the cursor will appear in the formula bar.) Press F4 and the selected cell address will change to reflect another type of cell reference. If you continue to press the F4 key, the cell address will vary each time, displaying the different types of cell references you can use in a formula. The types of cell references include relative, absolute, and two types of mixed cell references. Table 5.1 shows the types of cell references.

116

Table 5.1
Types of Cell References

Cell Reference	Description
A1	Relative cell reference. Formula adjusts to relative location when copied or moved.
$A$1	Absolute cell reference. Formula always refers to this cell regardless of where the formula is copied or moved.
A$1	Mixed cell reference. The formula always refers to row 1. The column adjusts to relative location when copied or moved.
$A1	Mixed cell reference. The formula always refers to column A. The row adjusts to relative location when copied or moved.

Mixed Cell References

In most cases, you either will want to have relative or absolute cell references in a formula. However, sometimes you will want to have the column reference of a cell address remain the same (absolute reference) and the row reference adjust to the relative position of the formula. A mixed cell reference enables you to have this flexibility. To mix cell references, place a dollar sign ($) in front of one cell component and not the other. For example, if you want the column reference to remain the same regardless of where the formula is copied, place a dollar sign in front of the column letter. If you want the row number to adjust depending on the row in which the copied formula is pasted, do *not* place a dollar sign ($) in front of the row number of the cell address.

The formula bar displays a formula in cell D11 using a mixed cell reference. The column reference is absolute. The row reference is relative.

117

Clearing and Deleting Cells

Excel has two separate commands for deleting cell contents and deleting cells. The commands are Edit Clear and Edit Delete. While the two commands sound similar, there is a difference between clearing and deleting a cell. The Edit Clear command is used to clear a cell's contents, including formatting, formulas, and notes. When you clear a cell, the contents are removed, but the cell is still in place on the worksheet. The Edit Delete command actually removes the cell from the worksheet and prompts you to move the surrounding cells to fill the space occupied by the deleted cell.

Part of the confusion with these two commands stems from the fact that the Delete key on your keyboard is assigned to the Edit Clear command. When you press the Delete key, the Edit Clear dialog box appears on your screen.

Clearing Cell Contents

The Edit Clear command provides four options for clearing cells.

The four options
are listed in the
Clear dialog box.

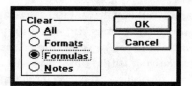

Each option is explained as follows:

All   Clears everything including formatting, formulas, and cell notes.

Formats   Moves any formatting from the cell.

Formulas   Clears formulas and maintains formatting and cell notes.

Notes   Clears only notes attached to the cell.

To clear a cell or range, follow the steps below:

1. Select the cell or range you want to clear.
2. Choose the Edit Clear command; or press Alt, E, A; or press Del.
3. The Clear dialog box appears. Select the option that represents what you want to clear from the cell. Formulas is the default setting.
4. Choose OK or press ↵Enter.

118

Deleting Cells

When you delete cells from the worksheet by choosing the **Edit Delete** command, Excel removes the cells and prompts you to move surrounding cells to fill the space of the deleted cells.

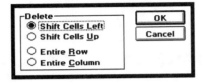

The Edit Delete dialog box appears when you choose the **Edit Delete** command.

The Delete dialog box provides the following four options for moving surrounding cells to fill the space of the deleted cells:

Shift Cells Left	Shifts surrounding cells to the left.
Shift Cells Up	Shifts surrounding cells up.
Shift Entire Row	Shifts entire row up.
Entire Column	Shifts entire column to the left.

To delete a cell or range, follow these steps:

1. Select the cell or range you want to delete.
2. Choose the **Edit Delete** command; or press Alt, E, D; or press Ctrl -(minus). The Delete dialog box appears on the screen.
3. Select the option in the dialog box that represents the direction you want to move the surrounding cells.
4. Choose **OK** or press Enter. Based on the option selected, surrounding cells shift to fill the deleted space.

If you do not want the surrounding cells to move to fill the deleted cells, use the **Edit Clear** command.

Inserting Cells

Inserting cells in a worksheet works the same as deleting cells. The **Edit Insert** command prompts you to move surrounding cells to make space on the worksheet for the new cells and inserts the blank cells. To insert a cell or range, follow these steps:

1. Select the cell or range where you want blank cells to appear.

5

119

Here, cells B2 to
B7 are selected.

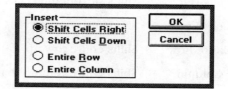

5

2. Choose the Edit Insert command; or press Alt, E, I; or press
   Ctrl + (plus).

The Insert dialog
box appears on
the screen.

```
┌Insert─────────┐      ┌──────────┐
│ ◉ Shift Cells Right │    │    OK    │
│ ○ Shift Cells Down  │    └──────────┘
│                     │    ┌──────────┐
│ ○ Entire Row        │    │  Cancel  │
│ ○ Entire Column     │    └──────────┘
└─────────────────────┘
```

3. Select the option in the dialog box that represents the direction you
   want to move the selected and surrounding cells to make room for the
   additional cells.

4. Choose OK or press ↵Enter. Based on the selected range, blank cells
   appear, and the selected cells and surrounding cells move according
   to the direction indicated in the Insert dialog box.

Selected cells shift
to the right.

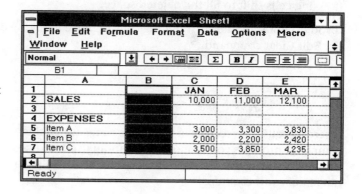

120

Inserting and Deleting Columns and Rows

Inserting and deleting cells takes care of some of your worksheet modifications. Sometimes, however, you will want to insert and delete column(s) and row(s). If you want to create additional space in the middle of a worksheet, you can insert a column or row that runs through the entire length or width of the worksheet. Conversely, if you have a column or row that is no longer necessary, you can delete the column or row rather than delete the cells. Follow these steps for inserting or deleting a column or row:

1. Select the entire column or row by clicking on the column or row heading, or press Ctrl+**space bar** to select the active column or ⇧Shift+**space bar** to select the active row.

2. Choose the **Edit Insert** command, or press Ctrl+ (plus) to insert a blank column or row through the worksheet.

   Choose the **Edit Delete** command, or press Ctrl - (minus) to delete a column or row from the worksheet.

Edit Insert and **Edit Delete** are widely appreciated commands. These commands also can cause problems if you are not careful. Remember that when you are inserting or deleting a column or row, the entire length or width of the worksheet is affected by the change. You may have formulas or data in cells in another section of the worksheet that you cannot see; these cells will be affected by the insertion or deletion. If a formula refers to a cell that has been deleted, the cell containing the formula will display the #REF! error value. To undo a deletion, choose the **Edit** menu and select the **Undo Delete** command immediately after making the deletion. This command reverses the action.

The **Edit Insert** command is a little more adaptable than the **Edit Delete** command. Formulas will adjust for cell address changes when you insert a column or row. However, the command can disorganize areas of the worksheet. Always double-check your worksheet to verify worksheet results when using the **Edit Insert** or **Edit Delete** commands.

Changing Column Width and Row Height

One of the more popular worksheet commands is the command for adjusting the width of a column. When data is in a cell, the data often gets cut off because the column is not wide enough to display the entire cell contents. If a cell cannot display an entire number or date, the cell will be filled with

########. After the column is widened sufficiently, the number or date appears in the cell. You can adjust the column width with the mouse or with the keyboard.

To adjust the column width with the mouse, follow these steps:

1. Select multiple columns by dragging over the column headings. If you are adjusting the width of a single column, this step is not necessary.

2. Position the mouse pointer on the right border of the column heading. The mouse pointer changes to a two-headed horizontal arrow when positioned properly.

3. Drag the arrow right or left to increase or decrease the column width, respectively. A light gray outline indicates the column width. Release the mouse button when the column is at the desired width.

To adjust the column width with the keyboard, follow these steps:

1. Select the active column by pressing Ctrl+space bar. Hold down ⇧Shift and use → or ← to select multiple columns. If you are adjusting the width of a single column, this step is not necessary.

2. Press Alt, T, C to choose the Format Column Width command.

The Column
Width dialog box
appears.

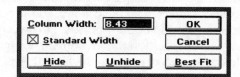

3. Enter the column width in the Column Width text box. (This number represents the column width in characters.)

4. Choose **OK** or press ↵Enter. All selected columns adjust to the new width.

Best Fit Column Width

The Best Fit column width command enables you to automatically adjust the column width to the widest cell in the column. To access the Best Fit command using the mouse, position the mouse pointer on the right border of the column heading and double-click. The column adjusts to the widest cell in the column.

122

To access the Best Fit command using the keyboard, press Alt, T, C to choose the Forma**t** **C**olumn Width command. Press Alt+B to select the Best Fit command button. The active column(s) will adjust to the widest cell in the column.

Row Height

Adjusting a row's height works much the same as adjusting a column's width. You can adjust the row height with the mouse or with the keyboard.

To adjust row height with the mouse, follow these steps:

1. Select multiple rows by dragging over the row headings. If you are adjusting the height of a single row, this step is not necessary.

2. Position the mouse pointer on the bottom border of the row heading. The mouse pointer changes to a two-headed horizontal arrow when positioned properly.

3. Drag the arrow down or up to increase or decrease the row height, respectively. A light gray outline indicates the row height. Release the mouse button when the row is at the desired height.

To adjust the row height using the keyboard, follow these steps:

1. Select the active row by pressing ⇧Shift+**space bar**. Hold down ⇧Shift and use ↑ or ↓ to select multiple rows.

2. Press Alt, T, R to choose the Forma**t** **R**ow Height command.

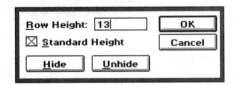

The Row Height dialog box appears.

3. Enter the desired height in the Row Height text box and press ↵Enter. (This number represents the row height in font point size.)

The row adjusts to the new height.

Hiding and Unhiding Columns and Rows

If you want to temporarily hide data that is in a column or row, you can hide the column or row when you do not want the data displayed on-screen or printed. Later, you can unhide the column or row when you want to have the hidden data back in view. The following steps explain how to hide and unhide a column or row:

1. Select the entire column or row by clicking on the column or row heading(s); or press Ctrl+**space bar** to select the active column or ⇧Shift+**space bar** to select the active row. Hold down ⇧Shift and use the arrow keys to select multiple columns or rows.

2. Choose the Format Column Width or Format Row Height command. The appropriate dialog box appears.

3. Choose the Hide button or press Alt H. The active column or row will be hidden from view.

To unhide a column or row, follow these steps:

1. Select the columns or rows bordering the hidden column or row on both sides.

Columns B and D
are selected to
unhide column C.

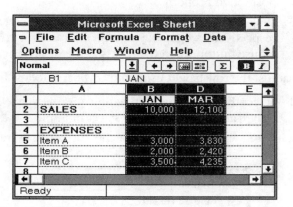

2. Choose the Format Column Width or Format Row Height command.

3. Choose the Unhide button or press Alt U. The unhidden column or row appears.

Finding and Replacing Cell Contents

Excel includes commands for finding specific data and for replacing specific data. The Formula Find command enables you to enter the data you want to find in the worksheet. Excel searches the worksheet until it finds the first cell containing the data. The Formula Replace command searches for the data and enables you to replace the found data with new data.

To use the Formula Find command, follow these steps:

1. Select the range of cells you want to search, or select a single cell if you want to search the entire worksheet.

2. Choose the Formula menu and select the Find command.

5

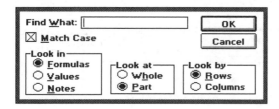

The Find dialog box appears.

3. Enter the data you want to find in the Find What text box.

4. Select the Look at, Look in, and Look by options to control how much of the cell contents must match the data entered in the Find What text box. Select the Match Case check box if you want the data to be sensitive to upper- or lowercase characters.

5. Choose OK or press ⏎Enter. Excel searches forward starting from the active cell. The first cell containing the data that matches the data entered in the Find dialog box is selected.

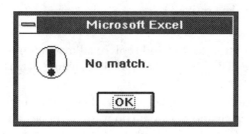

If the worksheet does not contain a match, a dialog box displays No Match. Choose OK or press ⏎Enter or Esc to clear the dialog box.

The Formula Replace command works similarly to the Find command. The Formula Replace command also enables you to replace the found data with new data. The command is beneficial if you have entered a formula in several cells and later the formula changes. You can use the Replace command to replace the old formula with the new formula in all cells containing the formula. To use the Formula Replace command, follow these steps:

1. Select the range of cells you want to search, or select a single cell if you want to search the entire worksheet.

2. Choose the Formula Replace command.

5

The Replace dialog box appears.

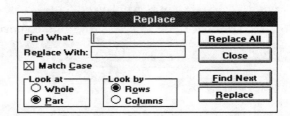

You can move the dialog box on the screen if it is covering data you want to see.

3. Enter the data you want to replace in the Find What text box.

4. Press Alt W or press Tab to select the Replace With text box; enter the text that will replace the current data.

5. Select the Look at and Look by options to control how much of the cell contents must match the data in the Find What text box.

Whole	Data in the Find What text box must match the entire cell contents.
Part	Data in the Find What text box can match part of the cell contents.
Rows	Searches for data by row.
Columns	Searches for data by column.

6. Choose the Replace All button to find and replace all matches in the range or worksheet. The dialog box clears and all matching data is replaced with the new data.

If you want more control over the replacements, choose the Find Next button to look at each match and decide if you want to replace the old data with the new. Choose the Replace button if you want to make the replacement in the found match. Choose the Close button when all replacements have been completed, or press Alt F4 or Esc to close the dialog box. If the worksheet does not contain a match for the data in the Find What text box, a dialog box displays the message No Match.

If you make a mistake with the replacement of data, close the Replace dialog box and choose the Edit Undo Replace command immediately. All replacements will be reversed to the original data.

Converting Formulas to Values

In previous sections of the book, you were introduced to formulas. You learned that the result of a formula, or the formula's value, is displayed in the cell, and the formula that is actually in the cell is displayed in the formula bar. Sometimes you will not be concerned with the formula after you have the value of the formula. If you want the formula to be a value in both the cell and the formula bar, you can convert the formula to its actual value. You can use one of two methods to convert a formula to its actual value. The first method converts a formula to its actual value in a single cell. The second method converts formulas to values in a range.

Converting a Single Cell

To convert a formula in a single cell to a value, follow these steps:

1. Select the cell containing the formula.
2. Press F2 to activate the formula bar.
3. Choose the Options Calculate Now command. The result of the formula replaces the formula in the formula bar.
4. Press ↵Enter and the formula is replaced by its value.

Converting a Range

To convert formulas in a range to values, follow these steps:

1. Select the range containing formulas you want to convert to values.
2. Choose the Edit Copy command. A marquee surrounds the selected range.
3. Choose the Edit Paste Special command.

The Paste Special
dialog box
appears.

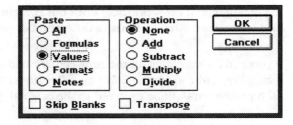

4. Choose the Values option button.

5. Choose **OK** or press ↵Enter. All cells in the range containing formulas are replaced with values.

Summary

This chapter covered many important worksheet features that are necessary for moving and copying data. You also learned step-by-step procedures for inserting and deleting cells, rows, and columns. Additionally, you learned to adjust the column width and row height. The chapter concluded with details for finding and replacing cell contents and converting formulas to values.

In this chapter, you were introduced to the following key information about Excel:

- The **Edit Cut** command enables you to move data from one location to another.

- The clipboard temporarily stores data you have cut or copied.

- The **Edit Paste** command enables you to retrieve data you have cut or copied to the clipboard.

- The **Edit Copy** command enables you to duplicate selected data. Copied data can be pasted more than once using the **Edit Paste** command.

- The application Control menu has a **Run** command that enables you to open the clipboard and view its contents.

- The **Edit Fill** commands enable you to copy the contents of the active cell to selected cells that are adjacent to the active cell. You can fill data down, right, up, or left. The Edit Fill Up (**w**) and Fill Left (**h**) commands appear on the **Edit** menu when you hold down the Shift key prior to choosing the **Edit** menu.

- A relative cell reference in a formula refers to a cell address that adjusts to its new location when the formula is copied or moved.

- An absolute cell reference in a formula refers to a cell address that remains the same regardless of where the formula is copied or moved. An absolute cell reference is indicated by a dollar sign ($) in front of the column address and a dollar sign in front of the row address.

- A mixed cell reference has one part of the cell address relative and the other part of the cell address absolute. Either the row address or column address is preceded by a dollar sign ($) to indicate which part is absolute.

- The Edit Clear command clears the cell contents; the Edit Delete command actually deletes the cell from the worksheet and shifts the surrounding cells to fill the space.

- The Delete key on your keyboard is assigned to the Edit Clear command, which clears cell contents.

- The Edit Clear command enables you to clear formulas, formats, cell notes, or everything from the selected cell(s).

- You can use the Edit Insert and Edit Delete commands to insert and delete cells, columns, or rows.

- You can select a column or row by clicking on the column or row heading.

- Inserting or deleting columns or rows affects the entire worksheet. You may accidently delete worksheet data or insert blank cells through sections of data that are out of view.

- A double-click on the right border of a column heading will automatically adjust the column width to the widest cell in the column.

- A cell will contain ####### if the column is not wide enough to display a number or date.

- You can adjust row height by dragging the bottom border of the row heading, or you can choose the Format Row Height command and enter the desired height.

- The Format Column Width and Format Row Height commands enable you to hide or unhide a column or row. To unhide a column or row, select the columns or rows that border the hidden column or row.

- The Formula Replace command searches cells to find specified data and enables you to replace the found data with new data.

- The Options Calculate Now command enables you to convert a single formula to its value. The Edit Paste Special command enables you to convert a range of copied formulas to their values.

5

129

Now that you are comfortable with the basics for modifying a worksheet, you are ready to move on to Chapter 6. Chapter 6, "Formatting a Worksheet," will introduce you to Excel features that enhance the appearance of your worksheet. You will learn how to format numbers, text, and cells. You also will learn how to create and format objects using the tool bar and the multiple formatting commands.

5

Formatting a Worksheet

This chapter deals with all aspects of the appearance of your worksheet. Whenever you format something, you change the appearance of it. If you change the format of text to bold, for example, you change the appearance of the text. When spreadsheets were first introduced, the end result was dull. Data appeared in a grid of rows and columns, and about the only formatting option was the alignment of text in a cell. Today you can produce a high-quality worksheet that includes text, graphics, colors, arrows, patterns, borders, and multiple fonts.

In Excel 3.0, Microsoft added a tool bar that enables you to draw objects, charts, and text boxes on a single worksheet. Icons on the tool bar enable you to make text bold, italicized, and centered. Multiple formatting commands have been added to enhance cells and objects with borders and patterns. You are no longer limited to using a worksheet just for analyzing data. Excel 3.0 now has presentation capabilities that produce impressive results.

This chapter covers formatting numbers, aligning cell contents, justifying cell contents, and changing fonts, cell borders, and patterns. This chapter also covers the tool bar in detail and concludes with procedures for creating a style.

Formatting numbers

Aligning cell contents

Changing fonts

Justifying paragraphs

Formatting cells

Key Terms in This Chapter

Formatting	The process of changing the appearance of text, numbers, cells, or objects.
Predefined formats	Formats that have already been created and that come standardized with Excel.
Custom format	A special format created by an individual user.
Tool bar	A group of icons, representing formatting commands and other Excel tools for enhancing a worksheet.
Objects	Graphical drawings created with tools from the tool bar.
Style	A combination of formatting commands.

6

Formatting Numbers

Because numbers are the most common items on a worksheet, Excel offers a variety of predefined formatting options you can apply to numbers. You may want a number to appear with a certain number of decimals in some cases and with no decimals in other places on the same worksheet. You may also want to express negative numbers in red or in parentheses. Often you may want to display currency symbols without having to type the symbol every time you enter a number. When you enter numbers, you do not need to be concerned with the way they look initially. After you have completed your entries, you can apply formatting to numbers to improve the way they look.

Follow these steps to format numbers:

1. Select the cells containing numbers you want to format.
2. Choose the Format Number command.

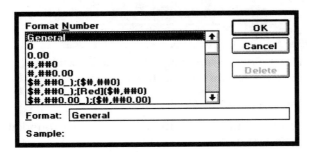

A dialog box appears, displaying a list of predefined number formats.

3. Use the scroll bar or ⬆ or ⬇ to move through the Format Number list. Select the format you want from the list. A sample of the selected format appears in the bottom section of the dialog box.

4. Choose **OK** or press ↵Enter. The selected format is applied to the selected cells.

Creating a Custom Number Format

After you choose the Format Number command, you see a list of predefined formats. Date and time formats are included at the end of the list. The list includes most of the common number formats. You may, however, have specific needs that require a number format that is not in the list. You may want a word or other text to appear after a number, for example. Excel enables you to create custom number formats to meet your specific needs. To create a custom format, refer to the formatting symbols outlined in table 6.1.

Table 6.1
Custom Number-Formatting Symbols

Symbol	Function
General	Default format for unformatted cells.
0	Placeholder for numbers. Uses extra zeros on either side of the decimal to force numbers to match the selected format. If the format chosen indicates two decimals, for example, .5 appears as .50.

continues

133

Table 6.1 *(continued)*

Symbol	Function
#	Placeholder for numbers. Does not use zeros to force the number to match the format.
. (decimal)	Placeholder for decimal point.
, (comma)	Separates numbers by thousands when surrounded by # or 0.
% (percentage)	Multiplies entry by 100 and displays number with a % sign.
E– E+ e– e+	Displays number in scientific notation, with E or e indicating the size of the exponent.
: $ – + () space	Displays the specified character.
\	Displays only the character following the backslash.
"text"	Displays the text contained in quotes.
*	Fills the remaining column width with the next character.
@	Places text at the location of the @ in the format.
?	Placeholder for digits. Spaces are inserted in place of insignificant zeros so that numbers still align correctly.
_(underscore)	Skips the width of the character following the underscore. Allows positive numbers to align correctly with negative numbers enclosed in (). For example, entering a _) at the end of a positive number format inserts a blank that is the width of the).
/ (slash)	Serves as a separator in fractions when a decimal fraction or a leading integer followed by a fraction is entered.
[color]	Displays cell contents in specified color.
[condition value]	Uses conditional statements, such as <, >, =, >=, <=, and <> within the number format to determine when a format will be used.

134

To create a custom number, follow these steps:

1. Choose the Format Number command.

2. To create a custom format that closely matches one of the predefined formats, select the predefined format. The formatting symbols appear in the Format text box, and a sample appears below the text box.

3. Select the Format text box or press [Alt][F]. The cursor appears in the text box. Use normal editing procedures to edit the selected format, or delete the selected format and create the custom format starting with a blank text box.

Table 6.1 lists the symbols used for custom formats.

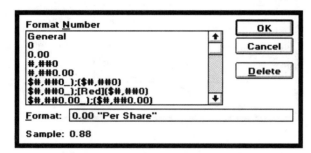

The custom format in the Format text box has been defined to display the text Per Share after a two-decimal number that has a zero in front of the decimal.

6

4. Choose OK or press [↵Enter]. The custom format appears at the end of the Format Number list. You can select and delete custom formats from the list. You cannot delete an Excel number format.

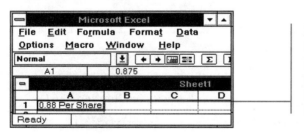

This is how the entered number .875 appears after custom formatting has been applied.

Date and Time Formats

If you enter 1-1-91 in a cell, Excel assumes that you are entering a date. The cell displays the number in a date format. (The default date format is 1/1/91.) If you enter 9:45, Excel assumes that you are referring to a time and displays a time format. To change to another date or time format, you can use the Format Number command to choose another format. The procedure for changing a date or time format is the same as changing a number format. The date and time formats are listed after the number formats. The time formats follow the date formats.

A list of some of the predefined date and time formats appears in the Format Number dialog box.

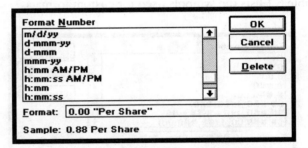

You can create custom date and time formats using the same procedures outlined for creating a custom number format. The only difference is that you use date and time symbols to create the custom format. The symbols for date and time are listed in table 6.2.

Table 6.2
Date and Time Symbols

Symbol	Format
m	Month as a number with no leading zeros (1–12).
mm	Month as a number with leading zeros (01–12).
mmm	Month as a three-letter abbreviation (Jan–Dec).
mmmm	Month as a full name (January–December).
d	Day of month as a number with no leading zeros (1–31).
dd	Day of month as a number with leading zeros (01–31).

Symbol	Format
ddd	Day of week as a three-letter abbreviation (Sun–Sat).
dddd	Day of week as a full name (Sunday–Saturday).
yy	Year as a two-digit number (00–99).
yyyy	Year as a four-digit number (1900–1999).
h	Hour with no leading zeros (0–23).
hh	Hour with leading zeros (00–23).
m	Minute with no leading zeros (0–59).
mm	Minute with leading zeros (00–59). If this format does not appear after the hour format, Excel functions as if you are referring to a month format.
s	Second with no leading zeros (0–59).
ss	Second with leading zeros (00–59).
AM/am/A/a	Displays the selected format from midnight until noon.
PM/pm/P/p	Displays the selected format from noon until midnight.

6

The shortcut keys for entering the current date and time and for applying a date format and time format are as follows:

Ctrl+; (semicolon)	Current date
Ctrl+: (colon)	Current time
Ctrl+#	Date format d-mmm-yy
Ctrl+@	Time format h:mm AM/PM

Aligning Cell Contents

Data appearing in a cell can be aligned to the left, right, or center of the cell. You can apply alignment formatting using the tool bar or the Format Alignment command. The steps for aligning data in a cell using both methods are outlined in the text that follows.

To align text using the tool bar, follow these steps:

1. Select the cell or range you want to align.

2. Click on the tool icon that represents the alignment you want to apply to the selection.

The three Align-
ment icons are
located on the
tool bar.

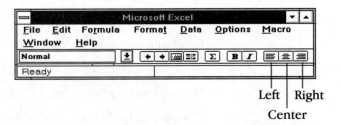

Left   Right

Center

To align text using the Format Alignment command, follow these steps:

1. Select the cell or range you want to align.

2. Choose the Format Alignment command.

The Format
Alignment dialog
box appears.

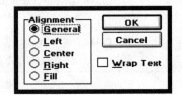

3. Choose General or press (Alt)(G) to align text to the left and numbers to the right. Choose Left, Center, or Right to align text or numbers accordingly. Choose Fill to fill the entire cell with the cell contents. Select the Wrap Text check box or press (Alt)(W) to make text wrap according to the width of the cell.

4. Choose OK or press (↵Enter).

Changing Fonts

In earlier versions of Excel for Windows, you were limited to four font choices. With Excel 3.0 you can use up to 256 fonts. Fonts are listed in a dialog box from which you can select a font type, choose a size for the selected font, and apply a style.

To change a font, follow these steps:

1. Select a cell, a range, or the entire worksheet. (To select the entire worksheet, click in the area intersecting the column and row headings, or press [Ctrl] [⇧Shift] +space bar.)

2. Choose the Format Font command.

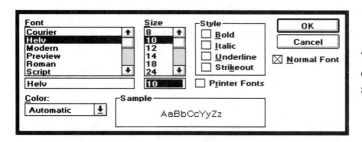

The Format Font dialog box appears.

3. Select the options you want to apply. Select the type of font you want from the Font list. The sizes available for the selected font appear in the Size list. Select the size you want, and select the Style check boxes that you want to apply to the selection. Select the Color list by clicking on the down arrow to display the list, or press [Alt] [C] and [Alt] [↓]. Use [↑] and [↓] to select a color from the list. The sample area of the dialog box shows you what the selected options look like.

    Note: Many fonts can be displayed on your screen but cannot be printed by your printer. If your printer cannot print a font that has been selected, it tries to match the font with the closest printer font available. To avoid problems with selecting fonts that your printer does not support, turn on the Printer Fonts check box. (Select the box or press [Alt] [R] so that an X appears in the box.) When the Printer Fonts check box is turned on, only fonts supported by your printer appear in the Font list.

    If the Normal Font check box is turned on, the default font and size are applied to the selection.

4. Choose OK or press [↵Enter] to apply the formatting and close the Format Font dialog box.

Justifying Paragraphs

Although spreadsheet applications were not intended to handle word processing tasks, some users try to incorporate large text entries in worksheet cells.
For those users, the Format Justify command comes in handy. The Format
Justify command enables you to select long text entries and spread the text
over a selected area. The long text entries are easier to edit if they are organized as paragraphs in a defined area. To enter text into a cell that stretches
over five columns and to confine this text to an area of three columns and
three rows, follow these steps:

1. Select the cell or range containing the text plus the columns and rows
   you want to define as the area for justification.

The selected area
defines how the
text will be
justified.

2. Choose the Format Justify command. The selected text is divided to fill
   the defined area.

This text has been
justified.

140

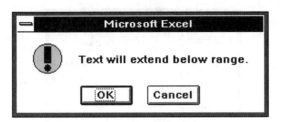

If the defined area is not large enough to hold the justified text, Excel displays an alert message.

If you choose OK, the text will extend beyond the defined area. If the text spills over into cells containing text, the existing text will move down to accommodate the justified text. If the text spills over into cells that contain numbers or formulas, however, the text will overwrite the numbers or formulas in the cells. If you accidentally overwrite cells containing numbers or formulas, choose the **E**dit Undo command immediately to reverse the Justification command.

With Excel 3.0, you can use the text box on the tool bar to create large blocks of text. In many cases, the text box provides a better method for working with long entries. Text that is entered in a text box automatically wraps according to the width of the text box, and the text adjusts when the text box is resized. The Text Box tool is covered in more detail later in this chapter.

Formatting Cells

So far most of this chapter has dealt with formatting numbers or text. This section deals specifically with applying cell formats. Applying cell formats includes adding a border around a cell or range of cells and filling a cell with a color or pattern.

The Border dialog box controls placing borders around a cell and placing a single or double underline below a series of numbers.

To apply a border to a cell or selected range, follow these steps:

1. Select the cell or range you want to format.

2. Choose the Format **B**order command.

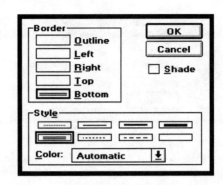

The Border dialog
box appears.

3. Choose the placement of the border by selecting Outline, Left, Right,
   Top, or Bottom. The Outline option puts a border around the outer
   edges of the selection. The Left, Right, Top, and Bottom options
   enable you to put a border along the specified edges of each cell in the
   selection.

   From the style area, select the type of border you want. On the keyboard, press [Alt][E] and use the arrow keys to select a style from the
   eight styles. To change the color of the border, choose the Color list by
   clicking on the down arrow, or press [Alt][C] and [Alt][↓] to display the
   list of colors. Select the Shade check box to make the selected cells
   shaded.

4. Choose OK or press [↵Enter].

In addition to adding borders to cells, you can enhance a cell with patterns
and colors. The Format Patterns dialog box enables you to choose foreground
and background colors and a pattern.

To format a cell with colors and patterns, follow these steps:

1. Select the cell or range you want to format.

2. Choose the Format Patterns command.

The Cell Shading
dialog box
appears.

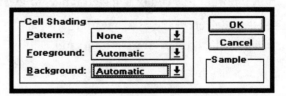

142

3. Choose the Pattern drop-down list by clicking on the down arrow. Press `Alt` `P` followed by `Alt` `↓` to display the list of patterns using the keyboard. Follow the same procedure for selecting the Foreground color list and the Background color list. If the foreground and background colors are the same, the cell displays a solid color. The sample box in the lower right corner of the dialog box shows you what the formatting looks like.

4. Choose **OK** or press `↵Enter`.

If you do not like the formatting you have chosen after it has been applied, select the **Edit Undo** formatting command before proceeding with another command. If you like the formatting and want to apply the same formatting to another area, select the new area and choose the **Edit Redo** formatting command immediately after the formatting has been applied.

Using the Tool Bar

The tool bar in Excel 3.0 enables you to create objects using the Drawing tools, to use text boxes for word processing, to view data in outline format, to apply formatting and styles, and to create pictures of worksheet data, charts, and buttons.

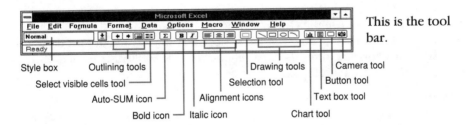

This is the tool bar.

The tool bar is one example of what graphical computing is all about. Although most of the icons on the tool bar represent Excel commands that also can be accessed from the menus, the tools on the tool bar itself can be accessed only with the mouse. Because Excel commands do not exist for drawing objects, buttons, or text boxes, you can use these tools only if you access them from the tool bar with the mouse.

The following sections cover some of the tool bar items that enable you to format a worksheet. The topics that follow include applying formatting, aligning data, drawing and formatting objects, moving and sizing objects, using a text box, and creating and applying a style.

Applying Formatting

In previous sections of this chapter, you learned that you can apply bold or italic formatting to text or numbers using the Format Font command. A much faster way to accomplish this task is to use the tool bar. Select the cells you want to format and choose the Bold icon to make the selection bold, or the Italic icon to make the selection italicized. If the formatting is turned on, the icon on the tool bar changes color, indicating that the option is turned on. If you decide that you do not want the formatting, select the icon again, and the formatting turns off, and the icon returns to its normal color.

The Format Alignment command provides you with options for making data centered, left-aligned, or right-aligned. These same options are available on the tool bar. From left to right, the three Alignment icons are the following: Left-aligned, Centered, and Right-aligned. The Alignment icons toggle on and off just as the Bold and Italic icons do.

Creating Objects

You easily can enhance a worksheet by adding objects to it. You may, for example, want to create a graphic, picture, or drawing using Excel's Drawing tools. Before you can draw objects, such as circles, squares, rectangles, lines and arcs, the tool bar must be turned on. Excel is set with the tool bar turned on. However, you can use the Options Workspace command to turn off the tool bar. The Workspace dialog box has a check box for turning on or off the tool bar. If an X appears in the Tool bar check box, the tool bar is turned on. You also can turn on and off the tool bar by pressing Ctrl+7.

The tool bar provides you with four Drawing tools, which are represented by icons. They are the Line, Rectangle, Oval, and Arc. When you combine them with the Shift key, the Rectangle and Oval icons can be used to create squares and circles, respectively. After you create objects, you can move, resize, and format them with color, patterns, and borders.

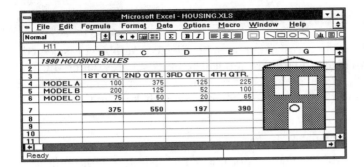

The house on this worksheet was created with the Drawing tools on the tool bar.

To create an object, follow these steps:

1. Select the Drawing tool that represents the object you want to create on your worksheet. The Drawing tool icon changes color when you select it. When you then position the mouse in the worksheet area, the mouse pointer changes to a small cross.

2. Position the cross in the area of the worksheet where you want to start drawing and click the left mouse button.

3. Drag the mouse until the object is the size you want and release the mouse button.

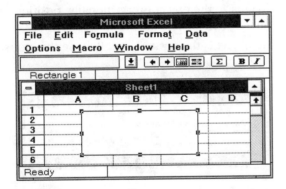

Black squares appear around this object, indicating that the object is selected and can be moved or resized.

6

Moving and Resizing Objects

For an object to be moved or resized, it must be selected. An object is selected when it appears with black squares around it. The black squares define the boundaries of the object and are used for resizing. To select an object, position the mouse pointer (arrow) next to the object and click the left mouse button once.

To move an object, follow these steps:

1. Select the object. Black squares appear around the object, indicating that the object is selected.

2. Position the mouse pointer inside the boundaries of the object and click the left mouse button.

3. Drag the object to the desired location and release the mouse button.

To resize an object, follow these steps:

1. Select the object. Black squares appear around the object. (These squares serve as handles for resizing the selected object.)

2. Position the mouse pointer on one of the black handles. The mouse pointer changes to a cross when properly positioned. To make the object wider or longer, position the mouse pointer over one of the middle handles. To resize the object proportionally, position the mouse pointer on one of the corner handles.

3. Drag the handle until the object is the desired size. Release the mouse button.

The rectangle object is being resized.

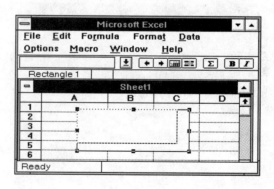

146

Formatting Objects

After an object is selected, you can format it by double-clicking on the object or using the Format **P**atterns command. Follow these steps to add color, patterns, or borders to an object:

1. Double-click on the object you want to format, or select the object and choose the Format **P**atterns command.

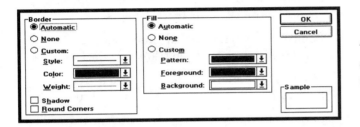

The Patterns dialog box appears.

2. Select from the dialog box the options you want to apply. The options are described in the following paragraph, and the custom features are detailed in table 6.3. The sample area in the lower right corner of the dialog box shows what the formatting will look like.

3. Choose **OK** or press ⏎Enter to apply the selected formatting and close the dialog box.

The Format Patterns dialog box is divided into two sections. The section on the left is the Border section, and it controls the type of border applied to the selected object. The section on the right is the Fill section, and it controls the area inside the border. The options available in both sections include Automatic, None, and Custom. Automatic applies the default settings, None means that the border or the inside area is invisible, and Custom enables you to select from three drop-down lists the specific options that you want to apply to either the border or the area inside the border.

The sample area in the lower right corner of the dialog box shows you how each choice looks.

If the selected object is a square or rectangle, two check boxes appear in the lower left corner of the dialog box. These check boxes enable you to have rounded corners or a shadow around the rectangle or square. Select the check box or press Alt+R or Alt+H to turn on rounded corners and shadows, respectively.

6

Table 6.3
Custom Options for Border and Fill

Option	Function
Border Style	Controls the style of the line or border. Enables you to choose from styles such as solid, dotted, and patterned.
Border Color	Controls the color of the line or border. Enables you to choose from a palette of colors.
Border Weight	Controls the thickness of the line or border. Enables you to choose a fine line or a thick line.
Fill **Pattern**	Controls the pattern inside the selected area. Enables you to choose from a list of patterns.
Fill **Foreground**	Controls the foreground color of the pattern or fills the selected object with a solid color if a pattern is not chosen. Enables you to choose from a palette of colors.
Fill **Background**	Controls the background color of the pattern or fills the selected object with a solid color if a pattern is not chosen. Enables you to choose from a palette of colors.

In this example, a rectangle is formatted with a thick border, a pattern on the inside, and rounded corners.

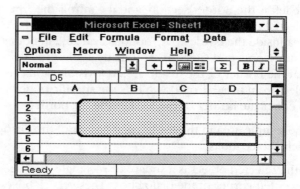

If a line is created and selected for formatting, the Format Patterns dialog box replaces the Fill section with an Arrow Head section. This section enables you to convert a line into an arrow.

148

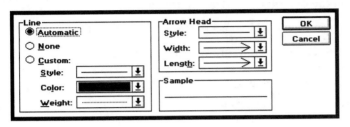

This dialog box shows the Arrow Head options available after a line is selected for formatting. The Style, Width, and Length options control the appearance of the arrow head.

Grouping Objects

If you are creating a graphic or picture, you might draw several separate objects. If you want to work with multiple objects as a single object, you can group the objects into a single object. To group objects, you must first select all the objects you want to group as a single object. To select multiple objects, hold down the Shift key as you point and click. To select multiple objects with the tool bar, use the Selection tool. The Selection tool is the single rectangular icon between the Alignment tools and the Drawing tools. If you choose the Selection tool and click and drag in the worksheet area, a light border appears on the screen, outlining the area you are selecting. If you drag over an area containing multiple objects, you select all objects inside the selection area.

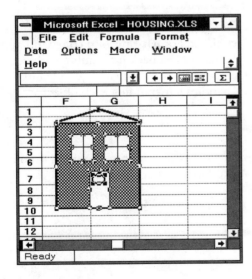

Here, multiple objects were selected with the Selection tool. You can format, move, and size multiple objects just as you do a single object.

149

To convert several objects into one object, you can select all objects that you want to be included in the one object and group them.

Follow these steps to convert multiple objects into a single object:

1. Select the objects that you want to group as a single object. Use the Selection tool on the tool bar, or hold down [⇧Shift] as you select each object with the mouse pointer.

2. Choose the Format Group command.

6

All selected objects appear as one object, with black handles outlining the area of the single object.

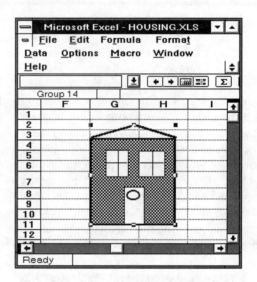

If a single grouped object is selected, the Format Ungroup command appears on the Format menu. To break a single object back into multiple objects, select the grouped object and choose the Format Ungroup command. Individual objects appear, with black handles surrounding each object.

Protecting Objects

When you turn on document protection, you can protect objects from being changed. Choose the **Options P**rotect Document command.

150

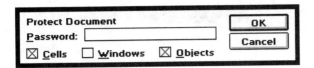

The Protect Document dialog box appears.

Select the **Objects** check box to prevent users from changing objects in the protected document. If the **Objects** check box is turned on, you cannot format, move, or size objects when document protection is turned on.

To have document protection turned on and still be able to change certain objects, you can unlock protection for selected object(s). You must unlock protection for objects before you turn document protection on. Select the object and choose the Format Object Protection command. If document protection is turned on, this command is dimmed.

The Object Protection dialog box appears.

Select the Locked check box to turn off object protection, and choose OK or press Enter. The selected objects are free of protection (these objects can be changed) when document protection is turned on. For more details on protecting a document, refer to the section in Chapter 4 titled "Protecting a Document."

Creating a Text Box

Before the invention of the text box, word processing in Excel was a bit cumbersome. Using the Text Box tool now makes word processing in a worksheet much easier. Select the Text Box tool and drag in the worksheet area to create a box of any size. After you release the mouse button, the cursor appears in the upper left corner of the text box, ready to accept the text you type. The text wraps according to the size of the box, just as word wrap functions in all word processors.

151

In this text box, text wraps within the box.

6

You can format, move, and resize a text box like any other object on a worksheet. When you resize a text box, the text automatically wraps to fit the new size of the box. You can apply formatting to all of the text in the text box or to individual words. If you want to make all the text bold, for example, select the text box and click on the Bold icon on the tool bar. If you want to make a single word inside the text box bold, move the mouse pointer inside the text box. The mouse pointer changes to an I-beam. Select the text you want to format by dragging the I-beam over the text. As long as the cursor appears inside the text box, you can use normal editing procedures.

You can select and move most objects on a worksheet by positioning the mouse pointer (arrow) inside the object. When the mouse pointer is positioned inside a text box, however, the pointer changes to an I-beam. To select and move a text box, position the mouse pointer (arrow) on the border of the text box.

Creating and Applying a Style

If you find yourself applying the same formatting to text over and over, you may want to save yourself a few keystrokes by creating a style that applies all the formatting with a single command. If, for example, you always make your titles Helvetica, 14-point, bold, and centered, you can create a style that applies all four formats for you. You can create a style by defining it in the Format Style dialog box, or you can create a style by selecting an example of the style you want to create. The two methods are outlined in the steps that follow.

152

To create a style by defining it in the Format Style dialog box, follow these steps:

1. Choose the Format Style command.

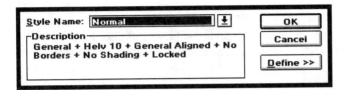

The Style dialog box appears, displaying the current style and a description of it.

2. Enter a name in the Style Name box for the style you want to create. Normal is the default style.

3. Choose the Define button.

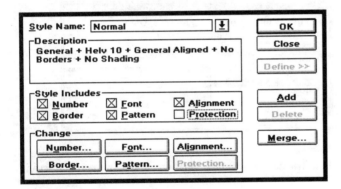

The dialog box expands to display the various formatting attributes.

4. In the Style Includes section, turn off the check boxes for the attributes you do not want to have in the style. As you turn off a check box, the attribute disappears from the description box. The check boxes correspond to the buttons below them in the Change section. If an attribute is turned off, the corresponding button is dimmed and unavailable.

5. Choose the button for the attribute that you want to change. The dialog box for the selected attribute appears.

6. Enter the changes you want to make. Choose OK or press ↵Enter to clear the attribute dialog box and return to the Style dialog box.

153

7. Choose **OK** or press [⏎Enter] after you have made all the necessary style changes. The dialog box closes, and the style is applied to any selected cells.

To create a style by example, follow these steps:

1. Select a cell containing the style you want to create.

2. Select the current style name in the Style list box on the tool bar, or choose the Format Style command and enter the name in the Style Name list box.

3. If you are using the tool bar, enter a name that identifies the selected style in the Style box and press [⏎Enter]. If you are using the Format Style command, enter the name in the Style Name box and choose **OK** or press [⏎Enter] The format is now defined and appears on the Style list.

After you create a style, the name of the style appears on the drop-down list in the Style menu on the tool bar.

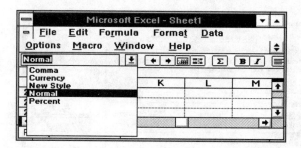

The name of the style also appears on the drop-down Style list in the Format Style dialog box.

To apply a style that has been created, follow these steps:

1. Select the cell or range to which you want to apply the style.

2. Click the down arrow to the right of the Style menu on the tool bar; or choose the Format Style command and click the down arrow to the right of the Style Name box or press [Alt][↓]. A list of defined styles appears.

3. Select the name of the style you want to apply from the list. If you are using the tool bar Style menu, the style is applied to the selected cell or range. If you are using the Format Style command, choose **OK** or press [⏎Enter] to clear the dialog box and apply the style to the selection.

Summary

This chapter dealt specifically with commands and features that enable you to improve the appearance of your worksheets. You learned about number formats, including date and time formats, and how to create custom number formats. You were introduced to formatting commands for alignment of text, changing fonts, and justification. The tool bar was explained, and you learned how to use the Drawing tools to create objects. You also learned how to format, move, resize, group, and ungroup objects. Finally, you learned how to use the text box to do word processing tasks, and you learned how to create and apply a style.

In this chapter, you were introduced to the following key information about Excel:

■ The Format Number command enables you to select from a list of predefined number, date, and time formats. You also can create custom number formats.

■ The Format Alignment command enables you to choose the Wrap text option so that cell contents wrap according to the column width.

■ The Format Font command enables you to change fonts and select a style and color for the font.

■ Turn on the Printer Fonts check box in the Format Font dialog box so that only fonts that are supported by your printer appear in the Font list.

■ You can add a cell border to put a single or double underline below a series of numbers.

■ The tool bar is a graphical representation of many Excel commands. You can access it only by using the mouse.

■ You can use the Drawing tools from the tool bar to create objects in the worksheet. The mouse is needed to create objects.

■ Multiple objects can be selected and grouped as a single object. If a grouped object is selected, the Format Ungroup command appears under the Format menu.

■ Double-clicking on an object brings up the Patterns dialog box, which enables you to format the border or the area inside the border.

■ The Format Object Protection command enables you to unlock selected objects when document protection is turned on.

■ You can only create a text box by using the Text Box tool on the tool bar. Text entered in a text box wraps according to the width of the box. A text box is an object, and it can be moved and resized.

6

155

■ Creating a style enables you to combine several formatting attributes and define and name a custom style. You then can apply the style to a selected cell or range.

■ You can apply a style from the Style drop-down list on the tool bar or from the Format Style dialog box.

The next chapter introduces you to Excel's Formula Paste Function command. This command enables you to access a list of over 140 built-in functions. Functions are predefined formulas that can save considerable time and increase accuracy in a worksheet that requires specific calculations. Chapter 7 explains what a function is, the various types of functions, and what each built-in function does.

6

Using Functions

Excel was designed with more than 130 built-in formulas called *functions*. A function is a predefined formula that will calculate selected data. You do not have to enter mathematical operators as you do with a formula. In many cases, entering a function rather than a formula saves you time and increases the accuracy of the results. You also can insert a function into a formula.

This chapter discusses what a function is, entering a function, and types of functions. The types of functions included in Excel range from simple mathematical functions for summing a group of numbers to complex trigonometric functions.

What is a function?

Entering a function

Types of functions

Key Terms in This Chapter

Function   A predefined formula consisting of a name and
                         arguments.

Argument   The data that a function acts upon to produce a
                         result.

Serial number   A date expressed in numbers based on the
                         calendar, starting with January 1, 1900, as day
                         number one.

Array   A range of values or formulas treated as one
                         group.

Annuity calculations   Calculations based on a series of even payments
                         over a specified time.

7

What Is a Function?

A function is a predefined formula that consists of a name and arguments. An
argument is the selected or entered data that the function acts upon to
produce a result. The function name is preceded by an equal sign (=) and
followed by an argument or a series of arguments. Function arguments are
enclosed in parentheses.

Here is an example of a simple function that sums a list of numbers.

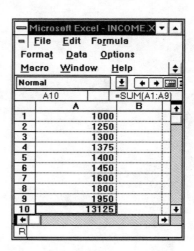

The name of the preceding function is SUM, and the argument is the range A1:A9. The result of this function is the sum of the values in cells A1 through A9. As with a formula, the result of the function appears in the cells. The function appears in the formula bar. This function contains one argument. Other functions, however, may contain several arguments and some functions have no arguments.

Entering a Function

You can enter a function in a cell by typing or using a command. The command method is the most accurate. If you type a function, you can make a mistake such as forgetting a comma or an argument. The command method enables you to paste placeholders as a reminder of what arguments are necessary to complete the function.

To enter a function using the Formula Paste Function command, follow these steps:

1. Select the cell where you want to enter the function.
2. Choose the Formula Paste Function command.

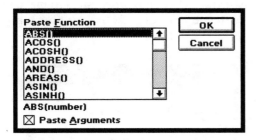

The Paste Function dialog box appears.

Function names are listed in alphabetical order in the Paste Function list. The list is alphabetically sensitive. If you press the first letter of the function name you want to access, the first function name beginning with that letter is selected. Use the scroll bar or ↑ and ↓ to scroll the list and select a function name.

Turn on the Paste Arguments check box if you want placeholders to appear in parentheses in the formula bar. The argument placeholders are only reminders of arguments that are necessary to complete the function. The argument placeholders must be selected and replaced with the actual arguments for the function to work properly.

3. Choose **OK** or press ⏎Enter. The function appears in the formula bar. If you chose to paste arguments, you will see the first argument placeholder in parentheses selected. Replace the argument placeholder with the required data. Select the other argument placeholders, and replace them by typing the data or selecting the cell(s) in the worksheet containing the data.

4. After the function is complete, select the check mark in the formula bar or press ⏎Enter. The result of the function appears in the cell. If you need to edit the function, it appears in the formula bar. Press F2 or click in the formula bar to make it active.

Some functions do not require an argument. For example the NOW( ) function inserts the current date in serial format; an argument is not required. Some functions require only one argument, and some functions require several arguments. Most functions have a limit of 14 arguments. If an argument can be repeated, an ellipsis (...) follows the argument name, indicating that the argument can be repeated up to the limit. If a function uses multiple arguments, commas separate the arguments.

One of the most common errors in functions is a missing comma. Another mistake is inserting spaces in the function. Do not put spaces anywhere in the function. If you need to edit a function, activate the formula bar by pressing F2 or click in the formula bar. Use normal editing procedures to make insertions or deletions. In some cases, if you have an error in your function, a message dialog box appears.

This message prompts you to correct the error in the formula bar.

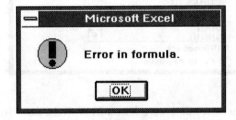

Choose OK or press Enter to clear the dialog box. The part of the function causing the error is selected in the formula bar. You then can determine what the error might be. Check for missing commas, too many commas, or blank spaces in the selected area.

Some functions include arguments that are mandatory and arguments that are optional. When you enter a function and choose the Paste Arguments option, the argument placeholders do not indicate which functions are mandatory and which ones are optional. This chapter gives a brief description of all worksheet functions and lists the arguments for each function. The optional arguments are italicized.

When you use the Formula Paste Function command, the Paste Arguments feature increases the accuracy of the function. First, the feature reminds you of the necessary arguments, so you are less likely to have a missing argument in the function. Second, the feature enables you to easily select the argument placeholder and replace it without having to worry about deleting a comma. To select an argument placeholder, position the mouse I-beam anywhere over the placeholder name and double-click. If you want to select an argument placeholder using the keyboard, position the cursor at the beginning of the placeholder, hold down the Shift key, and use the right-arrow key. After the argument placeholder is selected, you can replace it by typing in the data or selecting a cell or range on the worksheet containing the data. Table 7.1 lists the types of arguments and their description.

7

Table 7.1
Function Argument Types

Argument Type	*Description*
Value	A number or cell reference containing a value.
Logical	Result if formula is TRUE or FALSE.
Number	A number or numeric formula.
Text	Nonnumeric data. Text must be enclosed in quotation marks.
Array	A range of values treated as a single group.
Serial number	A date and time format.
Reference	A cell or range address.

Types of Functions

Excel has more than 130 built-in functions. These functions are grouped into the following categories:

Database	Mathematical
Date	Matrix
Financial	Statistical
Information	Text
Logical	Trigonometric
Lookup	

Database Functions

Excel includes 11 database functions that enable you to find average, minimum, and maximum numbers in the database. Other database functions include statistical functions that enable you to find the standard deviation and variance of a database population, the value of a field, a sum of numbers, a count of numbers, and a product of numbers.

The arguments for all database functions include database, field, and criteria. To define a database, use the **Data Set Database** command; to define the criteria range, use the **Data Set Criteria** command. The field names in a database are the names in the first row of the database. Field names are automatically defined when the database is defined. Refer to Chapter 11, "Managing Data," for more details on database commands. Table 7.2 lists the database functions.

Table 7.2
Database Functions

Function	Description
DAVERAGE(database,field,criteria)	Returns average of numbers.
DCOUNT(database,field,criteria)	Count of numbers.
DCOUNTA(database,field,criteria)	Count of nonblank cells.
DGET(database,field,criteria)	Value of a field.
DMAX(database,field,criteria)	Largest of numbers.
DMIN(database,field,criteria)	Smallest of numbers.

7

162

Function	Description
DPRODUCT(database,field,criteria)	Product of numbers.
DSTDEV(database,field,criteria)	Estimated standard deviation of a population based on sample.
DSTDEVP(database,field,criteria)	Standard deviation of a population based on the entire population.
DSUM(database,field,criteria)	Sum of numbers.
DVAR(database,field,criteria)	Estimated variance of a population based on a sample.
DVARP(database,field,criteria)	Variance of a population based on the entire population.

Date Functions

Excel uses a date calendar that starts with January 1, 1900, as day number 1. All dates from this date forward are numbered sequentially. The number of the day is the serial number for the date. For example, if you used a date function to find the serial number for July 4, 1991, the serial number returned is 33423. Excel also includes date functions for converting the day, month, year, and time to serial numbers. You also can use functions to convert a serial number to the actual date or time.

The date functions TODAY and NOW enable you to use the current date or the current date and time, respectively. The date and time are initially displayed as serial numbers but can be formatted to display a date or time format.

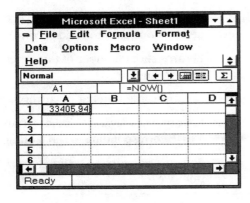

Here you see the serial number of a date using the NOW date function.

163

The NOW function is useful for documents that must always include the current date and time. If you use the NOW function, you do not need to change the date each time you print a document.

The date functions are listed in table 7.3.

Table 7.3
Date Functions

Function	Description
DATE(year,month,day)	Returns serial number of specified date.
DATEVALUE(date_text)	Returns serial number of date text.
DAY(serial_number)	Returns day, as an integer from 1 to 31, corresponding to serial number.
DAYS360(start_date,end_date)	Returns number of days between two dates.
HOUR(serial_number)	Returns hour, as an integer from 0 to 23, corresponding to serial number.
MINUTE(serial_number)	Returns minute, as an integer from 0 to 59, corresponding to serial number.
MONTH(serial_number)	Returns month, as an integer from 1 to 12, corresponding to serial number.
NOW( )	Returns serial number of current date and time.
SECOND(serial_number)	Returns second, as an integer from 1 to 59, corresponding to serial number.
TIME(hour,minute,second)	Returns serial number of time specified by hour, minute, and second.
TIMEVALUE(time_text)	Returns serial number of time specified by time_text.
TODAY( )	Returns serial number of current date.
WEEKDAY(serial_number)	Returns weekday, as an integer from 1 to 7, corresponding to serial number.
YEAR(serial_number)	Returns year corresponding to serial number.

7

164

Financial Functions

Excel has several built-in financial functions that calculate payments on a loan, depreciation, present and future values, internal rate of returns, net present value, and other annuity calculations. An annuity function performs a calculation based on a series of even payments over a specified time. The factors involved in solving most annuity problems are PV (present value) or FV (future value), NPER (number of periods), PMT (payment each period), and RATE (periodic interest rate).

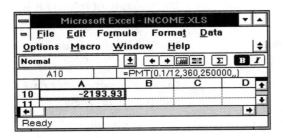

This PMT function determines the monthly payment on a mortgage of $250,000, over a 30-year period, at an annual interest rate of 10 percent.

The arguments for the PMT function are nper, rate, pv, fv, and type. Type and future value are optional arguments. The number of periods in the argument is 360, which is the total number of months for the loan. The periodic interest rate is the annual interest rate divided by 12. The interest rate must be in months because the payments are in months. The present value is the amount of the loan. The result of this function is 2193.93 per month. Because this is an outflow of cash, the number appears in the cell as a negative number.

Type and FV are optional arguments and are not included in this calculation. (Optional arguments are italicized in this book.) Type can be 0 or 1. Zero assumes the cash flow is at the end of the period. One assumes cash flow is at the beginning of the period. If no type is entered, zero is assumed. FV is the value at the end of the period.

Table 7.4 lists financial functions.

Table 7.4
Financial Functions

Function	Description
DDB(cost,salvage,life,period,*factor*)	Double-declining balance method of depreciation.
FV(rate,nper,pmt,*pv,type*)	Future value of an investment.
IPMT(rate,per,nper,pv,*fv,type*)	Interest payment for a specified period.
IRR(values,*guess*)	Internal rate of return for list of values.
MIRR(values,finance_rate, reinvest_rate)	Modified internal rate of return.
NPER(rate,pmt,pv,*fv,type*)	Number of periods for payments or investment.
NPV(rate,value1,value2,....)	Net present value for list of values.
PMT(rate,nper,pv,*fv,type*)	Periodic payment for an investment.
PPMT(rate,per,nper,pv,*fv,type*)	Payment on the principal for a given period.
PV(rate,nper,pv,*fv,type*)	Present value of investment.
RATE(nper,pmt,pv,*fv,type,guess*)	Interest rate per period.
SLN(cost,salvage,life)	Straight-line method of depreciation.
SYD(cost,salvage,life,per)	Sum-of-years' digits method of depreciation.
VDB(cost,salvage,life,start_period, end_period,*factor,no_switch*)	Depreciation for partial period.

7

Information Functions

You can use Excel's built-in information functions to analyze cells, columns, rows, ranges, and areas. Segments of a worksheet may need to be analyzed before performing a calculation, function, or macro.

Excel includes nine IS functions in the information category. The IS functions enable you to test the type of entry in a cell or range; the functions return a logical value of TRUE or FALSE. If the cell meets the condition of the function, the value of the cell is TRUE. If the cell does not meet the function condition, the value is FALSE. For example, if you want to determine whether a cell is blank, you can use the ISBLANK function. If the cell is blank, the value is TRUE; otherwise, the value of the cell is FALSE. The IS functions are generally used with IF functions to establish a cell or range contents.

Microsoft Excel - INCOME.XLS	

```
 File   Edit   Formula   Format   Data
 Options   Macro   Window   Help

Normal
        A3            =IF(ISTEXT(B9),"Cell B9 contains
                      text.","Cell B9 does not contain
  1                   text.")
  2                                  $10,000    $11,0
  3  Cell B9 does not contain text.
  4
  5                                    3000        3
  6                                    2000        2
  7                                    3500        3
  8
  9                                    8500        9

Ready
```

The IF and ISTEXT functions are combined to establish whether cell B9 contains text.

7

The IS and ISTEXT functions are entered as a combined function in cell A1. The IF function includes arguments to define value_if_true and value_if_false. The value_if_true argument is defined as a message, "Cell B9 contains text." The value_if_false argument is defined as a message, "Cell B9 does not contain text." If the result of the function in cell A1 is true (cell B9 does contain text), cell A1 displays the message Cell B9 contains text. If the result of the function in cell A1 is false (cell B9 does not contain text), cell A1 displays the message Cell B9 does not contain text. You must enter text arguments in quotation marks.

The other types of IS functions include ISBLANK, ISERR, ISERROR, ISLOGICAL, ISNA, ISNONTEXT, ISNUMBER, ISREF, and ISTEXT. These information functions are listed in table 7.5.

Table 7.5
Information Functions

Function	Description
ADDRESS(row_num,col_num, abs_num,a1,sheet_text)	Returns text reference of a single cell.
AREAS(reference)	Number of areas in reference.
CELL(info_type,reference)	Cell information including contents, formatting, or location.
COLUMN(reference)	Column number of reference.
COLUMNS(array)	Number of columns in reference.
INDIRECT(ref_text,a1)	The contents of a reference in the form of text.
INFO(type_num)	Information about current operating system.
ISBLANK	Returns TRUE if value is blank.
ISERR	Returns TRUE if value is any error value except #N/A.
ISERROR	Returns TRUE if value is any error value.
ISLOGICAL	Returns TRUE if value is logical value.
ISNA	Returns TRUE if value is error value #N/A.
ISNONTEXT	Returns TRUE if value is not text.
ISNUMBER	Returns TRUE if value is number.
ISREF	Returns TRUE if value is reference.
ISTEXT	Returns TRUE if value is text.
N(value)	Argument converted to a number.
NA( )	The error value #N/A.

7

168

Function	Description
OFFSET(reference,rows,cols, height,width)	Returns a reference offset by a specified number of rows and columns.
ROW(reference)	Row number of reference.
ROWS(array)	Number of rows in reference.
T(value)	Argument converted to text.
TYPE(value)	Number indicating the data type of a value.

Logical Functions

Excel's logical functions are used frequently for testing conditions and making decisions. The IF function enables you to set conditions for a cell or range. You can combine the IF function with other logical functions, such as AND and OR, to test for multiple conditions.

The IF function is one of the most common logical functions used to test cell values and formulas. The IF function has two sets of arguments.

The Select Arguments dialog box appears if you choose the IF function with Paste Arguments turned on.

The dialog box lists the two sets of arguments. The first argument set enables you to return a value for TRUE if the condition is met or a value for FALSE if the condition is not met. The second argument set enables a logical test and returns a result if the condition is met. If the condition is not met, the active cell displays FALSE.

The logical functions are listed and described in table 7.6.

Table 7.6
Logical Functions

Function	Description
AND(logical1,*logical2,...*)	True if every argument is TRUE.
FALSE( )	Logical value FALSE.
IF(logical_test,value_if_true, *value_if_false*)	Value_if_true if logical test is TRUE; Value_if_false if logical value is FALSE.
NOT(logical)	Reverses TRUE and FALSE logicals.
OR(logical1,*logical2,...*)	True if any argument is TRUE.
TRUE( )	Logical value TRUE.

Lookup Functions

Lookup functions are used to retrieve a value or cell reference from a table or an array. Examples of lookup functions include LOOKUP, MATCH, and various INDEX functions. Table 7.7 lists the lookup functions.

Table 7.7
Lookup Functions

Function	Description
CHOOSE(index_num,value1,*value2,...*)	Chooses a value from a list corresponding to the index number.
HLOOKUP(lookup_value, table_array,row_index_num)	Looks across the top row of range until value is met.
INDEX(reference,row_num, column_num,*area_num*)	Returns a cell reference within specified area at intersection of specified column and row.
INDEX(array,*row_num,column_num)*	Returns value of cell referenced in array at intersection of specified column and row.
LOOKUP(lookup_value, lookup_vector,result_vector)	Value in table selected by lookup value.

Function	Description
LOOKUP(lookup_value,array)	Value in array selected by lookup value.
MATCH(lookup_value, lookup_array,*match_type)*	Cell address in array of lookup value.
OFFSET(reference,rows,cols, *height,width*)	Returns a reference offset by a specified number of rows and columns.
VLOOKUP(lookup_value, table_array,col_index_num)	Looks down the first column of range until value is found.

Mathematical Functions

Excel's built-in mathematical functions enable you to perform standard arithmetic operations, including SUM and PRODUCT. Other mathematical functions enable you to round and truncate numbers. These types of mathematical functions are the basis for using mathematical functions in building a worksheet.

You can use three mathematical functions to round a number to certain specifications. The INT function rounds a number to the nearest integer. The TRUNC function truncates a number to its next lower integer, and the ROUND function rounds a number up or down. The built-in mathematical functions are listed in table 7.8.

Table 7.8
Mathematical Functions

Function	Description
ABS(number)	Absolute value of number.
EXP(number)	e to the power number.
FACT(number)	Factorial of number.
INT(number)	Number rounded down to the nearest integer.
LN(number)	Natural logarithm of number.

continues

171

Table 7.8 *(continued)*

Function	Description
LOG(number,base)	Logarithm of number in base.
LOG10,(number)	Base 10 logarithm of number.
MOD(number,divisor)	Remainder of number divided by divisor.
PI( )	Value of pi.
PRODUCT(number1,*number2*,...)	Product of numbers.
RAND( )	Random number between 0 and 1.
ROUND(number,num_digits)	Rounds number to specified number of digits.
SIGN(number)	Sign of number.
SQRT(number)	Square root of number.
SUM(number1,*number2*,...)	Total of arguments.
SUMPRODUCT(array1,array2,...)	Sum of product of corresponding array elements.
TRUNC(number,num_digits)	Changes number to an integer by truncating the decimal portion.

Matrix Functions

Matrix functions are used primarily for solving more complex problems that involve several unknown variables in an array. An *array* is a rectangular range of values or formulas that are treated as a single group. The matrix functions are listed in table 7.9.

Table 7.9
Matrix Functions

Function	Description
MDETERM(array)	Returns determinant of array.
MINVERSE(array)	Returns inverse of array.
MMULT(array1,array2,...)	Returns product of two arrays.
TRANSPOSE(array)	Transposes rows and columns in an array.

7

Statistical Functions

Statistical functions enable you to find the average, minimum, maximum, standard deviation, or variance of a selected group of values. The statistical functions were discussed earlier in the database functions section. Other statistical functions that are not database functions include the TREND, LINEST, LOGEST, and GROWTH functions. You can use these functions to calculate lines and curves that fit test data. Table 7.10 lists the statistical functions built into Excel.

Table 7.10
Statistical Functions

Function	Description
AVERAGE(number1,*number2,...*)	Average of defined range.
COUNT(value1,*value2,...*)	Total number in defined range.
COUNTA(value1,*value2,...*)	Total of nonblank cells in range.
GROWTH(known_y's,*known_x's, new_x's,const)*	Values on exponential trend.
LINEST(known_y's,*known_x's, const,stats)*	Parameters of linear trend.
LOGEST(known_y's,*known_x's, const,stats)*	Parameters of exponential trend.
MAX(number1,*number2,...*)	Largest number in defined range.
MEDIAN(number1,number2,...)	Middle value in defined range.
MIN(number1,*number2,...*)	Smallest number in defined range.
STDEV(number1,*number2,...*)	Standard deviation for a sample population.
STDEVP(number1,*number2,...*)	Standard deviation of entire population.
TREND(known_y's,*known_x's, new_x's,const)*	Calculates values on linear trend.
VAR(number1,*number2,...*)	Variance for sample population.
VARP(number1,*number2,...*)	Variance for entire population.

7

Text Functions

Excel includes a number of built-in text functions that help you find text in a cell or range. The functions are listed in table 7.11.

Table 7.11
Text Functions

Function	Description
CHAR(number)	Returns character corresponding to ASCII code number.
CLEAN(text)	Removes characters that are not printed.
CODE(text)	Returns ASCII code of the first character.
DOLLAR(number,*decimals*)	Rounds number to specified decimals and converts the number to text in a currency format.
EXACT(text1,text2)	Compares text and returns logical of TRUE if text is the same.
FIND(find_text,within_text, *start_at_num*)	Returns location of matching text.
FIXED(number,*decimals*)	Rounds number to specified decimals and displays it as text.
LEFT(text,*num_chars*)	Returns leftmost number of characters from text.
LEN(text)	Returns the number of characters in the text string.
LOWER(text)	Changes text to all lowercase.
MID(text,start_num, num_chars)	Returns number of characters specified in text extending from starting number.
PROPER(text)	Changes text to lowercase with first character capitalized.

7

Function	Description
REPLACE(old_text,start_num, num_chars,new_text)	Replaces old text characters specified with new text.
REPT(text,num_times)	Repeats text specified number of times.
RIGHT(text,*num_chars)*	Returns number of characters for the right end of the text string.
SEARCH(*find_text,* within_text,*start_num*)	Returns position of matching text.
SUBSTITUTE(text,old_text, new_text,*instance_num*)	Replaces old text with new characters.
T(value)	Returns text when value is text; returns blank when value is not text.
TEXT(value,format_text)	Converts number value to formatted text value.
TRIM(text)	Removes excess spaces from text.
UPPER(text)	Changes text to all uppercase.
VALUE(text)	Converts numeric text to number.

Trigonometric Functions

Excel includes several trigonometric functions used primarily to build complex scientific and engineering formulas. The built-in functions for creating trigonometric formulas are outlined in table 7.12.

Table 7.12
Trigonometric Functions

Function	Description
ACOS(number)	Returns arccosine of a number.
ACOSH(number)	Returns inverse hyperbolic cosine of a number.

continues

175

Table 7.12 *(continued)*

Function	Description
ASIN(number)	Returns arcsine of a number.
ASINH(number)	Returns inverse hyperbolic sine of a number.
ATAN(number)	Returns arctangent of a number.
ATAN2(x_num,y_num)	Returns arctangent given the x- and y-coordinates.
ATANH(number)	Returns inverse hyperbolic tangent of a number.
COS(number)	Returns cosine of an angle.
COSH(number)	Returns hyperbolic cosine of a number.
SIN(number)	Returns sine of an angle.
SINH(number)	Returns hyperbolic sine of a number.
TAN(number)	Returns tangent of an angle.
TANH(number)	Returns hyperbolic tangent of an angle.

Summary

In this chapter, you were introduced to functions. You learned what a function is and how to use functions to improve accuracy in formulas. You also learned what an argument is and how to paste argument placeholders in a function.

This chapter provided several tables outlining the different types of functions and what each function does. The tables provided you with the arguments that are necessary to produce a result using a function.

In this chapter, you were introduced to the following key information about Excel:

■ Excel has more than 130 built-in functions that enable you to do mathematical, financial, statistical, database, logical, date, lookup, matrix, information, text, and trigonometric calculations.

■ A function consists of a name preceded by an equal sign (=) and followed by arguments in parentheses.

■ An argument is data that the function acts upon to produce a result. Some arguments are mandatory. Some arguments are optional.

■ The Formula Paste Function command provides an alphabetical list of all built-in functions. This command enables you to insert a function in a cell.

■ If you are not sure which arguments are required for a function, you can turn on the Paste Arguments check box in the Formula Paste Function dialog box. The Paste Arguments option provides temporary placeholders as reminders of which arguments are necessary.

■ Arguments are separated by commas. Missing commas and spaces cause many of the errors that occur when using functions.

■ Argument placeholders must be replaced with actual data that is entered in the formula bar or selected from the worksheet.

■ Database functions enable you to perform statistical calculations and analyze data in a database. Database functions help you calculate average, minimum, maximum, standard deviation, and variance.

■ The NOW function is a date function. You can use the NOW function to enter the current date and time. You can use the TODAY function to enter the current date only.

■ The PMT function is one of the built-in financial functions you can use to determine the monthly payment on an investment based on a specified periodic interest rate, a specified number of periods, and the present value of the investment.

■ Excel includes financial functions for determining internal rate of return and depreciation.

■ Information functions enable you to analyze a cell's contents, columns, rows, ranges, and areas.

■ You can use IS functions to test the type of entry in a cell and return a logical value of TRUE or FALSE.

■ You can use logical functions, such as IF, AND, and OR, to test cell values and formulas.

■ TRUNC, INT, and ROUND are mathematical functions that enable you to round a number according to defined specifications.

■ You can use text functions to help you find text in a cell or range.

7

Chapter 8 deals with various aspects of printing a worksheet. The chapter introduces you to the Excel commands for setting up the printer, previewing a document before it is printed, and adjusting margins and columns in the Preview mode. You will learn how to define a print area, define titles to be printed on every page, change the printer orientation, and create headers and footers on a document.

7

Printing a Worksheet

Excel 3.0 has various features for printing a worksheet or chart. Using Excel's print commands, you can prepare your worksheet or chart data for an impressive presentation by customizing the appearance of data on the page. Excel produces high-quality output when you use a laser printer.

This chapter covers the steps involved when you use Excel's printing commands. In this chapter, you will learn how to set up a printer, define a print area, use the **File Page Setup** command, and preview a document before it is printed.

Setting up the printer

Setting up the page

Previewing a document

Changing margins and columns

Printing a document

Key Terms in This Chapter

Printer driver	File that defines the printer you are using and enables your computer to communicate with the printer.
Default setting	Controls the way all documents are printed.
Portrait orientation	Prints the document down the length of the paper.
Landscape orientation	Prints the document across the width of the paper.
Header	Text, date, page numbering, and formatting in the top margin of each page of a document.
Footer	Text, date, page numbering, and formatting in the bottom margin of each page of a document.
Print area	Defined section to be printed.
Manual page break	Determines the end of a page. Inserted with a command.
Print titles	Information that appears across the top or along the left margin of each page of a document.
Preview mode	Overview of the print area that enables you to see what the page will look like when printed.

8

Setting Up the Printer

When you are installing Windows on your computer, you are prompted to choose a printer from a list. After you select a printer, Windows installs a file called a *printer driver*. The printer driver is needed for the computer to understand the type of printer you are using. You may define several printers to produce various types of output.

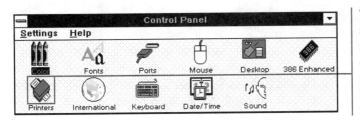

To add a printer after you have installed Windows on your computer, access the Printer icon in the Control Panel.

After you have defined a printer in the Windows environment, you can print from all applications, using the settings defined by the printer driver. To make changes to the settings you originally defined in the printer driver, use the File Printer Setup command. You can select among printers that have been defined and make changes to the original settings.

To use the File Printer Setup command, follow these steps:

1. Choose the File Printer Setup command.

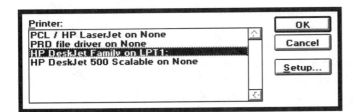

A dialog box appears, listing the installed printer drivers.

8

The active printer is selected in the list, along with the port to which the printer is assigned.

2. To switch to another installed printer, select the printer from the list. Choose OK or press ↵Enter to make the selected printer active. To change the default settings of the selected printer, proceed to the next step.

3. Choose the Setup button to change the active printer's default settings.

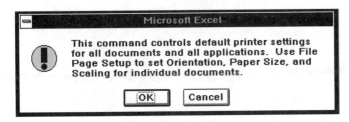

This dialog box appears, reminding you that settings chosen in the Setup dialog box control the default settings.

181

All documents will be affected by the printer changes. Choose **OK** or press ⏎Enter to acknowledge the message and continue. Choose **Cancel** or press Esc to cancel the command.

If you continue, the Printer Setup dialog box appears with the current settings.

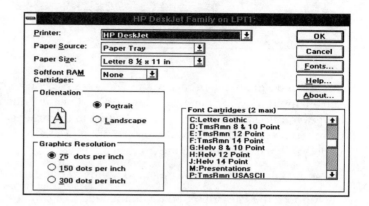

4. Choose the settings you want to change. The options are described in table 8.1.

5. After you have selected all settings, choose **OK** or press ⏎Enter. The Setup dialog box disappears, and you return to the Printer List dialog box.

6. Choose **OK** or press ⏎Enter to confirm the printer changes and clear the dialog box.

Table 8.1
Printer Settings

Printer Setting	Description
Printer	Identifies the current printer driver.
Paper Source	Sets manual or automatic paper feed.
Paper Size	Sets paper sizes, including letter, legal, European, and envelope.
Softfont RAM Cartridges	Allocates memory for softfont cartridges.
Orientation	Portrait option prints document down the length of the paper. Landscape option prints document across the width of the paper.
Graphics Resolution	Defines quality of graphics based on dots per inch.

Printer Setting	Description
Font Cartridges	Lists font cartridges and enables you to select two that your computer is using.
Fonts Button	Displays the Font Installer dialog box and enables you to install fonts.
Help Button	Displays a Help window with topics pertaining to the active printer driver.
About Button	Displays general information about the active printer driver.

Setting Up the Page

The preceding section explained how to change the default settings of a printer. When you change default settings, the change affects all documents. Sometimes you may, however, want to change certain printer settings for a single document only.

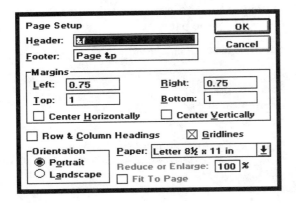

The Page Setup dialog box controls the way the document appears on the page.

The File Page Setup command enables you to modify certain printer settings and affect the active document only. The File Page Setup command also provides capabilities for adding headers and footers to a document, changing margins, turning worksheet gridlines on or off, and positioning a document on a page. Table 8.2 outlines the options that the File Page Setup command gives you.

Table 8.2
Page Setup Options

Option	Description
Header	Specifies text, page numbering, date, and formatting at the top of each page.
Footer	Specifies text, page numbering, date, and formatting at the bottom of each page.
Margins	Controls amount of space between left, right, top, and bottom edges of the paper and the printed document.
Center Horizontally, Vertically	Centers the document between margins.
Gridlines	Turns worksheet gridlines on or off.
Size (charts only)	Sizes chart according to screen size, to page size, or to full page size, adjusting height-to-width ratio.
Orientation	Portrait option prints document down the length of the paper. Landscape prints document across the width of the paper.
Paper	Specifies letter, legal, ledger, or envelope paper sizes.
Reduce/Enlarge	Specifies percentage of reduction or enlargement. Available only on printers that support this feature.
Fit To Page	Compresses document to fit on a single page. Printer must be PostScript-compatible to support this feature.

8

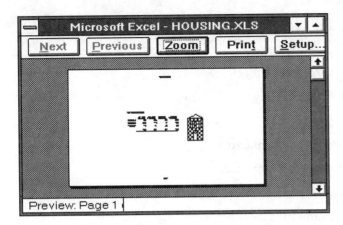

The Page Setup dialog box was used to center the print area horizontally and vertically, change the orientation to Landscape, and remove gridlines.

Creating Headers and Footers

A header or footer creates a consistent look across all the pages of a document. You can use a header, for example, to have a title at the top of each page. And you can use a footer to automatically number each page at the bottom. Headers and footers appear .50" from the top or bottom of the paper and .75" from the left or right edge of the paper.

A header or footer can include text, a page number, the current date, and formatting such as bold, italics, centering, and alignment. Excel uses codes to assign formatting. All codes begin with an ampersand (&) and are followed by a letter. The default header setting is &f, which prints the file name centered at the top of the page. The default footer setting is Page &p, which prints the word *Page* followed by the page number centered at the bottom of the page. Table 8.3 lists the other header and footer codes.

Table 8.3
Header and Footer Codes

Code	Description
&L	Left-aligns following characters.
&C	Centers following characters.
&R	Right-aligns following characters.
&B	Boldfaces following characters.

continues

185

Table 8.3 *(continued)*

Code	Description
&I	Italicizes following characters.
&U	Underlines following characters.
&S	Prints following characters in strikeout style.
&D	Prints the current date.
&T	Prints the current time.
&F	Prints the name of the file.
&P	Prints the page number.
&N	Prints the total number of pages. Used with another code. Example: Page &P of &N produces Page 1 of 5.
&P+number	Adds number to page number. Example: &P+2 prints the number 3 on page 1.
&P–number	Subtracts number from page number. Example: &P–2 prints the number 1 on page 3.
&&	Prints a single ampersand.
&"fontname"	Assigns font to following characters.
&nn	Assigns font point size to following characters. Indicate a two-digit number when using this code.

Here, the Page Setup dialog box has header codes that left-align the current date and boldface and center the word *Report*.

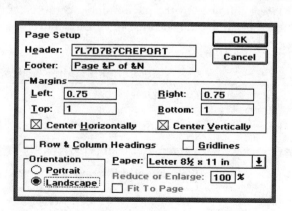

The footer code displays the page number followed by the total page count. The footer may read Page 1 of 5, for example.

186

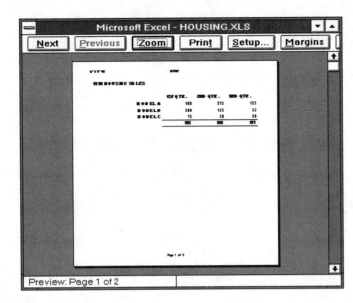

This document includes a customized header and footer.

Excel's on-line Help includes header and footer codes. If you cannot memorize these codes and want to see a list of codes without having to refer to a book, press F1 to access Help and use the Search button to locate the topic header and footer codes. You also can directly access this Help topic by choosing the File Page Setup command and pressing F1. A Help window displays the File Page Setup command with the topic headers and footers underlined. Select the topic by clicking on it, or use the Tab key and press Enter. The Help window displays a list of the header and footer codes.

Defining the Print Area

To print a portion of a worksheet, define that portion as a print area. To print multiple nonadjoining sections of your worksheet on the same page, select the sections and define the multiple sections as a single print area. If you do not define a print area, Excel assumes that you want to define the entire worksheet as the print area.

To define a print area, follow these steps:

1. Select the range you want to print. To select multiple nonadjoining ranges using the mouse, hold down Ctrl as you select the other ranges. Excel will print each range on a separate page.

    To select multiple ranges using the keyboard, after the first selection press ⇧Shift F8 to change to Add mode. Move to a corner of the next

8

section. Press ⇧Shift and the arrow keys to select the next section. Repeat this procedure until you have selected all the sections you want to print.

2. Choose the Options Set Print Area command. This command names the selection Print_Area. The area is surrounded by a dashed border that indicates the area to be printed.

The selection is shown after it has been defined as the print area.

	A	B	C	D	E	F	G
		JAN	FEB	MAR	APR	MAY	
1							
2	Sales	$10,000	$11,000	$12,100	$13,310	$14,641	
3							
4	Expenses						
5	Item A	3,000	3,300	3,630	3,993	4,392	
6	Item B	2,000	2,200	2,420	2,662	2,928	
7	Item C	3,500	3,850	4,235	4,659	5,124	
8							
9	Total Expenses	8,500	9,350	10,285	11,314	12,445	
10							
11							
12	Net Income	$1,500	$1,650	$1,815	$1,997	$2,196	
13							
14							
15							

Microsoft Excel - INCOME.XLS — File Edit Formula Format Data Options Macro Window Help — Normal — A1 — Ready

Inserting Page Breaks

If you select an area for printing that cannot fit on a single page, Excel inserts automatic page breaks. Page breaks appear as dashed lines surrounding the area to be printed. If you are not satisfied with the location of the automatic page break, you have the option of inserting manual page breaks. A manual page break enables you to control where a page ends. After you insert a manual page break, the automatic page break readjusts downward to affect pages below. To insert a page break, select the cell below and to the right of the location where you want the page to break. Choose the Options Set Page Break command. A manual page break appears above and to the left of the active cell. Manual page breaks appear on the screen as bold dashed lines; manual page breaks also are darker than automatic page breaks.

To insert a horizontal page break only, select the cell in Column A just below the gridline where you want the page to end. Then, choose the Options Set Page Break command. To insert a vertical page break only, select a cell in Row 1 to the right of the gridline where you want the page to end. Then, choose the Options Set Page Break command.

8

188

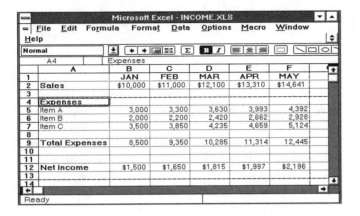

In this example, a manual horizontal page break was inserted above the Expenses section.

You can delete a manual page break by selecting the cell below and to the right of the page break intersection. If the correct cell is selected, the Options menu displays the Remove Page Break command rather than the Set Page Break command. An automatic page break cannot be removed.

You can remove all manual page breaks in a worksheet after the entire worksheet is selected. To do so, follow these steps:

1. Select the entire worksheet by clicking in the blank cell at the intersection of the row and column headings, or press Ctrl+Shift+space bar. The entire worksheet is selected.

2. Choose the Options Remove Page Break command.

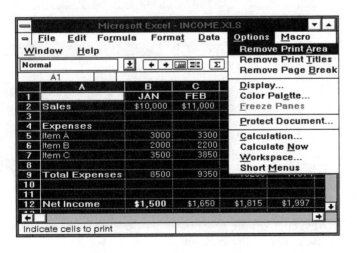

Here, the entire worksheet is selected, and the Remove Page Break command is displayed.

8

189

After you select the command, all manual page breaks disappear.

Defining Print Titles

You may find yourself confronted with a common printing problem: trying to print an area that cannot fit on a single page. Suppose that, for example, you are printing a list with headings at the top of the list, and the list spills over to two pages. The second page of the list does not include the headings, and the data may be difficult to understand without the headings. To avoid entering the headings again for the second page, define the row(s) containing the headings as a title row. After the row is defined as a title, the data in the defined row(s) or column(s) appears on every printed page.

To define titles for every page of a document, follow these steps:

1. Select the entire row(s) containing the data you want to appear as titles across the top of each printed page. Or, if you want the data to appear as titles down the left margin of each printed page, select the entire column(s). If you want titles to appear across the top and down the left margin of each printed page, select both the row(s) and column(s) containing the data you want to use as titles.

8

The data in the selected row will be defined as print titles.

	A	B	C	D	E	F	G
2							
3	**Part No.**	**Price**	**Quantity**				
4	678999	$52.95	23				
5	679000	$52.90	26				
6	679001	$52.85	29				
7	679002	$52.80	32				
8	679003	$52.75	35				
9	679004	$52.70	38				
10	679005	$52.65	41				

Microsoft Excel - Sheet3

File Edit Formula Format Data Options Macro Window Help

Normal   A3   Part No.

Ready

To select an entire row, click on the row heading, or press Alt+**space bar**. To select an entire column, click on the column heading, or press Ctrl+**space bar**.

2. Choose the Options Set Print Titles command to define titles to be printed on each page. This command names the selection Print_Titles.

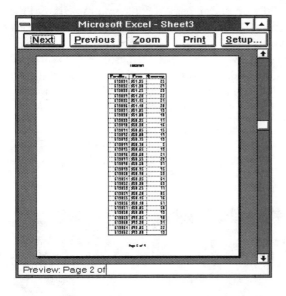

The defined titles appear at the top of each page.

8

You may be puzzled if you select the entire row or column when defining titles. Remember that row selection determines the titles that appear across the top of each page. The column selection determines the titles that appear down the left margin of each page. If the print area you define does not contain data in the row or column defined for titles, a title will not appear. If, for example, row 3 is selected and set as Print Titles, and only cells A3 through D3 contain data, only the data that is defined for printing in columns A through D will have titles. If a range of F5:H9 was defined as the print area, titles will not appear because cells F3 through H3 are blank.

If you define print titles, do not select the titles when you define the print area. If the titles are defined and you also select the titles as part of the print area, the titles will appear twice on the first page.

The Options Set Print Titles command is replaced by the Remove Print Titles command when the entire worksheet is selected. To select the entire worksheet, click in the blank cell at the intersection of the row and column headings, or press Ctrl+Shift+space bar. Choose the Options Remove Print Titles command to clear titles that have been set.

191

Previewing a Document

Because a worksheet is actually one large grid of cells, you may have difficulty visualizing what a document will look like when you print it. Excel's **File Print Preview** command enables you to view your document before it is printed. In Preview mode, you have a bird's-eye view of what the document will look like on the page. The preview feature also includes options that enable you to change the margins of the document, change column width, and zoom in on a section of the document to view a section up close. The next section covers the Print Preview features.

After you have defined a print area with the **Options Set Print Area** command, you can view the area to be printed by choosing the **File Print Preview** command.

Here is the
Preview window.

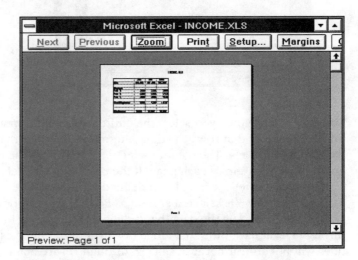

Scrolling

The buttons across the top of the window include **Next** and **Previous**. You can use these buttons for moving from one page to the next in Preview mode. If you are previewing a document that is a single page, the **Next** and **Previous** buttons are dimmed. If you are previewing multiple pages, the **Next** button is available only if a page follows the page you are viewing. The **Previous** button is available only if a page precedes the page you are viewing.

You also can use the vertical scroll bar on the right side of the window to move to another page. Or, you can use the PgUp, PgDn, and arrow keys to move to another page in Preview mode.

Zooming

In Preview mode, you may not be able to see the exact detail of your document. If you need a close-up view of the document, you can zoom in and view enlarged sections of it.

To zoom with the mouse, follow these steps:

1. Position the mouse over the section you want to see enlarged and click once. The mouse pointer changes to a magnifying glass when positioned over any part of the document.

2. Use the vertical and horizontal scrolls to move to other sections while maintaining the enlarged view.

3. Click the left mouse button once to zoom out and see the entire page.

To zoom with the keyboard, follow these steps:

1. Press Alt Z to choose the Zoom button.

2. Use the arrow keys to move to other sections while maintaining the enlarged view.

3. Press Alt Z to zoom out and see the entire page.

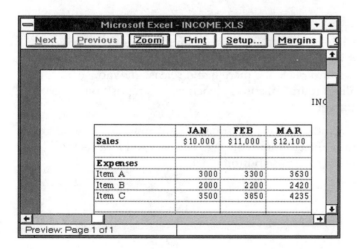

Here is a document enlarged in Preview mode.

Changing Margins and Column Widths

You can change margins using the **F**ile Page Se**t**up command. You can change column widths using the Forma**t C**olumn Width command. You also can adjust margins and column widths using the mouse in Preview mode. After you choose the Margins button, light gray boundaries appear around the document, with black rectangular handles marking the left, right, top, and bottom margins. Square handles also appear along the top of the page, with lines indicating the width of each column.

Margin and column width markers appear when the Margins button is selected and boundaries are turned on.

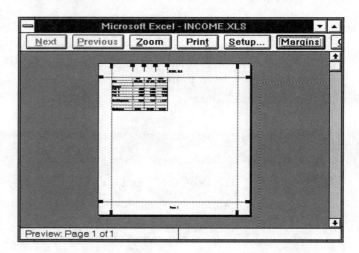

To adjust the margins, click on the left, right, top, or bottom handle that represents the respective margin. The mouse pointer changes to a cross bar when properly positioned on the margin handle. Drag the marker to the position where you want to place the margin and release the mouse button. The page automatically is redrawn, and the document is repositioned according to the changed margin.

To adjust the column width, click on the square handle and drag it to increase or decrease the width of the column. The page redraws and reflects the change after you release the mouse button.

8

194

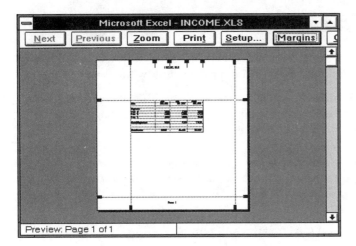

This document is repositioned after the left margin is modified and a column width is increased.

Turn off the margin and column width boundaries by choosing the Margins button. If you like the way your document looks, you can proceed directly to the printer by choosing the Print button.

The Print dialog box appears.

Choose the print options you want, or accept the default settings by choosing OK, or press Enter.

To make changes, such as adding a header or footer, turning off gridlines, or centering the document on the page, choose the Setup button. The Page Setup dialog box appears, and you can make the necessary changes before printing your document.

If you do not like the way your document looks in Preview mode and you need to return to the document to make some changes, choose the Close button to exit Preview mode and return to the active document.

195

Printing a Document

After setting up the printer and document, you are ready to execute the File Print command. To complete the printing process, follow these steps:

1. Choose File Print. The Print dialog box appears. This dialog box controls the number of copies you print, the number of pages, and the quality of the printing. You also can choose to print only the worksheet or macro sheet, only cell notes attached to cells, or both the document and the cell notes. The dialog box is set up to print one copy of all pages of the worksheet or macro sheet unless you choose other options.

2. To preview the document you are about to print, select the Preview check box to turn on the Preview option mode.

3. Select the options you want, or accept the default settings.

4. Choose OK or press ⏎Enter. If you did not select the Preview option, printing begins. If Preview was selected, you enter Preview mode. You can execute the Print command in the Preview mode.

8

Summary

This chapter introduced you to many aspects of printing in Excel. You learned how to change default printer settings and control the way a page is set up before you print. You also learned how to insert and remove manual page breaks, define print titles and print areas, and add headers and footers to a document. You learned about print preview and the options included in Preview mode for zooming, changing margins, and adjusting column widths.

In this chapter, you were introduced to the following key information about Excel:

■ The File Printer Setup command enables you to switch to another printer or change default printer settings.

■ Default settings control the way all documents are printed with the active printer.

■ The File Page Setup command enables you to change settings that affect only the active document.

■ Headers and footers are created in the Page Setup dialog box using codes to define such options as the date, page numbering, and formatting.

196

■ The **Options Set Print Area** command defines the selected range as the area to be printed.

■ Excel creates automatic page breaks if the area to be printed cannot fit on a single page. Automatic page breaks appear as dashed borders that outline the end of one page and the beginning of the next page. Automatic page breaks cannot be deleted.

■ You can insert manual page breaks with the **Options Set Page Break** command.

■ You can remove manual page breaks using the **Options Remove Page Break** command. This command appears only if the active cell is positioned in the proper location below and to the right of the manual page break intersection.

■ The **Options Set Print Titles** command defines data in rows or columns as headings that appear on each page of a multiple-page document.

■ The **File Print Preview** command gives you a bird's-eye view of a document before it is printed. The Preview mode also enables you to zoom in and out for a close-up view.

■ You can adjust margins and column widths in Preview mode by dragging the boundary markers.

■ The **File Print** command enables you to choose the number of copies to print and the number of pages to print.

8

Chapter 9 will introduce you to specific commands and techniques for working with multiple documents. The chapter will explain how to arrange open documents on the screen and save the screen as a workspace file. You will learn how to link data in one document to another document. You also will learn how to consolidate data from multiple worksheets onto a single worksheet. Chapter 9 also covers how to save an Excel file to another file format and how to import a file from another file format.

Working with Multiple Documents

T his chapter covers the fundamentals of working with multiple documents. In Excel, you can have several documents open at one time. This capability enables you to create smaller worksheets that are easier to work with and see the documents at the same time. The first part of this chapter deals primarily with arranging multiple documents as a workspace. A workspace saves the layout of open documents, such as the size of the window, the position of the window, and workspace settings.

In earlier chapters you learned about the Edit Cut, Copy, and Paste commands. These commands make it possible to share data across multiple documents. This chapter carries the concept of sharing data one step further by explaining how to link data. *Linked data* are items of data that are connected. If the data changes in one location, any data associated or linked to the changed data automatically updates to reflect the change.

Other Excel features that simplify working with multiple documents include consolidating data, saving to other file formats, and importing data from other file formats.

Arranging multiple files

Creating a workspace file

Linking files

Consolidating data

Saving to file formats

Importing from file formats

Key Terms in This Chapter

Workspace file	A file that stores file names, window positions, and workspace settings.
External reference	A formula that refers to a location outside the active worksheet.
Supporting worksheet	A file that supplies data to another worksheet.
Dependent worksheet	A file that depends on data from another worksheet.
Destination area	The section of a document in which data from other worksheets is consolidated.
Source area	Selected data in a document that is consolidated in an area of another document.

Arranging Multiple Worksheets

Excel enables you to have multiple documents open at the same time. Because of this capability, you may want to create small worksheets rather than try to fill a single worksheet with various types of data. You can have as many worksheets open as your computer's memory can accommodate. All open worksheets are listed under the Window menu.

The Window menu lists four open worksheets.

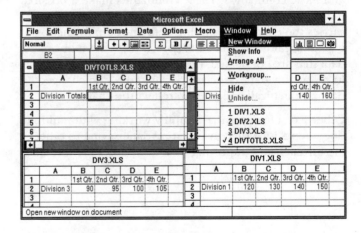

200

You can move from one open file to the next by selecting the file name from the Window menu or by pressing Ctrl+F6. You can move and size a window if it is in the restored position.

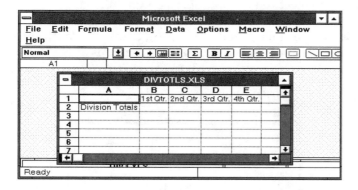

If a window is in the restored position, the window has a border that can be used to resize the window.

Refer to Chapter 2, "Getting Started," for details on how to move and size a window.

If you want to have all open files evenly displayed on-screen, you can choose the Window Arrange All command. This command automatically arranges all open files in the Excel application window.

9

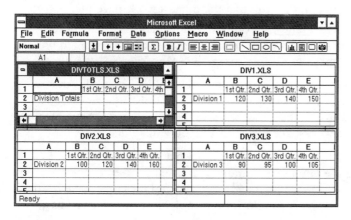

Four open files are displayed on-screen after the Arrange All command is chosen.

All open files are in the restored position and can be moved and sized to your specifications. You may, for example, need to view certain sections of each of the open files. By moving, sizing, and scrolling, you can position the windows to display the sections you want to view in each window.

Creating a Workspace File

Each time you open multiple files, you can spend considerable time trying to arrange the multiple files to meet your desired specification. Instead of constantly having to arrange the files after you open them, you can save the arrangement. After you have the files arranged on-screen exactly the way you want them, save the screen as a workspace file. Follow these steps to save a workspace file:

1. Choose the File Save Workspace command.

The Save
Workspace As
dialog box
appears.

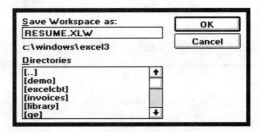

2. Enter a name for the workspace in the text box, or accept the proposed name of RESUME.XLW. Excel automatically adds the extension XLW to the file name, indicating that the file is a workspace file.

3. Choose **OK** or press ⏎Enter. If you have made changes to any of the files that make up the workspace, Excel prompts you to save each file. Respond to each message dialog box by choosing Yes, No, or **Cancel**

When you create a workspace file, it does not include the actual files that make up the workspace. The workspace file includes only the names of the files, the position and size of the windows, and the workspace settings. Do not assume that saving the workspace file saves the individual files.

You open a workspace file the same way you open a worksheet, chart, or macro sheet. Choose the File Open command and select or enter the file name. Workspace files end with the extension XLW. All files that make up the workspace appear on-screen in the position in which they were saved as a workspace file.

9

Linking Worksheets

The **Edit Cut, Copy,** and **Paste** commands were introduced earlier in the book. These commands use the clipboard to share data within the same document or across multiple documents. Cell contents can be cut or copied to the clipboard, and pasted in another location. If the shared data changes in one location, however, you have to change the data in the other locations to ensure that the data is consistent. To avoid having to make these multiple changes, you can link data. Linked data updates automatically to reflect any changes.

When you build a formula in a cell that references other cells containing values, the cell addresses appear in the formula. If you refer to a cell located on another worksheet, the cell address is preceded by the name of the worksheet. A reference to a cell or range in another worksheet is called an *external reference*.

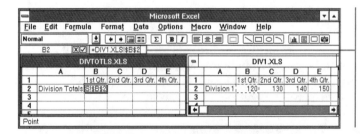

In the external reference in the formula bar, the file name is followed by an exclamation point (!) and the cell address.

Creating an External Link

When you use linked files, you will work with supporting and dependent worksheets. The file containing the original data is the *supporting worksheet*. The file that contains the formula with the external reference is referred to as the *dependent worksheet*.

You can create an external reference on the dependent worksheet by selecting a cell and entering an equal sign (=). Then, select the data on the supporting worksheet to create an external reference. If you know the name of the supporting worksheet and the cell address you want to select, you can enter the external reference from the keyboard. If you do not know the exact location of the data you want to link, the selection method may be more accurate.

To link a formula in the dependent worksheet to data in a supporting worksheet with the selection method, follow these steps:

1. Open the dependent and supporting worksheets.

2. Select a cell in the dependent worksheet to build a formula. Type = (an equal sign) to begin the formula.

3. Activate the supporting worksheet by selecting it from the Window menu, or by pressing [Ctrl] [F6] until the supporting worksheet is in view, or click on the worksheet if it is in view.

4. Select the cell that will be linked to the dependent worksheet.

5. Activate the dependent worksheet by selecting it from the Window menu, by pressing [Ctrl] [F6], or by clicking on the worksheet if it is in view. The external reference formula appears in the formula bar.

6. Click on the check mark in the formula bar, or press [↵Enter] to complete the formula. The data in the linked cell appears in the active cell. The formula bar displays the external reference.

When a formula has an external reference that does not involve a calculation, a function, a relative cell reference, or a named formula, the reference is called a *simple external reference*. Supporting worksheets for simple external references do not have to be open. Dependent worksheets can access the data from disk if the supporting worksheet is closed. If a supporting worksheet is closed, the formula bar displays the entire path of the supporting worksheet.

9

The formula bar displays the entire path of the simple external reference when the supporting document is not open.

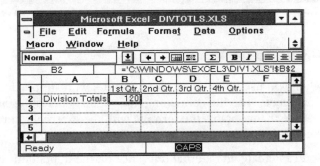

If a formula contains an external reference that involves a calculation, function, relative cell reference, or named formula, the reference is called a *complex external reference*. If a dependent worksheet has a complex external reference, the supporting worksheet must be open. Examples of complex external references are listed in table 9.1.

Table 9.1
Complex External References

Reference	Description
=EAST.XLS!$B$11*4	Reference contains a calculation.
=EAST.XLS!B11	Reference contains a relative cell reference.
=SUM(EAST.XLS!$B$11:$F$11)	Reference contains a function.
=EAST.XLS!Total	Total is a named formula.

Changing, Updating, and Opening Linked Worksheets

After you create a worksheet containing data that is linked to another worksheet, you need to know some Excel commands for controlling linked worksheets. This section covers the **File Links** command and the steps for changing, updating, and opening linked worksheets.

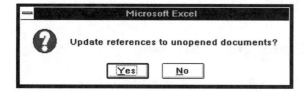

When you open a dependent worksheet that contains a reference to an unopened supporting worksheet, a message dialog box appears.

The dialog box asks if you want to update references to unopened documents. If you respond **Yes** to the message, Excel checks the unopened document. Excel updates the document you are opening with the latest values from the unopened document(s). If you respond **No**, the unopened document(s) are not checked for changes in data.

If the worksheet you are opening contains complex external references to an unopened document, #REF! appears in all cells containing a complex external reference. To recalculate cells containing complex external references, open the referenced document.

205

To change, update, or open a support document, follow these steps:

1. Choose the File Links command. This command is available only if the active document is linked to another document.

The File Links dialog box lists the names of the supporting documents with the type of link specified in the Link Type box.

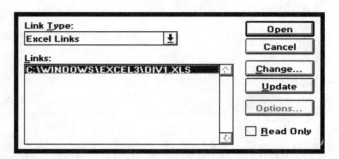

2. Select the supporting document from the list that you want to open, change, or update.

3. Choose the Open button or press ⏎Enter if you want to open the selected supporting document. Choose the Change button if you want to redirect the link to another file. Choose the Update button if you want to update the dependent document with information from the supporting document without opening the supporting worksheet.

Linking with the Paste Link Command

With Excel's Paste Link command, you can link a range of data in a supporting worksheet to a corresponding range in a dependent worksheet. To link a range of cells, follow these steps:

1. Open the supporting and dependent worksheets.

2. Activate the supporting worksheet.

3. Select the range you want to link to the dependent worksheet.

4. Choose the Edit Copy command. A marquee appears around the copied data.

5. Activate the dependent worksheet by selecting the file from the Window menu, by pressing Ctrl F6, or by clicking on the window if it is in view.

6. Select the first cell of the range you want to paste.

7. Choose the Edit Paste Link command. The cells are filled with the copied cells from the supporting worksheet.

9

If the data in the supporting worksheet changes, the linked data in the dependent worksheet updates automatically. The **Edit Paste Link** command treats the pasted area as an array. Individual formulas cannot be modified.

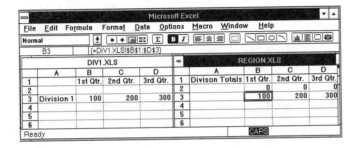

A range of cells is pasted into the dependent worksheet.

The formula bar displays braces around the linked data, indicating that the active cell is part of an array.

Consolidating Data

Consolidation summarizes results from multiple worksheets onto a single worksheet. You may, for example, want to sum totals from different divisions of a company onto a single report. The single report is referred to as the *destination area*. The worksheets containing the division totals are referred to as the *source areas*.

If the destination and source areas share a similar format and contain common category labels, you can consolidate data based on category.

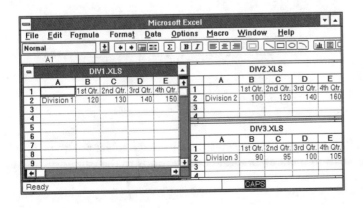

These worksheets have the same labels.

207

Consolidated data is not linked. If data in the source area changes, the data in the destination area does not update to reflect the change. You do have the option, however, to create linked data with the **D**ata Co**n**solidate command. To consolidate data from multiple worksheets into a single worksheet, follow these steps:

1. Open the destination and source worksheets.

2. Activate the destination worksheet and select the area that will contain the consolidated data.

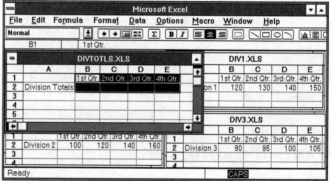

The destination
area is selected.

3. Choose the **D**ata Co**n**solidate command.

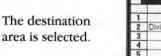

The Consolidate
dialog box
appears.

4. If you are consolidating data based on category labels, select the **T**op Row and/or **L**eft Column check box that corresponds to the category labels you want in the destination area.

9

208

5. Select the **Reference** text box. (The cursor blinks in the text box when the text box is selected.) Activate the first source worksheet containing data to be consolidated. You can move the Consolidate window if it is covering data you want to select.

6. Select the data from the source area that you will consolidate in the destination area. If you are consolidating by category, you must include the category labels in the source area selection.

7. Choose the **Add** button to add the first source reference to the All Reference list in the dialog box. Repeat steps 6 and 7 until all source areas have been added to the list.

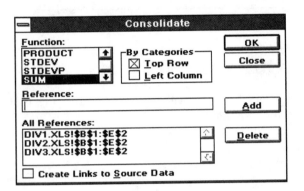

Three source areas have been added in the Consolidate dialog box.

8. Select the function you want to use to consolidate the selected source areas. SUM is the default function.

9. If you want to link the destination area to the source areas, select the Create Links to **S**ource Data check box.

10. If you want to delete a source area from the list, select the reference and choose the **D**elete button.

11. Choose **OK** or press ⏎Enter to clear the dialog box and proceed with the data consolidation. Choose the Close button or press Esc to close the Consolidate dialog box and return to the active document.

9

The destination area includes consolidated data from three source areas. The data was consolidated by Top Row category labels.

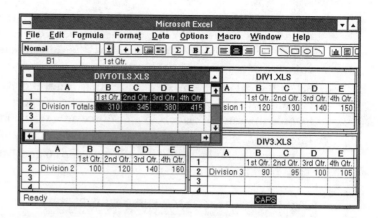

Saving Files to Other File Formats

Sometimes you might share worksheet files with others who are using another application. To make Excel files compatible with other applications, save the Excel files to a file format that the other application can understand. Excel provides the capability to save to several application file formats. The file formats are described in table 9.2.

Table 9.2
File Formats

Format	Description
Normal	Standard Excel file format.
Template	Assigns XLT extension to documents you want to be used as a template.
SYLK	Symbolic Link format.
Text	Text DOS (tab delimited) format.
CSV	Text DOS Comma Separated Values format.
WKS	Lotus 1-2-3 version 1.x format.
WK1	Lotus 1-2-3 version 2.x format.
WK3	Lotus 1-2-3 version 3.x format.
DIF	Data Interchange Format (VisiCalc).
DBF 2	dBASE II format.

9

210

Format	Description
DBF 3	dBASE III format.
DBF 4	dBASE IV format.
Text Macintosh	Macintosh text (tab delimited) format.
CSV Macintosh	Macintosh Comma Separated Values format.
CSV OS/2 or DOS	Comma Separated Values format (DOS & OS/2).

To save an Excel file to another file format, follow these steps:

1. Choose the File Save As command.

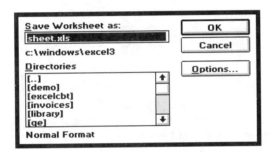

The File Save As
dialog box
appears.

2. Enter a file name in the text box if you are saving the document for the first time.

3. Choose the Options button.

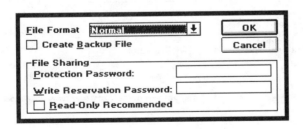

The File Format
dialog box
appears.

4. Select the File Format list by clicking on the down arrow, or press Alt ↓.

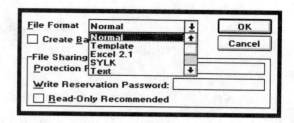

The list of
possible file
formats appears.

5. Select the file format you want from the list.

6. Choose **OK** or press [Enter]. You return to the File Save As dialog box.

7. The file name appears with the extension of the selected file format.

8. Choose **OK** or press [Enter].

Importing a File from Another File Format

Excel has two-way compatibility with other applications. Not only can you
export Excel files to another file format, but you can import other file formats
into Excel. The file formats listed in table 9.2 also can be imported by Excel.
Suppose that you are handed a document that has been created in Lotus 1-2-3.
Rather than recreate the same document in Excel, you can open the 1-2-3 file
into an Excel spreadsheet. Follow these steps:

1. Choose the File **O**pen command.

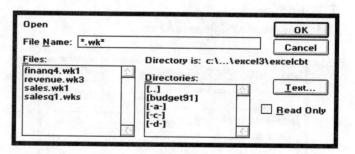

The Open dialog
box appears.

2. Choose the directory or drive where the Lotus 1-2-3 file is located from
the Directories list box.

3. Enter ***.WK*** in the File Name text box. All files in the current directory
with a Lotus 1-2-3 extension appear in the Files list box.

212

4. Select the file you want to open from the Files list box, or enter the name of the file in the File Name text box.

5. Choose **OK** or press ⏎Enter to open the file into Excel.

Most applications have the capability to be saved as a text file. Once a file is saved in a standard text file format, the file can be imported into an Excel worksheet. Each line in a text file appears in a row. Columns of data are divided by a comma or tab. When a text file is imported, you can specify whether data should be delimited by tabs or commas, and the original source of the text file. To import a text file format, follow these steps:

1. Choose the **File Open** command.

2. Choose the **Text** button.

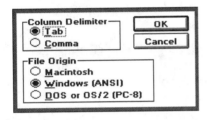

This dialog box appears.

3. Select the Column delimiter option, **Tab** or **Comma**. Choose the File Origin: **Macintosh**, **Windows**, or **DOS** or OS/2.

4. Choose **OK** or press ⏎Enter. You return to the File Open dialog box.

5. Select the file from the Files list or enter the name of the file in the File Name text box.

6. Choose **OK** or press ⏎Enter.

Summary

In this chapter, you learned how to work more efficiently with multiple documents. You learned how to link data in one worksheet with data in another worksheet, and consolidate data from several worksheets into a single worksheet. In addition to learning techniques for working with multiple documents, you learned to import and export Excel files to other file formats.

In this chapter, you were introduced to the following key information about Excel:

■ The **Window Arrange All** command evenly tiles all open windows.

213

- The File Save Workspace command enables you to save the arrangement of files on your screen.

- A workspace file includes only the file name, not the actual file.

- A formula can refer to data in another file. The referenced data is called an *external reference*.

- An external reference involves a supporting worksheet and a dependent worksheet. The supporting worksheet contains the original data that is referred to by the dependent worksheet. The dependent worksheet contains the formula that refers to data in the supporting worksheet.

- A simple external reference is one that involves only an absolute reference.

- A complex external reference involves a calculation, function, relative cell address, or named formula.

- The File Links command enables you to change, update, or open the supporting worksheet.

- The Edit Paste Link command enables you to link ranges. Pasted areas are treated as an array and cannot be modified.

- The Data Consolidate command enables you to summarize data from multiple worksheets into a single worksheet.

- The File Save As command has an Options button that enables you to save an Excel file to another file format.

- Excel can import files that were created in another application.

The following chapter introduces you to charting—one of Excel's most exciting and powerful features. In Chapter 10, you will learn how to create a chart as a separate document and how to create a chart on a worksheet. You also will learn how to change to another chart type, add chart objects to enhance a chart, and format a chart. The chapter also provides instructions for creating a picture chart. When you create picture charts, you present data in the form of graphic images or pictures.

9

214

Charting

Data can be interpreted much faster if it is represented in a graphical format. A chart provides a graphical format that has a greater visual impact than rows of numbers in a worksheet. A chart can communicate results that are recognized with a quick glance. Without a chart, each piece of data would have to be analyzed to draw a conclusion.

Charting data in an Excel worksheet is a simple process. You select data and press the Chart key. The chart is linked to the selected data. If the underlying data changes, the chart updates automatically to reflect the change. Once a chart is created, Excel offers many features to enhance and edit the chart. You can choose from among several chart types including column, bar, area, line, pie, and scatter charts. Excel 3.0 offers four 3-D chart types that you can rotate and elevate. Each chart type includes several predefined charts that you can select from the Chart gallery.

This chapter covers the steps involved in selecting a chart type and creating, enhancing, formatting, modifying, and printing a chart. This chapter also provides instructions for creating a picture chart.

A picture chart uses graphic drawings, pictures, or clip art to chart data rather than lines, columns, or bars. You can stack the pictures or stretch them to represent a certain number.

Key Terms in This Chapter

X-axis	The horizontal (category) axis on a chart.
Y-axis	The vertical (value) axis on a chart.
Chart tool	The Excel tool used to create a chart on a worksheet.
Attached text	Text on a chart that is fixed to a position and cannot be moved.
Chart object	An item added to a chart. The item can be moved, sized, and formatted.
Patterns dialog box	The dialog box that appears when you double-click on a chart object. Enables you to choose a border format and patterns for the area inside the border for most chart objects.
Legend	A guide near the chart that identifies the data in the chart.
Chart overlay	An Excel feature that creates a combination chart enabling you to compare data on a single chart.
Data series	A collection of data from a worksheet.

10

Creating a Basic Chart

Charts are based on selected data in a worksheet. Once data is selected on a worksheet, creating a chart is as simple as pressing a single key. Excel displays the selected data in a column chart, which is the default chart type. Later in this chapter, you will learn how to change the default chart type and enhance your chart with objects and formatting.

To create a chart, follow these steps:

1. Select the worksheet data you want to chart. If you are unsure of the procedures for selecting data, refer to Chapter 3 for more detailed instructions.

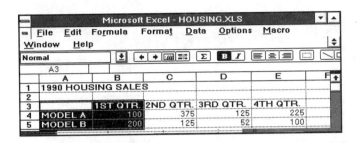

This selected data will be charted on a worksheet.

2. Press the Chart key, F11 (or Alt F1). Or, choose the File menu and select the New command. Select Chart from the dialog box, and choose OK or press ←Enter.

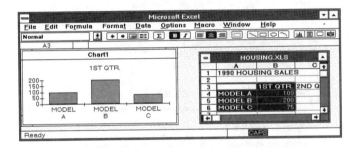

The selected range of data has been charted.

The chart is linked to the selected worksheet data. If the data changes, the chart adjusts to reflect the change.

When Excel charts the selected data, Excel assumes that the category (X) axis runs along the longest side of the selection.

10

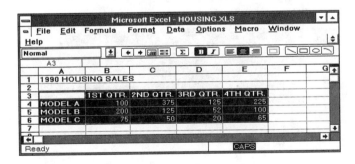

If the selected range is wider than it is tall, the data in the top row is displayed on the X-axis (horizontal axis).

217

Data in the first
row of the
selection is
displayed on
the X-axis.

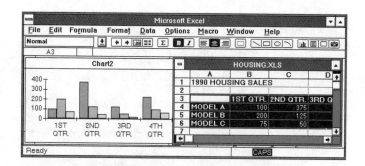

If the selected
range is longer
than it is wide,
the data in the
left column is
displayed on
the X-axis.

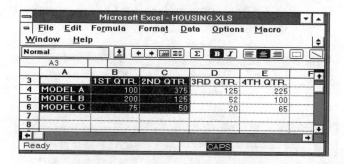

10

Data in the left
column of the
selection is
displayed on
the X-axis.

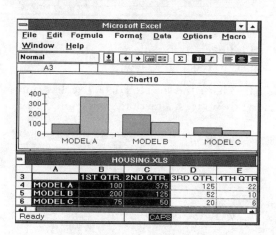

If the selection is equal in length and width, Excel assumes that the category (X) labels are contained in the first row of the selection.

On some occasions, a dialog box appears on-screen and requests more information about plotting data.

The dialog box lets you state what the first row of data in the selection contains.

Choose one of the options: First Data Series, Category (X) Axis Labels, or **X**-Values for XY Chart. Choose OK or press Enter to clear the dialog box and proceed with the chart.

The chart appears in a separate window that has a menu bar different than the menu bar on a worksheet. The commands on the menu bar apply to the chart. For example, the chart menu bar includes the Chart and Gallery menus, which are not included on the worksheet menu bar. The Format menu on the chart menu bar is different than the Format menu on the worksheet menu bar. The Format menu on the chart menu bar contains formatting commands that pertain to charts. The chart commands are outlined in table 10.1

Table 10.1
Chart Commands

Command	Action
Gallery Preferred	Applies to the active chart the format you defined with the **G**allery Se**t** Preferred command.
Gallery Set Preferred	Changes the default chart format to one that you specify.
Chart Attach Text	Inserts text near a chart object, such as the title, an axis, a data series, or an overlay.
Chart Add Arrow	Adds (or deletes) an arrow on a chart.
Chart Add Legend	Adds (or deletes) a legend on a chart.

continues

10

Table 10.1 *(continued)*

Command	Action
Chart Axes	Hides or displays the category (X) and value (Y) axes.
Chart Gridlines	Displays or hides major and minor gridlines attached to the category and value axes.
Chart Add Overlay	Adds (or deletes) a second chart over the current main chart to create a combination chart.
Chart Edit Series	Creates, edits, or deletes a data series on an active chart.
Chart Select Chart	Selects all elements of a chart, enabling Edit commands to affect all aspects of the chart.
Chart Select Plot Area	Selects a chart's plot area, enabling Format Patterns to affect all elements in the area bounded by the axes.
Chart Protect (Unprotect) Document	Protects (or unprotects) a chart's data series, formatting, and window from change. Provides password protection.
Chart Color Palette	Customizes colors in the color palette and copies color palettes between open documents.
Chart Calculate Now	Recalculates all open worksheets, and then redraws all open charts supported by those worksheets when manual calculation is on.
Chart Short (Full) Menus	Full Menus sets menus to display all options. Short Menus sets menus to display only the most-used options, which speeds command selection and makes Excel simpler for new users.
Format Patterns	Sets the style, weight, color, and pattern of selected chart object.
Format Font	Changes the font for selected chart text.
Format Text	Sets the alignment and orientation of text in a chart.

10

Command	Action
Format Scale	Controls the scale setting for each axis on the active chart.
Format Legend	Changes the position of the chart's legend.
Format Main Chart	Sets the active main chart's type and formatting; enables you to change chart types without losing custom formatting.
Format Overlay	Sets the active overlay chart's type and formatting.
Format 3-D View	Controls the angle at which you view the data in a 3-D chart.
Format Move	Enables you to move selected chart objects.
Format Size	Enables you to resize chart arrows and unattached text boxes in a chart.

Creating a Chart on a Worksheet

In the previous section, you learned how to create a chart that was a separate document from the worksheet document. In many cases, you will want the worksheet data and chart on separate pages. Sometimes, however, you will want to have your worksheet data and the chart that represents the data on the same page. Excel provides you with a Chart tool on the tool bar that enables you to plot selected data on the worksheet.

To create a chart on a worksheet, follow these steps:

1. Select the data to be charted.

10

Charting

This data is selected.

	A	B	C	D	E	F
1	1990 HOUSING SALES					
2						
3		1ST QTR.	2ND QTR.	3RD QTR.	4TH QTR.	
4	MODEL A	100	375	125	225	
5	MODEL B	200	125	52	100	
6	MODEL C	75	50	20	65	

2. Choose the Chart tool on the tool bar.

This is the Chart tool on the tool bar.

3. Position the cross-hair on the worksheet area in the upper left corner where you want the chart to start. Drag diagonally toward the lower right corner until the border defines the area you want the chart to occupy. Release the mouse button. A chart of the selected data appears in the area.

A chart is created on the worksheet.

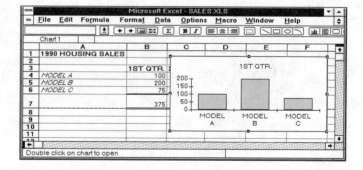

222

Moving a Chart

When you create a chart on a worksheet, the position and size may not suit you. If you want to make changes, you can move and resize the chart.

To move a chart on a worksheet, follow these steps:

1. Select the chart by clicking on it. The chart is enclosed by boundary lines with small black handles.

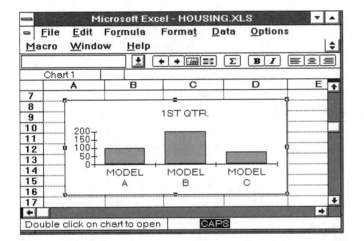

The selected chart is enclosed by small black handles.

2. Position the mouse pointer (arrow) inside the chart area and drag it to the desired location.

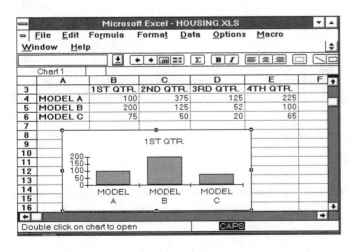

The selected chart can be moved around on a worksheet.

10

223

Sizing a Chart

When a chart is selected on a worksheet, the chart appears enclosed by boundary lines with six small black squares called *handles*. The black squares are used for sizing the area. The corner handles are used to size the chart proportionally. The handles in the middle between the corner handles are used to increase or decrease the chart horizontally or vertically.

To resize the chart, follow these steps:

1. Select the chart.
2. Position the cell pointer on one of the black square handles. The cell pointer changes to a cross-hair when properly positioned on the handle.
3. Drag the handle until the chart reaches the desired size. The corner handles size the chart proportionally. The middle handles size the chart horizontally or vertically.

This chart has been resized proportionally.

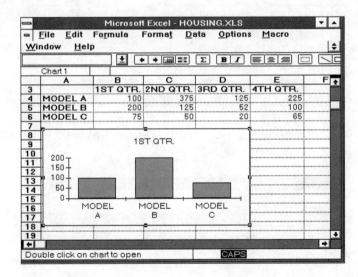

10

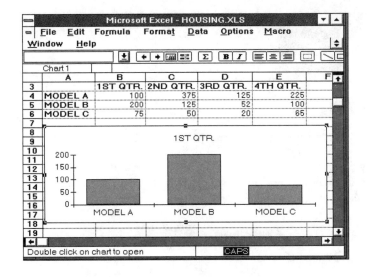

This chart has been resized horizontally.

Selecting a Chart Type

The first section of this chapter discusses charts that appear in separate windows. The separate Chart window displays a menu bar with Chart commands for choosing other chart types, enhancing, and formatting. When you create a chart on a worksheet, you will notice that the worksheet menu bar does not include the Chart commands. If you want to change to another chart type, enhance the chart, or format the chart, you must display the worksheet chart in a Chart window, position the mouse pointer (arrow) on the chart, and double-click. The chart appears in a Chart window with the chart menu bar and Chart commands. The changes you make to the chart in the Chart window appear on the worksheet chart.

Excel uses a column chart as its default chart type. If you want to change to another chart type after the chart is created, you must go to the Chart gallery. The Chart gallery is a collection of the various types of charts. Your choices include seven 2-D chart types and four 3-D chart types. To select a chart type, you must be in a Chart window. If the Chart window is not the active window, choose the Window menu and select the chart document, or press Ctrl+F6 until the Chart window is active.

The steps for selecting a chart type are as follows:

1. Choose the Gallery menu and select the chart type you want: Bar, Area, Column, Line, Pie, Scatter, Combination, 3-D Area, 3-D Column, 3-D Line, and 3-D Pie.

10

225

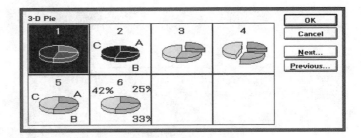

Predefined chart formats for the selected chart type appear in a dialog box.

2. Choose the style you want by double-clicking on the example, or select the chart and choose **OK** or press ⏎Enter. To view other chart types in the gallery, choose the Next or Previous button.

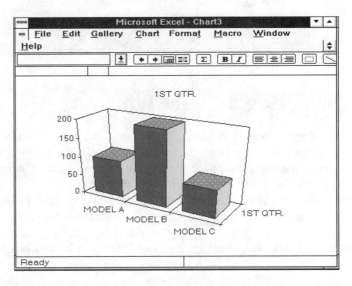

This is an example of the 3-D column chart number 7.

10

Setting the Preferred Chart Type

As mentioned earlier, the default chart type is a two-dimensional column chart. The column chart is set as the preferred chart type. If you consistently use a chart type other than the column chart, change the preferred chart type to the style you use most frequently. For example, if you consistently use a line chart to chart data from a particular worksheet, you can change the column chart to a line chart and set the line chart as the preferred chart type. Once a chart is set as the preferred chart type, the preferred chart type appears each time a chart is created. The preferred chart also can include formatting and enhancements.

Use the following steps to set a preferred chart type:

1. From the Chart window, choose the chart type you want using the Gallery menu. Select the predefined format you want.

2. Add any custom formatting or enhancements you want.

3. Choose the Gallery menu and select the Set Preferred command.

The preferred chart type applies to all charts created in the active document. If you change to a chart type other than the preferred chart type, you can return to the preferred chart type by selecting the Gallery Preferred command.

Enhancing and Formatting a Chart

The chart menu bar includes a number of commands to enhance a chart. The chart commands enable you to add text, arrows, legends, overlays, and gridlines. You can format a chart object by double-clicking on the object, or choosing from the Format menu.

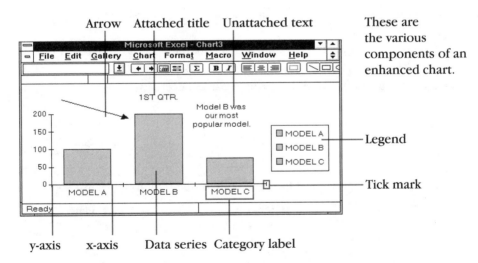

Adding chart enhancements and formatting chart objects are described in the following sections.

Adding Text to a Chart

You can add text to a chart in the form of a title or a label attached to an axis or a data point. *Attached text* is centered and fixed to the option selected and cannot be moved. You can attach text to the horizontal (X) axis, the vertical (Y) axis, or a data series chart marker. To attach text to a chart section, display the Chart window and follow these steps:

1. Choose the Chart menu and select the Attach Text command.

The Attach Text To dialog box appears.

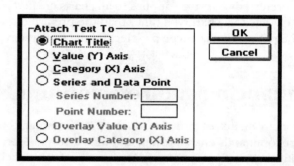

2. Choose the type of text you want to add. The attached text options are described in table 10.1.

3. Choose **OK** or press ⏎Enter to clear the dialog box and attach text to the chart.

4. Edit the attached text in the formula bar as necessary.

Table 10.1
Attached Text Options

Option	Function
Chart Title	Centers a title in the plot area.
Value (Y) Axis	Attaches a Y on the vertical Y-axis. (This option changes to Value (Z) Axis for 3-D charts.)
Category (X) Axis	Attaches an X on the horizontal X-axis.
Series (Y) Axis	Attaches a Y on the vertical series axis.
Series and Data Point	Attaches a number representing a data point.

10

228

Option	Function
Overlay Value (**Y**) Axis	Attaches a Y on the overlay vertical axis.
Overlay Category (**X**) Axis	Attaches an X on the overlay horizontal axis. (Overlay options are not available for 3-D charts.)

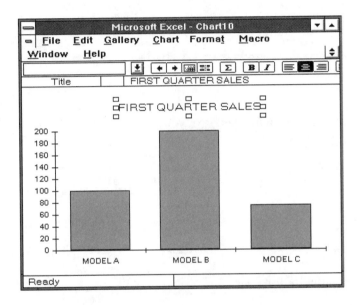

If attached text is selected, it is surrounded by white square handles, indicating that it cannot be moved.

10

Adding Unattached Text

The preceding example explained how to attach text to certain points on a chart. The attached text is fixed to the chosen point and cannot be moved. Some charting situations may require you to include text that can be moved on the chart. For example, you may want to position text in the form of a brief note or label to explain a specific point on the chart. If you want to include text on a chart that is not attached and can be moved, follow these steps:

1. Enter text when the formula bar is clear. (The formula bar is clear when nothing on the chart is selected. Text appears in the formula bar as it is being entered.)

   For example, type **Model B was our most popular model**.

2. Click on the check mark in the formula bar or press ↵Enter.

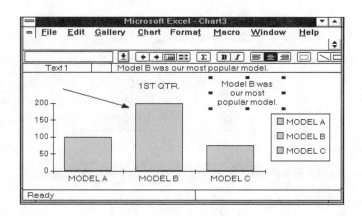

The unattached text appears in the center of the chart plot area surrounded by black squares. You can move the text anywhere on the chart.

Deleting Text

If you want to delete attached or unattached text, you must delete the text in the formula bar. Use the following steps to delete text:

1. Select the attached or unattached text on the chart. Attached text is surrounded by white handles when selected. Unattached text is surrounded by black handles when selected. The selected text appears in the formula bar.

2. Activate the formula bar by clicking in the formula bar area when the cell pointer changes to an I-beam, or press F2. The cursor appears in the formula bar.

3. Select all the text in the formula bar.

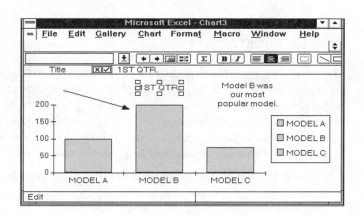

The chart title is selected and appears in the formula bar.

230

4. Press ⌷Del⌷.

5. Click on the check mark in the formula bar or press ↵Enter. The selected text disappears from the chart.

Formatting Text

You can format text by changing alignment, orientation, font, point size, or style, or by adding a border or pattern. Follow these steps to format text:

1. Select the text you want to format by clicking on it with the mouse, or press ← or → until the text you want is selected. The selected text is surrounded by square handles.

2. Choose the Format menu and select the Text command.

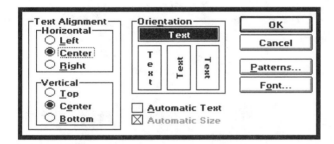

The Text Alignment dialog box appears.

3. Choose from among the Horizontal and Vertical alignments to position the text within its text border. The text can be centered, left-aligned, or right-aligned within the area containing the text.

4. Choose the orientation style you want from among the text orientation choices. You can rotate selected text to a vertical or sideways orientation. If the selection is too long to display vertically, the text wraps to additional columns.

5. For unattached text, choose the Automatic Size check box if you want the border to fit exactly around the text and automatically adjust when the text is changed. Automatic Size is turned off if you resize the area of the unattached text. If you want the text border size to remain fixed, keep Automatic Size turned off.

   If the selected text is attached text, such as a chart title or data series marker, the Automatic Size check box appears dimmed because the attached text area cannot be resized.

10

231

The Automatic Text check box is available only when attached text is selected. This check box enables you to restore attached text to the default text.

6. Choose the Patterns button if you want to access the Format Patterns dialog box and select border and area patterns to apply to the selected area.

7. Choose the Font button if you want to access the Format Font dialog box and change the font, point size, and style of the selected text.

8. Choose OK or press [⏎Enter] to clear the dialog and apply the text formatting.

The Text Align-
ment dialog box
was used to
format the text in
this chart.

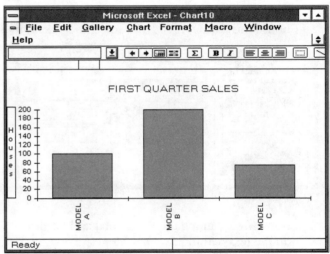

Adding a Pattern and Border to Text

You can add a background pattern and border to selected text to enhance its appearance. The Patterns dialog box appears whenever you double-click on a chart object.

The Format Patterns dialog box is divided into two sections. The section on the left is titled Border and controls the type of border applied to the selected object. The section on the right is titled Area and controls the area inside the border. The options available in both sections include Automatic, None, and Custom. Custom enables you to select from three drop-down lists specific formatting options that you can apply to either the border or the area inside the border.

232

To format text with patterns and a border, follow these steps:

1. Double-click on the text you want to format or select the text; then choose the Format Patterns command.

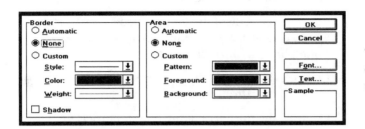

The Patterns dialog box appears.

2. Choose the border style you want from the options on the left side of the dialog box. The options are described in table 10.2.

3. Choose the background, foreground, and pattern you want from the drop-down lists on the right side of the dialog box. The options are described in table 10.2.

    To display a drop-down list using the mouse, click on the down arrow to the right of the list box.

    To display a drop-down list with the keyboard, press Alt and the underlined letter of the option to activate the option. Then press Alt↓.

    The list for the selected option drops down to display the choices. Click on the selection you want to make, or use the arrow keys to move through the list until the choice you want is selected. The sample area in the lower right corner of the dialog box displays what your choices will look like.

4. Choose OK or press ↵Enter to clear the dialog box and apply the formatting.

10

Table 10.2
Patterns Dialog Box Options

Option	Function
Automatic (Border)	Apply default border settings.
Automatic (Area)	Apply default fill settings.
None (Border)	Make border invisible.

continues

233

Table 10.2 *(continued)*

Option	*Function*
None (Area)	Make inside area invisible.
Border Style	Controls the style of the line or border. Enables you to choose from styles including solid lines, dotted lines, and pattern lines.
Border Color	Controls the color of the line or border. Enables you to choose from a palette of colors.
Border Weight	Controls the thickness of the line or border. Enables you to choose a fine line or a thick line.
Fill Pattern	Controls the pattern inside the selected area. Enables you to choose from a list of patterns.
Fill Foreground	Controls the foreground color of the pattern or fills the selected object with a solid color if a pattern is not chosen. Enables you to choose from a palette of colors.
Fill Background	Controls the background color of the pattern or fills the selected object with a solid color if a pattern is not chosen. Enables you to choose from a palette of colors.
Shadow	Shadows the background of the border.

10

In this example, text is formatted with a rectangular border with a shadow.

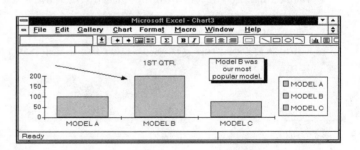

Selecting Fonts

In the Font dialog box, you can choose from among installed screen fonts and printer fonts. The font list in the dialog box includes a number of fonts with point sizes corresponding to each font type. You also can choose a style for a font such as bold, italic, or underline.

To format selected text by changing the font, follow these steps:

1. Select the text you want to format.

2. Choose the Format menu and select the Font command.

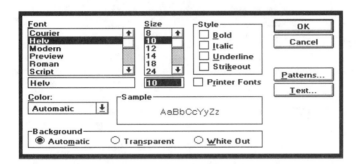

The Font dialog box appears.

3. Choose the Font, Size, Style, Color, Background, and other formatting options available in the dialog box. You can see what your selected options will look like in the sample area.

   Note: Many fonts can be displayed on your screen but cannot be printed on your printer. If your printer cannot print a font that has been selected, your printer will try to match it with the closest printer font available. To avoid problems with selecting fonts that your printer will not support, turn on the Printer Fonts check box. (Select the box or press (Alt) (R) so that an X appears in the box.) When the Printer Fonts check box is turned on, only fonts supported by your printer are displayed in the Font list.

4. Select the Patterns button if you want to access the Patterns dialog box. Use the Patterns option to apply a border and patterns to the inside area of the selected object.

5. Select the Text button if you want to access the Text Alignment dialog box. The Text option controls text alignment and orientation.

6. Choose OK or press (↵Enter) to clear the dialog box and apply the selected formatting.

10

235

Several fonts were used to enhance this chart text.

Adding an Arrow

You may want to draw attention to a particular section of a chart. You can add an arrow to emphasize a region of a chart. You also can combine an arrow with unattached text to explain a result.

Use the following steps to add one or more arrows to a chart:

1. Choose the Chart menu and select the Add Arrow command.

   An arrow appears in the center of the plot area, surrounded on each end with a black square handle. The handles are used for sizing the arrow.

10

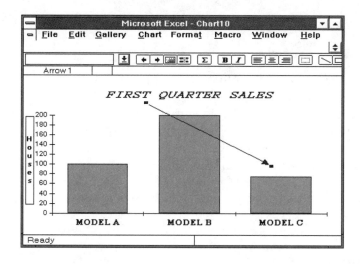

The selected arrow appears with small black squares at each end.

2. Choose the Chart Add Arrow command again if you want to have multiple arrows on your chart.

The Add Arrow command on the Chart menu changes to Delete Arrow when an arrow on the chart is selected. (An arrow is selected if it is enclosed by small black handles at each end.) If you want to add multiple arrows on a chart, make sure that an arrow is not selected. The Add Arrow command appears on the Chart menu as long as an arrow is not selected.

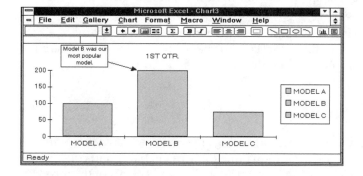

10

In this example, an arrow and unattached text are combined on a chart.

To delete an arrow from a chart, follow these steps:

1. Select the arrow you want to remove.

2. Choose the Chart menu and select the Delete Arrow command. The selected arrow disappears.

Moving an Arrow

To move an arrow, follow these steps:

1. Select the arrow by clicking on it, or press ⬆ or ⬇ until the arrow is selected.

2. With the mouse, position the mouse pointer on the arrow and drag it to the desired location. Then release the mouse button when the arrow is placed in the desired location.

   With the keyboard, choose the Format menu and select the Move command. Next, use the arrow keys to move the arrow to the desired location. Then press ⏎Enter when the arrow is placed in the desired location.

Sizing an Arrow

The handles on each end of a selected arrow are used to change the length of the arrow and rotate the arrow. To change the size of the arrow, follow these steps:

1. Select the arrow by clicking on it, or press ⬆ or ⬇ until the arrow is selected.

2. With the mouse, position the mouse pointer on one of the sizing handles at the end of the arrow. Drag the handle until the arrow is at the desired size. Use the handle to rotate the arrow until the arrow is pointing in the desired direction.

   With the keyboard, choose the Format menu and select the Size command. Next, use the arrow keys to change the arrow to the desired size. Then press ⏎Enter when the arrow is the desired size.

Formatting an Arrow

Excel provides several options for formatting an arrow, including converting an arrow into a straight line. The formatting options enable you to control the line Style, Color, and Weight, and the Style, Width, and Length of the arrow head. The Arrow Head Style option enables you to exclude the arrow head, which makes the arrow a straight line.

To format an arrow, follow these steps:

1. Double-click on the arrow with the mouse, or choose the Format menu and select the Patterns command.

238

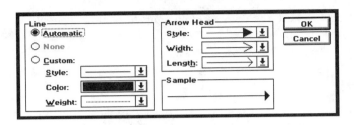

The Patterns
dialog box
appears.

2. Choose the formatting option you want to set the style of the arrow in, including the shaft and arrow-head length and width. You can see in the sample area what the selected options will look like when applied.

3. Choose **OK** or press ⏎Enter to clear the dialog box and apply the selected formatting.

Adding a Legend

A *legend* is used in a chart to identify the data in the chart. Legends usually are necessary for understanding the way the data is presented. In the section on creating a chart, you learned that the labels on the horizontal (X) axis are created using the data from the long side of the selected data. A legend is created from the short side of the selected data.

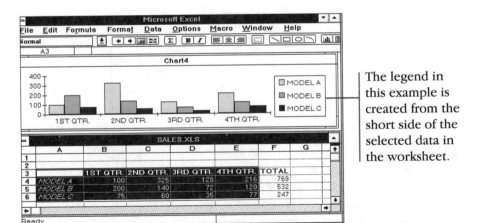

The legend in this example is created from the short side of the selected data in the worksheet.

To add a legend to a chart, choose the Format menu and select the Add Legend command. The legend appears on the right side of the chart. After a legend has been added to a chart, the command changes to `Delete Legend`. A chart can have only one legend.

Moving a Legend

When the legend is selected, it is enclosed by small black handles indicating that the legend can be moved. To move the legend to another location on the chart, position the mouse pointer on the legend and drag it to the desired location. Then release the mouse button. Or, with the keyboard, choose the Format menu and select the **Move** command. Press the arrow keys until the legend reaches the desired location and press Enter.

Formatting a Legend

You can move a legend on a chart with the mouse or keyboard command. You also can position a legend to a specific location in the chart area.

To change the position of a legend, follow these steps:

1. Select the legend by clicking on it, or press ⬆ or ⬇ until the legend is enclosed by small black handles.

2. Choose the Format menu and select the **Legend** command.

The Legend dialog box appears.

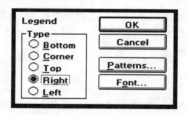

3. Choose the **Bottom**, **Corner**, **Top**, **Right**, or **Left** position.

4. Choose the **Patterns** button if you want to access the Patterns dialog box. Then choose from among the formatting options.

5. Choose the **Font** button if you want to access the Font dialog box, and select from among the formatting options.

6. Choose **OK** or press ⏎Enter to clear the dialog box and apply the selected formatting.

As with most chart objects, double-clicking on the legend displays the Patterns dialog box.

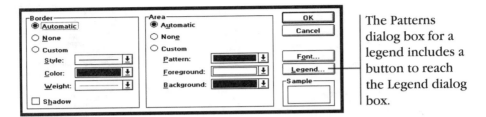

The Patterns dialog box for a legend includes a button to reach the Legend dialog box.

Customizing Axes

When a chart is created, it has a horizontal (X) axis and a vertical (Y) axis. A 3-D chart has an additional (Z) axis. These axes can be removed or formatted to meet specific charting requirements.

If you want to remove an axis from the chart, choose the Chart menu and select the Axes command.

The Axes dialog box appears.

10

The check boxes in the Axes dialog box indicate which axes are turned on. If you want to remove an axis, select the check box to remove the X. The axis disappears from the chart.

Formatting an Axis

You can format an axis to enhance its appearance. To format a chart axis, follow these steps:

1. Double-click on the axis to select it, or select the axis and choose Format Patterns.

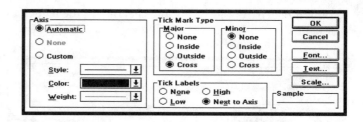

The Patterns
dialog box
appears.

2. Choose the formatting options you want from the dialog box.

3. Choose the Font button if you want to access the Font dialog box with
   more formatting options.

4. Choose the Scale button if you want to access the Scale dialog box.
   The dialog box displays more formatting options. (The Scale dialog
   box is discussed in more detail in the section that follows.)

5. Choose **OK** or press ↵Enter to clear the dialog box and apply the axis
   formatting.

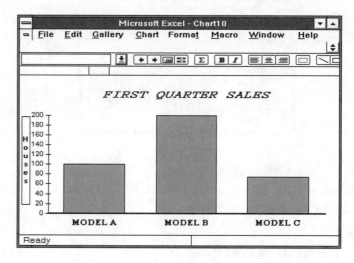

The horizontal
axis has been
formatted.

Scaling an Axis

When an axis is selected, you have access to the Scale formatting command.
Depending on which axis is selected, the Scale command offers options that
pertain to the selected axis.

10

If the horizontal (X) category axis is selected, the **Scale** command enables you to control where the vertical (Y) axis will intersect the (X) axis, the number of categories between tick marks and tick labels, and other formatting options.

If the vertical (Y) value axis is selected, the **Scale** command enables you to control minimum and maximum values, major and minor units, and where the horizontal (X) axis will intersect the (Y) axis.

<table>
<tr><td>

Category (X) Axis Scale

Value (Y) Axis Crosses
at Category Number: [1]

Number of Categories
Between Tick Labels: [1]

Number of Categories
Between Tick Marks: [1]

[X] Value (Y) Axis Crosses Between Categories
[ ] Categories in Reverse Order
[ ] Value (Y) Axis Crosses at Maximum Category

[OK] [Cancel] [Patterns...] [Font...] [Text...]
</td><td>

This Scale dialog box appears when the horizontal (X) category axis is selected.
</td></tr>
</table>

<table>
<tr><td>

Value (Y) Axis Scale

Auto
[X] Minimum: [0]
[X] Maximum: [500]
[X] Major Unit [500]
[X] Minor Unit [100]
[X] Category (X) Axis
Crosses at: [0]

[ ] Logarithmic Scale
[ ] Values in Reverse Order
[ ] Category (X) Axis Crosses at Maximum Value

[OK] [Cancel] [Patterns...] [Font...] [Text...]
</td><td>

This Scale dialog box is displayed when the vertical (Y) value axis is selected.

10
</td></tr>
</table>

To apply scale formatting to a selected chart axis, follow these steps:

1. Choose the chart axis by clicking on it, or press ↓ or ↑ until the axis is selected.

2. Choose the Format menu and select the Scale command. (The Scale command is available only when an axis is selected.) A dialog box appears.

3. Choose the scale options you want for the selected axis.

4. Choose the Patterns button if you want to access the Patterns dialog box. This dialog box provides more formatting options you can apply to the numbers on the axis.

5. Choose the Font button if you want to access the Font dialog box. This dialog box provides more formatting options you can apply to the numbers on the axis.

6. Choose OK or press ⏎Enter to clear the dialog box and apply the scale formatting.

The vertical axis has been scaled.

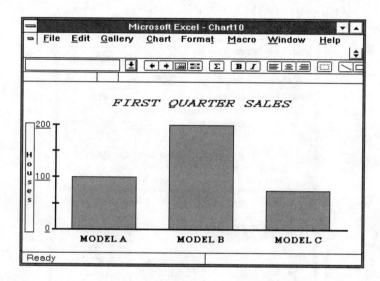

10   Adding Gridlines

You can add gridlines to a chart to help identify the value of a chart marker. Use the Chart Gridlines command to create horizontal or vertical gridlines.

To add major gridlines to a chart, follow these steps:

1. Choose the Chart menu and select the Gridlines command.

The Gridlines dialog box appears.

244

2. Select the type of gridlines you want on the chart.

   Choose Category gridlines if you want the gridlines to start from the horizontal (X) axis and extend vertically.

   Choose Value gridlines if you want the gridlines to start from the vertical (Y) axis and extend horizontally.

   If you are adding gridlines to a 3-D chart, the Z-axis gridlines options are available.

3. Choose **OK** or press ⏎Enter.

After you have added gridlines to a chart, you can format the lines. To format gridlines follow these steps:

1. Double-click on one of the gridlines, or select a line and choose the Format Patterns command. The Patterns dialog box appears. Choose a line style, color, and line weight.

2. Choose **OK** or press ⏎Enter to clear the Patterns dialog box and apply the selected formatting.

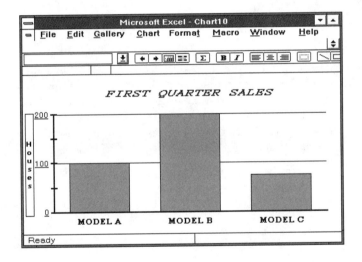

This chart displays Y-axis major gridlines.

10

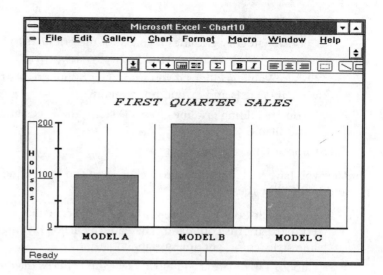

This chart displays X-axis minor gridlines.

Adding a Chart Overlay

You may want to use a chart to compare data. You may, for example, want to compare income with expenses on a single chart. A chart overlay enables you to create a combination chart. The selected data is divided evenly with the first half of the data assigned to the main chart in the background. The second half of the data is assigned to the overlay and is displayed in the foreground. If an odd number of data series exists, the main chart receives the additional data series. After you add an overlay, you can format it.

To create a chart overlay, choose the Chart menu and select the Add Overlay command. A combination chart displays two sets of data.

10

246

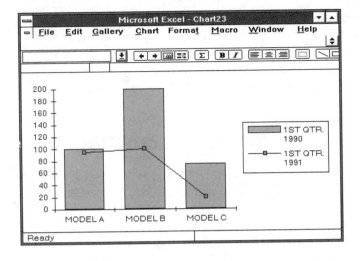

In this example, a column chart is the main chart with a line chart overlay.

When you add a chart overlay to the main chart, the Add Overlay command changes to `Delete Overlay` on the Chart menu. Choose this command to remove the overlay and return all the data to the original main chart.

If an overlay has been added to a chart, a command appears on the Format menu that enables you to apply formatting to the overlay chart.

Use the following steps to format the chart overlay:

1. Choose the Format menu and select Overlay.

The Overlay dialog box appears.

247

2. If you want to change the overlay chart to another chart type, choose the Overlay Chart Type drop-down list in the dialog box, and select the type of chart you want for the overlay.

3. Choose other overlay formatting in the dialog box. The available formatting options will vary depending on the type of overlay selected.

4. Choose OK or press ⏎Enter.

This chart has a formatted overlay.

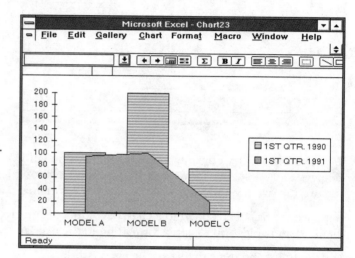

Changing the Main Chart Type

Earlier in this chapter you were introduced to the Chart gallery. The Chart gallery enables you to change to another chart type. If you have added formatting to a chart and decide that you want to change to another chart type, the Gallery menu removes all formatting when you select another chart type. If you want to change to another chart type and preserve your formatting, use the the Format Main Chart command.

To change the main chart type and preserve any formatting you have done, follow these steps:

1. Select Format Main Chart.

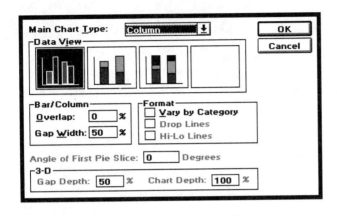

The Format Main
Chart Type menu
dialog box
appears.

2. Choose the chart type you want from the Main Chart Type drop-down
    list.
3. Choose other chart formatting from the dialog box. The available
    formatting options will vary depending on the type of chart selected.
4. Choose **OK** or press ⏎Enter when you have completed your
    selections.

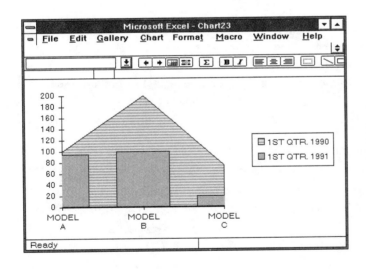

10

Formatting is
preserved when
the main chart
type is changed.

Editing and Adding a Data Series

A *data series* represents a collection of data from a worksheet. If a data series is selected on a chart, a white square appears in the center of all related data markers. The formula bar displays the external reference to the worksheet and the location of the data represented by the data series. If you want to edit the data series or add a new series to the chart without re-creating the chart, Excel provides the **C**hart **E**dit **S**eries command for making changes and additions of a series to a displayed chart. You also can format data series markers, such as columns, bars, and lines, with the Forma**t** **P**atterns command.

To modify or add a series to a displayed chart, follow these steps:

1. Choose the **C**hart menu and select the Edit **S**eries command.

The Edit Series dialog box appears. All data series are listed in the Series list box.

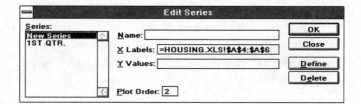

2. From the list, select the data series you want to edit, or choose New Series to add a new data series to the chart.

3. Enter a name into the **N**ame text box, or select a cell from the referenced worksheet if you want to name the data series.

   Select the **X** Labels text box if you want to change the category labels on the horizontal (X) axis. The data you select on the worksheet replaces the selected data in the text box.

   Select the **Y** Values text box if you want to change the values on the vertical (Y) axis.

   A Z Value text box appears in the dialog box if you are editing a 3-D chart.

   Enter a number in the **P**lot Order box if you want to change the order of the data series.

4. Choose the **D**elete button if you want to remove a selected series from the chart. Choose the **D**efine button if you want to define an edited or new data series and continue with additional changes.

10

5. Choose **OK** or press `↵Enter` to accept the changes and clear the dialog box. The chart updates to display the changes. Choose the Close button if you want to cancel the changes you made and clear the dialog box.

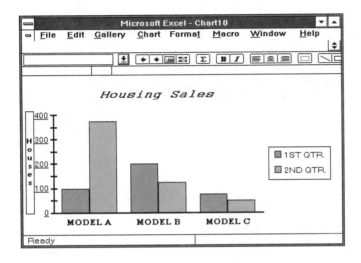

This existing chart contains a new series.

A chart uses data series markers, such as columns, bars, lines, and pie wedges, to represent underlying values. As with most chart objects, you can format a data series marker with the Format **P**atterns command. If you want to change the color, pattern, or border style of a data series marker, follow these steps:

1. Double-click on the data series marker, or select the marker and choose the Format **P**atterns command.

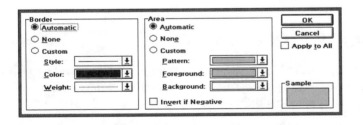

The Format Patterns dialog box appears.

2. Choose the border style from the options on the left side of the dialog box. Choose the background, foreground, and pattern from the drop-down lists on the right side of the dialog box. The options are described in table 10.2. The sample area shows what the selected formatting options will look like when applied.

10

251

3. Select the Apply to All check box if you want to apply the selected formatting to all data series markers in the chart.

4. Select the Invert if Negative check box if you want to reverse the foreground and background colors that represent negative values in a bar, column, area, or pie chart.

5. Choose **OK** or press ⏎Enter to clear the dialog box and apply the selected formatting.

This column chart has formatted data series markers.

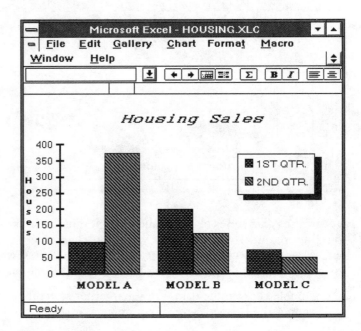

Formatting the Plot Area

In addition to formatting chart objects, you can format the area enclosed by the horizontal (X) and vertical (Y) axes. This area is called the *plot area*. If you want to format the plot area, follow these steps:

1. Double-click anywhere in the plot area, or select the plot area by choosing the **Chart Select Plot Area** command.

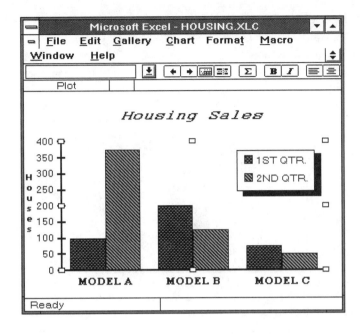

White squares
enclose the plot
area when the
area is selected.

Then choose the Format Patterns command.

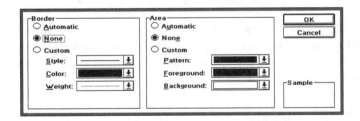

The Patterns
dialog box
appears.

10

2. Choose the border style from the options on the left side of the
   dialog box. Choose the background, foreground, and pattern from the
   drop-down lists on the right side of the dialog box. The options are
   described in table 10.2. The sample area shows what the selected
   formatting options will look like when applied.

3. Choose **OK** or press ⏎Enter to clear the dialog box and apply the
   selected formatting.

This chart has a
formatted plot
area.

Formatting the Chart Background

The chart plot area is defined by the horizontal and vertical axes. A chart has
an area outside the plot area. This area is the chart background. The chart title
and legend are displayed in the chart background. When the chart background
is selected, the entire chart area is selected. If you want to format the chart
background, follow these steps:

1. Double-click anywhere outside the chart plot area, or select the chart
   background by choosing the Chart Select Chart command.

10

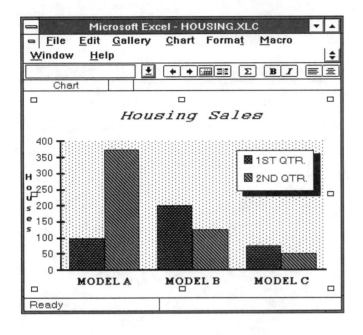

The entire chart area appears enclosed by white squares when the area is selected.

Then choose the Format Patterns command.

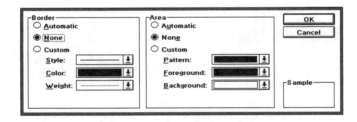

The Patterns dialog box appears.

10

2. Choose the border style from the options on the left side of the dialog box. Choose the background, foreground, and pattern from the drop-down lists on the right side of the dialog box. The options are described in table 10.2. The sample area shows what the selected formatting options will look like when applied.

3. Select the Shadow check box if you want a shadow to appear in the background of the chart area.

4. Choose the Font button if you want to access the Font dialog box and change the font for all text and numbers in the chart.

255

5. Choose **OK** or press ⏎Enter to clear the dialog box and apply the selected formatting.

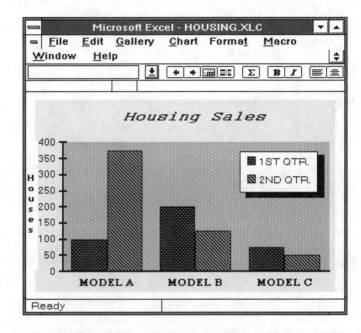

This chart has a formatted chart background.

Copying a Chart to the Clipboard

10

You may want to use an Excel chart in another application, such as a word processor. The clipboard is used to copy information from one application and place it in another application. Because all Windows applications support the clipboard, you will find sharing information with other applications easy. The commands for copying information to the clipboard and extracting the copied information from the clipboard are the same in all Windows applications. Some non-Windows applications also support extracting information from the clipboard. Refer to the non-Windows application's documentation for procedures to extract data from the clipboard.

The clipboard is described in detail in Chapter 5, "Modifying a Worksheet." You may want to refer to this chapter if you are not familiar with the clipboard. To copy a chart to the clipboard, follow these steps:

1. Select the entire chart by clicking anywhere outside the chart plot area, or choose the Chart Select Chart command. The chart appears enclosed by white squares when it is selected.

2. Choose the Edit menu and select the Copy command. A marquee appears around the chart, indicating that the chart has been copied to the clipboard.

3. Activate the application in which you want to place a copy of the chart.

4. If you are using a Windows application, choose the Edit menu and select the Paste command. The chart appears in the application.

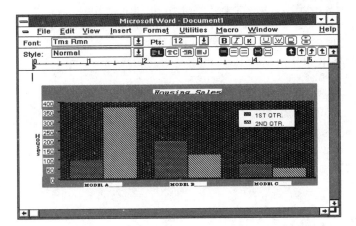

This Excel chart was pasted from the clipboard in a Word for Windows document. The chart appears stretched because it is fitting into the application's current margins.

If you are using a non-Windows application, refer to the application's documentation for the procedures to extract information from the clipboard.

10

Rotating and Elevating a 3-D Chart

3-D charting is an impressive feature included in Excel 3.0. In addition to displaying charted data in a three-dimensional format, you can rotate and elevate the 3-D chart to get the exact view you want. If you are working with a 3-D chart, the Format menu displays a command for 3-D View.

To rotate or elevate a 3-D chart, follow these steps:

1. Choose the Format 3-D View command.

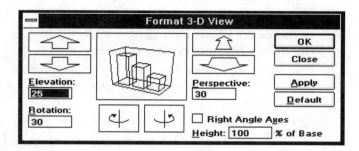

The 3-D View
dialog box
appears.

2. Click on the arrows in the dialog box to control the angle and elevation of the chart, or enter a number into the appropriate text box. The sample displays the changes as you are making them.

3. Select the Apply button if you want to apply the changes and leave the dialog box open to make additional changes.

4. Select the Default button if you want to set the selected angle and rotation as the default chart view.

5. Choose OK or press ⏎Enter if you want to apply the changes and close the dialog box. Or, choose the Close button if you want to cancel any changes you made.

Creating a Picture Chart

10

In addition to creating charts with Excel's predefined chart formats, you can create picture charts. If you are preparing a chart for a presentation to a group of bankers, for example, you may want to use a chart displaying dollar bills. Picture charts can be created by copying a picture or graphic image to the clipboard and pasting it into a bar, column, or line chart.

Follow these steps to create a picture chart:

1. Activate the document or application containing the picture you want to use for a picture chart. You can create a picture in Excel using the Drawing tools, or you can use clip art or graphic images from another application.

2. Copy the picture to the clipboard using the Edit Copy command or the application's command for copying.

3. Activate the Excel chart you want to use for the picture chart. The chart must be a bar, column, or line chart.

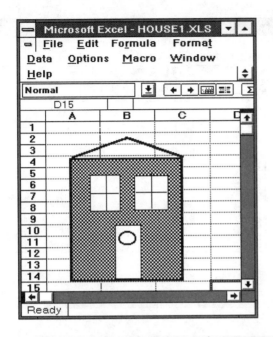

This picture was created on an Excel worksheet with the Drawing tools on the tool bar.

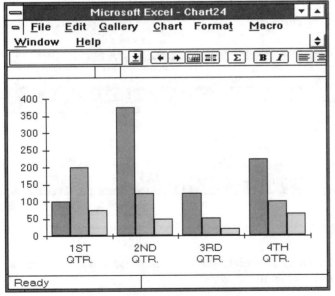

The column chart can be changed to a picture chart.

4. Select a data series marker by clicking on it, or press the arrow keys until the data series marker is selected. A white square appears in the middle of the marker when it is selected.

259

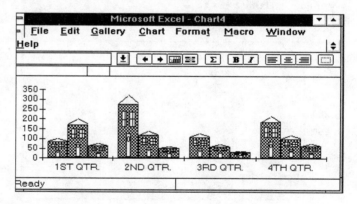

A picture will
replace the
selected data
series markers.

5. Choose the **Edit Paste** command. The data series markers are replaced
   by the picture on the clipboard.

This picture chart
was created by
using a picture of
a house.

You can format a picture chart to stretch, stack, or stack and scale the pictures.
To format a picture chart, follow these steps:

1. Double-click on the picture marker, or choose the Format menu and
   select the **Patterns** command.

10

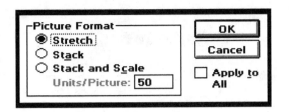

The Patterns
dialog box
appears.

2. Choose the option to Stretch, Stack, or Stack and Scale the picture according to the Units per Picture number.

3. Select the Apply to All check box if you want all data series markers to display the picture marker.

4. Choose OK or press ⏎Enter to clear the dialog box and apply the formatting.

To remove the picture and return to the original chart format, follow these steps:

1. Select a Data Series marker.

2. Choose the Edit Clear command or press Del.

The Clear dialog
box appears.

3. Select the Formats option.

4. Choose OK or press ⏎Enter. The chart returns to its original format.

Printing a Chart

Printing a chart is not much different than printing a worksheet. You do not, however, have to define a print area when you print a chart document.

To print a displayed chart, follow these steps:

1. Choose the File Printer setup command if you need to change to another printer or define default printer settings.

2. Choose the File Page Setup command.

10

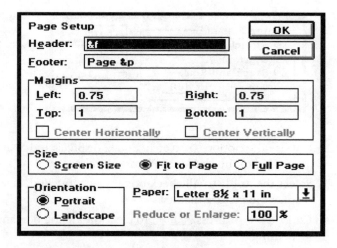

The Page Setup
dialog box
appears.

3. Choose the chart size button for the option you want.

   Screen Size prints the chart the same size as it is on the screen.

   The Fit to Page option prints the chart as large as possible while retaining the height-to-width ratio.

   The Full Page option prints the chart to fit the page, adjusting the height-to-width ratio as necessary.

4. Choose OK or press ↵Enter when you have completed your selections in the Page Setup dialog box.

5. Choose the File Print Preview command if you want to view the chart in preview mode before it is printed.

6. Choose the File Print command. The Print dialog box appears.

7. Choose OK or press ↵Enter to accept the settings and begin printing the chart document.

The printing commands, including Printer Setup, Page Setup, and Print Preview, are discussed in greater detail in Chapter 8.

Summary

In this chapter, you were introduced to many components of charting. This chapter covered topics related to creating and formatting a chart. You learned how to create a chart in a separate Chart window, and you learned how to create a chart on a worksheet. This chapter instructed you on how to add titles, legends, arrows, attached text, unattached text, and gridlines to enhance the appearance of a chart. You learned how to format all chart objects using the formatting commands and various dialog boxes, including the Patterns, Font, Text, Scale, and Arrow dialog boxes. You also learned how to rotate and elevate 3-D charts. You were introduced to picture charts and the steps required to convert a chart into a picture chart.

Charting is a very extensive feature in Excel. This chapter focused primarily on charting basics. If you want to explore charting in more depth and experiment with some of Excel's advanced charting features, you may want to read Que's book *Using Excel 3.0 for Windows*, Special Edition.

In this chapter, you were introduced to the following key information about Excel:

- A chart is a graphical representation of data selected from a worksheet. The chart is linked to the underlying data and updates when the data changes.
- The Chart key (F11) charts selected data in a separate chart window.
- The Chart tool on the tool bar creates a chart of selected data on a worksheet.
- If selected data is wider than it is long, the labels in the first row of the selection appear on the horizontal (X) axis.
- The Gallery menu on the chart menu bar lists the various 2-D and 3-D chart types available. A display of predefined chart formats appears when you select a chart type from the Gallery menu.
- The Chart menu includes commands for adding a legend, text, arrows, and gridlines.
- Attached text is fixed to a location and cannot be moved.
- Unattached text can be entered when the formula bar is blank.
- To delete text from a chart, you must select the text and delete it in the formula bar.
- Double-clicking on most chart objects displays the Format Patterns dialog box.
- The Format Text command controls alignment and orientation of text.
- The Format Font command controls font types, point size, style, color, and background.
- The Printer Fonts check box in the Fonts dialog box should be turned on to display only fonts that your printer can print.
- All formatting dialog boxes include buttons that display other relevant formatting dialog boxes.

10

263

■ You can format an arrow to be a straight line by selecting the arrow head style that is a straight line.

■ The Format Legend command enables you to position the legend at a specified location on the chart. You also can move a legend manually by dragging it to a desired location.

■ The Format Scale command enables you to set where the horizontal and vertical axes will cross.

■ You can add a chart overlay to create a combination chart.

■ If you want to change to another chart type and preserve your custom formatting, you must use the Format Main Chart command.

■ You can edit a data series and add a new series with the Chart Edit Series command.

■ You can create a picture chart by copying a picture, clip art, or graphic image to the clipboard, and pasting it into a bar, column, or line chart.

■ The File Page Setup command enables you to choose how to print the chart on a page.

Now that you have had an opportunity to experiment with some of Excel's charting capabilities, you are ready to tackle Excel's data management capabilities. Chapter 11 will introduce you to Excel's database features. The chapter covers how to create and define a database, find records in a database, and extract records that meet a specified criteria.

10

Managing Data

With Excel, you easily can enter, edit, find, and extract database information. Once information is organized into a database format, you can use database commands to locate data that meets certain criteria. You can sort a database to put data into a specific order, and you can extract and analyze data.

This chapter explains what a database is and how to create a database, including how to enter data into a database form. Defining a database, criteria, and extract ranges also is covered. You learn how to sort a database, search for records meeting a specified criteria, and extract records from a database that meet a specified criteria.

Building a database

Defining a database

Adding records

Deleting records

Sorting a database

Searching for records

11

Key Terms in This Chapter

Database	A range of cells on a worksheet consisting of records organized into categories.
Record	A row of cells containing related information in a database.
Fields	Columns that represent categories in a database.
Field names	Labels in the first row of a database that define the database categories.
Database form	A form that displays field names and text boxes for data entry, and buttons for adding, deleting, and finding records.
Criteria	A defined pattern or detail used to find matching records.
Criteria range	A defined range that includes field names plus a row for specified criteria.
Extract range	A selected or defined range that includes field names plus selected cells to contain copied data.

What Is a Database?

A *database* is a defined range of records organized by categories. A telephone directory is an example of a database. Each individual entry in a telephone directory is a record. Each record has a person's last name, followed by a first name or initial, followed by an address, followed by a phone number. All entries in a telephone directory are organized in the same sequence.

Each row in a database represents a record. A record contains related information. The information on each line in a telephone directory, for example, is related. The phone number for XL Computer Consulting, Inc., is listed on the same line as the company name. In a database, all records are organized with related information in a single row.

A database also consists of *fields*. Each column in a database represents a field. The fields in a database identify the categories of information that are required in each record. The first row of a database must contain labels that identify what the database categories are. These labels are referred to as *field names*.

Each field name is entered into a separate column in the top row of the database. In a telephone directory, the field names would be Last Name, First Name, Address, and Phone Number.

11

Microsoft Excel - Sheet1				
File **Edit** **Formula** **Format** **Data** **Options**				
Macro **Window** **Help**				
Normal				
G7				
	C	D	E	F
1				
2				
3	Last Name	First Name	Address	Phone
4	Bush	Millie	Pennsylvania Ave.	555-1212
5	Brenner	Buddy	Santa Cruz Ave.	555-7353
6	Geiger	Lucy	Vineyard Ave.	555-2244
7				
Ready				

This is an example of a telephone directory database with field names and a few sample records.

You can construct a database with an Excel worksheet. If you are comfortable entering data on a worksheet, you will have no problem creating a database. With an Excel command, you can define as a database any selected area on an Excel worksheet. Before you define an area, however, you must organize the data in a database format.

A database consists of field names and records. You enter individual records in a row. Each column in a database has a unique field name that determines the type of information required for each record. You enter the field names in the first row of the database. You enter records in the rows immediately following the field names. You select the field names and records and define them as a database. Once you define the database, you can use Excel commands to search, sort, extract, and analyze data in the database.

Planning and Building a Database

Before you actually begin building a database, think through how you will use your database. Time spent planning a database saves you time later. If you are planning to sort a database by last names, for example, you will want to create a separate category (field name) for LAST NAME, rather than entering the full name in a single field called NAME. If you are likely to sort data by ZIP code, do not include the ZIP code with an address. Create a separate field in the database for ZIP codes.

267

11

A database can use an entire worksheet, if necessary. If a database is created on an existing worksheet, consider where the database will be positioned. Keep the area below the database clear. Because a database expands downward, you can run into problems if the cells below your database contain data. Position a database on a worksheet where you can safely insert columns and rows. You may need to modify your database to include additional columns or rows. When a column or row is inserted into a worksheet, the column or row is inserted through the entire worksheet. Data in sections surrounding the database may be affected by inserting a column or row.

The first row of the database must contain the field names. The field names identify the categories of information required in each record.

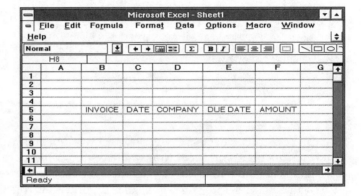

A field name can contain up to 255 characters. Keep field names as brief as possible, however. Field names must be text and should not contain numbers. (If a field name contains a number, the entire field name must be enclosed in quotation marks for Excel to interpret the name as text.) A field name must be unique—you cannot have two fields with the same field name.

Enter records in the first row below the field names. All related information must be entered in a single row. Records can include text, numbers, formulas, and functions. Every record must have the same fields, but you do not have to enter data into all fields.

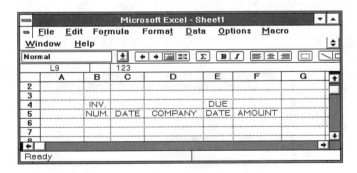

	A	B	C	D	E	F	G
3							
4							
5		INVOICE	DATE	COMPANY	DUE DATE	AMOUNT	
6		123	5-May	XYA & Assoc.	4-Jun	6,200.00	
7		124	10-May	Big Blue Inc.	9-Jun	10,000.00	
8		125	15-May	XL Consulting	14-Jun	2,000.00	
9		126	20-May	SLM & Co.	19-Jun	730.00	
10							
11							

This is an example of a database of outstanding invoices.

The field names, INVOICE, DATE, COMPANY, DUE DATE, and AMOUNT are entered in row 5. Four records have been entered in rows 6 through 9. The data entered in the records includes dates, text, numbers, and formulas. The formula takes the DATE field in column C and adds 30 days to calculate the DUE DATE.

To start building a database, enter the field names in the section of the worksheet where you want to start the database. A database can appear in any section of a worksheet. Make sure that, however, the area below the database is clear of any data so that the database can expand without interfering with other worksheet data.

You can use more than one row to enter field names. This method is useful if you want to keep the column width as narrow as possible to view more of the database on the screen. If you use two rows for the field names, you can select only the row directly above the first record when the database is defined.

	A	B	C	D	E	F	G
2							
3							
4		INV.			DUE		
5		NUM.	DATE	COMPANY	DATE	AMOUNT	
6							
7							

Field names are entered in two rows to accommodate smaller column widths.

To automatically adjust columns to the widest cell in the column, select the columns you want to adjust and double-click on the right border of the column heading, or choose the Forma**t** **C**olumn Width command and select the **B**est **F**it button. Chapter 5, "Modifying a Worksheet," covers changing the column width in greater detail.

The field names define the type of information needed for each record. After you enter field names in the first row, you can begin to enter records.

The first record is entered in the first row below the field names.

	A	B	C	D	E	F	G
2							
3							
4		INV.			DUE		
5		NUM.	DATE	COMPANY	DATE	AMOUNT	
6		123	5-May	XYZ & Assoc.	4-Jun	6,200.00	
7							

Defining a Database

A database consists of field names and records. After you have entered field names and records, the range of data in a worksheet must be defined as a database. Otherwise, Excel will not organize the selected data in a database format. When you define a database, Excel refers to the data in the selected area when you select database commands. Excel includes specific database commands, such as Find and Extract. These commands are effective only after you have defined a database.

If you have not defined a database and you select a database command, this dialog box appears.

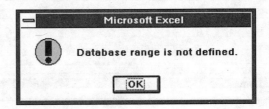

To define a database, follow these steps:

1. Select the field names and records that follow.

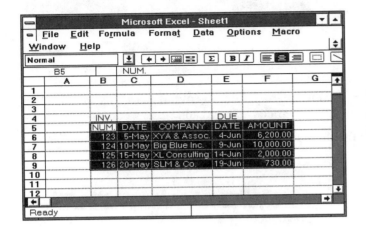

Field names and
records are
selected.

2. Choose the **Data** menu and select the Set Database command. Excel names the selected range Database.

3. Press [F5] or choose the **Edit GoTo** command to display the GoTo dialog box.

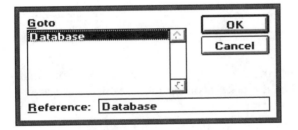

Select Database
from the list.

4. Choose **OK** or press [↵Enter]; the database is selected.

Adding Records

Excel offers two methods for adding records to a database: you can add records into blank cells or rows, or you can use a form to add records. When you add records into blank cells or rows, you enter data just as you would enter data in a worksheet. You can use the data form method to enter new records after the database has been defined. The data form displays the field names. A text box appears by each field name that requires an entry. The form presents an organized view of the data and makes data entry easier and more accurate. Both methods are described in the following sections.

11   Using the Data Form To Add a New Record

Before you define a database, you enter records into worksheet cells. After you define a database with the Data Set Database command, Excel creates a form that lists each field name followed by a text box for you to enter database information. You can use the database form to enter data as long as the field names and one row of data have been selected and set as a database.

To enter data using the database form, follow these steps:

1. Choose the Data Form command.

A dialog box appears display-ing the field names and text box to the right of each field name.

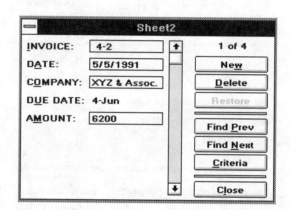

2. To add a new record to the database, choose the New button. A blank form appears, assigning the next record number. New records are added to the end of the database.

3. Enter data into each text box. Press [Tab] to move forward to the next field name text box. Press [Shift][Tab] to move backward to the preceding text box.

4. Press [Enter] after you have entered the data. Another blank form appears, enabling you to enter another new record.

5. Choose the Close button to clear the form and return to the worksheet.

Inserting a Record in the Worksheet

The preceding instructions explained how to add a new record to a database using the database form. The new record is added to the end of the database. The database form automatically extends the database to include the

272

additional records at the end of the database. If you add a record at the end of the database on the worksheet, however, the record is not included in the database unless you redefine the database with the **D**ata Set Database command to include the additional record.

To add a record to the database on the worksheet, insert blank cells in the database. You can insert a blank row if you are certain that data surrounding the database will not be affected by the insertion. Inserting cells in the area inside the database allows the database to expand and include additional records. You don't have to redefine the database when cells or records are inserted in the defined database area.

Use the following steps to insert cells and data into a database:

1. Select the cells inside the database area where you want to insert an additional record. Be sure to select all cells included in the record.

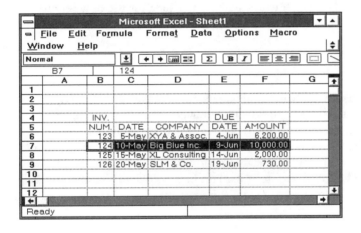

Blank cells will be inserted above the selected cells.

2. Choose the **E**dit **I**nsert command.

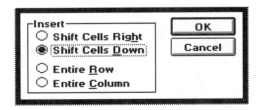

The Insert dialog appears.

3. Choose the Shift Cells Down option.
4. Choose **OK** or press ⏎Enter.

11

Selected cells
move down when
blank cells are
inserted.

	A	B	C	D	E	F	G
1							
2							
3							
4		INV.			DUE		
5		NUM.	DATE	COMPANY	DATE	AMOUNT	
6		123	5-May	XYA & Assoc.	4-Jun	6,200.00	
7							
8		124	10-May	Big Blue Inc.	9-Jun	10,000.00	
9		125	15-May	XL Consulting	14-Jun	2,000.00	
10		126	20-May	SLM & Co.	19-Jun	730.00	
11							
12							

5. Select the first cell in which you want to enter data for the new record.

Deleting Records

You can edit a database directly in the database form or on the worksheet.
When deleting database records, the data form is usually easier to use and
more accurate. When you use the form, however, you are limited to deleting
one record at a time. The worksheet method enables you to select more than
one record to delete. You may inadvertently, however, select a record you do
not want to delete. The following steps explain how to delete a record using
the form and how to delete a record from the worksheet.

Deleting a Record from the Data Form

To delete a record from the data form, follow these steps:

1. Choose the Data Form command. The database form appears.

2. Choose the Find Next or Find Prev button or press ↑ or ↓ to move
to the record you want to delete.

274

11

3. Choose the Delete button when the record you want to delete appears in the form. The records below the deleted record will be renumbered to account for the deleted record.

4. Choose the Close button to return to the worksheet.

Deleting a Record from the Worksheet

To delete a record from the worksheet, follow these steps:

1. Select the cells containing the record you want to delete. Be sure to select all cells included in the record.

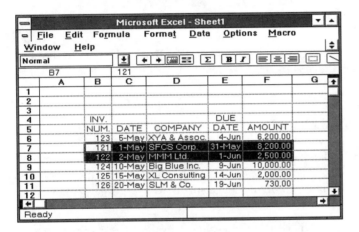

Database records are selected for deletion on the worksheet.

2. Choose the Edit Delete command.

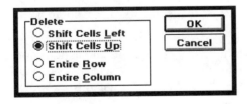

The Delete dialog box appears.

3. Select the Shift Cells Up option.

11

The records
below move up to
fill the deleted
cells.

```
 ═                    Microsoft Excel - Sheet1              ▼ ▲
 ▭  File   Edit   Formula   Format   Data   Options   Macro
    Window    Help                                           ♦
 Normal            ┃  ±  ┃ ← → ▦ ▦ ┃ Σ ┃ B I ┃ ≣ ≡ ≣ ┃ ▯ ┃ ◥
       B7        ┃      124
        A    B     C      D        E     F      G   ┃ ↑
  1
  2
  3
  4         INV.                 DUE
  5         NUM. DATE  COMPANY  DATE  AMOUNT
  6          123  5-May XYA & Assoc.  4-Jun   6,200.00
  7          124 10-May Big Blue Inc.  9-Jun  10,000.00
  8          125 15-May XL Consulting 14-Jun   2,000.00
  9          126 20-May SLM & Co.    19-Jun     730.00
 10
 11
 12                                                 ↓
 ←                                                  →
 Ready
```

You also can delete the entire row, if you are certain that other data in the
worksheet will not be affected by the row deletion.

Sorting a Database

An Excel database provides you with flexibility so that you can organize data to
meet your needs. Excel sorts databases based on fields. Any field name you
have created in the database can be used as a sort field for reorganizing the
database.

The sorting capability also lets you select a second sort field and a third sort
field, enabling you to perform a sort within a sort. If, for example, you are
sorting names in a telephone directory and several people have the same last
name, your second sort can be based on the first name. If several people have
the same last name and the same first name, the third sort could be based on
the address.

Make sure that you choose the File Save **As** command and assign another
name to the active document before sorting a database. This command
enables you to have two copies of the document. You can work with one copy
while the other copy remains intact.

Follow these steps to sort a database:

1. Select the records you want to sort. Do not select the database field
   names. Make sure that you select all columns of each row.

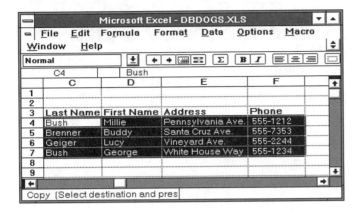

11

Only the records in a database are selected for sorting.

2. Choose the **Data Sort** command.

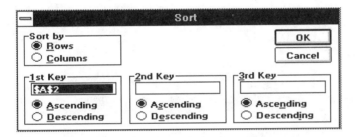

The Sort dialog box appears.

3. The 1st Key sort text box is selected. You must replace the cell address in this text box with the address of any cell in the column that contains the field on which you want to sort. If, for example, you want to sort on the Last Name field and Last Name is in column C, click on any cell in column C, or enter a cell address that includes column C as part of the cell address. Click on a cell in the worksheet, or enter a cell address in the text box.

4. Select the **Ascending** or **Descending** option for the order in which you want to sort the selected records. The **Ascending** option sorts the rows from A to Z. The **Descending** option reverses this order and sorts from Z to A. Numbers are sorted from the largest negative number to the largest positive number when the **Ascending** option is selected. Ascending is the default selection.

5. Press Tab⇥ or click in the 2nd Key text box if you want to perform a secondary sort within the 1st Key sort. Activate the 3rd Key text box if you want to sort on a third field.

11

In this example, the selected records will be sorted alphabetically according to Last Name. The second sort key will be First Name.

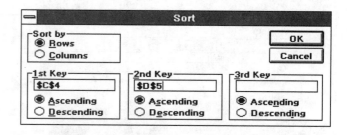

6. Choose **OK** or press ⏎Enter.

The selected records are sorted according to the selected options in the Sort dialog box.

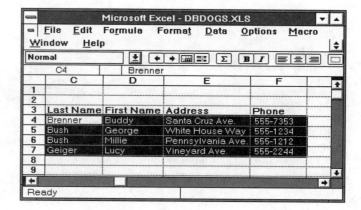

If you perform a sort that is incorrect, choose the **Edit Undo** command to reverse the sort and return to the original database list.

One of the most common sorting errors occurs in the selection process. A sort is performed on only the selected cells. If you did not select all the records or all the fields within the records, the sort could create a potential disaster. For example, if you perform a sort and you don't select the last column containing the invoice amount, the sorted data will be misaligned with the correct invoice amount. The selected data is reorganized when a sort is performed, while the unselected data remains in its original order.

The Undo command is a handy safety net. You can use the command to reverse most mistakes. The Undo command remembers only the last action you performed, however. If you do not catch the mistake right away, the Undo command cannot help you. Hopefully, you will catch your mistake before you save the document. If so, you can close the document without saving the

278

11

changes. Then, you can reopen the document as it existed originally. If you save the document with a mistake, locate the previous version of the document in a backup copy.

If you are sorting a database and you want the flexibility to return the database to its original order, you can automatically number each record sequentially before you start the sort. After the sort, you can perform a sort on the numbers. The selected records return to their original order.

Excel includes a data series command that simplifies automatically numbering a long list.To number a list of records in a database so that you can return to a previous order, follow these steps:

1. Enter the number **1** in the cell of a column on one side of the database.

2. Select the cell that contains the number plus the cells below through the height of the database.

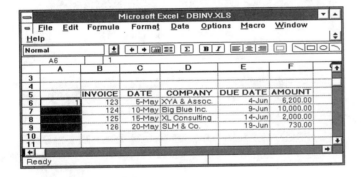

The selected cells will be numbered sequentially, starting with 1.

3. Choose the Data Series command.

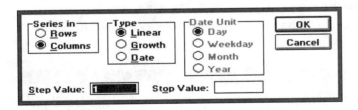

The Data Series dialog box appears.

4. Choose **OK** or press ⏎Enter. The default settings in the Data Series dialog box take the first number in the selection and steps 1 through the end of the selection.

279

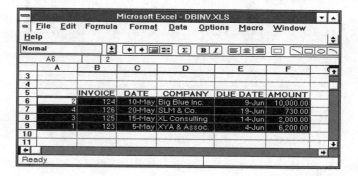

The **Data Series** command automatically numbers the selected cells.

5. Continue sorting the database, using the sorting procedures described earlier. Make sure that you include the column containing the numbers in the selection of records to be sorted.

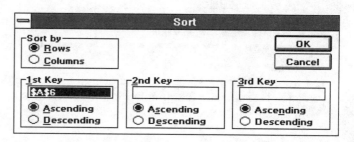

These records are sorted by company.

6. To return the records to their original order, select the records to be sorted, including the column containing the numbers.

7. Choose the **Data Sort** command. The Sort dialog box appears.

8. Select a cell in the column that contains the numbers. This cell appears as the **1st** Key sort.

Records are sorted by the numbers in Column A.

9. Choose **OK** or press ⊣Enter to clear the dialog box.

11

	Microsoft Excel - DBINV.XLS					
File	**Edit**	**Formula**	**Format**	**Data**	**Options**	**Macro**	**Window**

Help

Normal

A6 | 1

	A	B	C	D	E	F	
3							
4							
5	INVOICE	DATE	COMPANY	DUE DATE	AMOUNT		
6	1	123	5-May	XYA & Assoc.	4-Jun	6,200.00
7	2	124	10-May	Big Blue Inc.	9-Jun	10,000.00
8	3	125	15-May	XL Consulting	14-Jun	2,000.00
9	4	126	20-May	SLM & Co	19-Jun	730.00
10							
11							

Ready

The selected records are sorted in ascending numerical order, which is the order the records were originally in.

Searching for Records

Excel includes database commands that enable you to find specific records in a database and extract duplicate copies of records from a database. A database is often used to search for records that meet a specified criteria. Criteria is a pattern or specific details you want a record to match. Once you establish criteria, you can use Excel commands to find records that match the criteria, or you can extract duplicates of records that match the criteria.

Finding Records

You can define the pattern or criteria you want a record to match using the data form, or you can define a criteria range on the worksheet and use the **Data Find** command. The data form provides the quickest and easiest method for finding records that satisfy criteria. If you want to find records that match more complex criteria, however, you must define a criteria range on your worksheet and use the **Data Find** command.

Finding Records from the Data Form

To find records from the data form, follow these steps:

1. Choose the **Data Form** command.

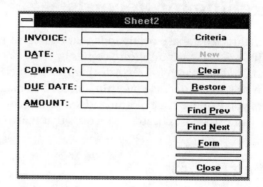

The database
form dialog box
appears.

2. Choose the Criteria button.

A blank Criteria
form appears.

3. Select a text box.

Enter the criteria
or pattern you
want to search
for.

You can enter multiple criteria.

11

4. Choose the Find Next button after you have entered the criteria.

```
┌──────────────────────────────────────────┐
│ ▬            DBINV.XLS                     │
├──────────────────────────────────────────┤
│ INVOICE:   [123      ] [↑]    1 of 4       │
│ DATE:      [5/5/1991 ]    ┌──────────┐     │
│ COMPANY:   [XYA & Assoc.] │   New    │     │
│ DUE DATE:  4-Jun          ├──────────┤     │
│                           │  Delete  │     │
│ AMOUNT:    [6200     ]    ├──────────┤     │
│                           │ Restore  │     │
│                           ├──────────┤     │
│                           │Find Prev │     │
│                           ├──────────┤     │
│                           │Find Next │     │
│                           ├──────────┤     │
│                      [↓]  │ Criteria │     │
│                           ├──────────┤     │
│                           │  Close   │     │
│                           └──────────┘     │
└──────────────────────────────────────────┘
```

The first record to match the defined criteria appears in the form.

If no matches exist, you hear a beep.

5. Choose the Find Prev button if you want to search backward through the database to find a match.

6. Choose the Close button to clear the dialog box.

Finding Records from the Worksheet

Searching for data with the database form is the best method to use if the criteria you want to define is simple. If, however, you want to search for complex or calculated criteria, you should create a criteria range on your worksheet. Defining a criteria range is very similar to defining a database range. A criteria range consists of field names and at least one blank row for entering the criteria.

Use the following steps to define a criteria range:

1. Select the field names that you want to use from the row of database field names.

2. Choose the Edit Copy command.

283

11

Copying the field names from the database field names reduces the chance of error.

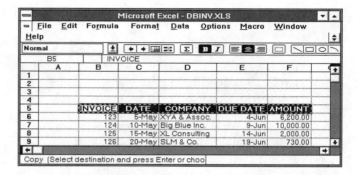

The field names in the criteria range must match the field names in the database.

3. Select a cell at the beginning of the area you want to use as the criteria range.

The criteria field names will start in the selected cell.

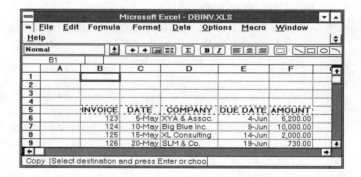

4. Choose the **E**dit **P**aste command to paste the field names in the top row of the criteria range.

Field names from the database were copied to the criteria range.

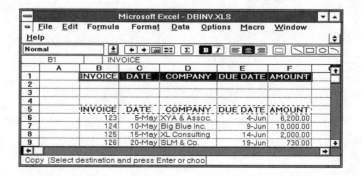

284

5. Select the pasted field names plus one blank row of cells directly below the criteria field names.

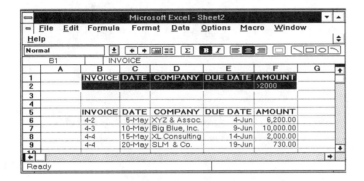

11

The criteria range is selected.

6. Choose the Data Set Criteria command. Excel assigns the name Criteria to the selected range.

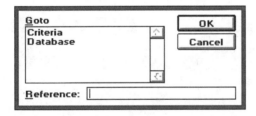

The GoTo dialog box displays the range name Criteria.

Use the blank row below the field names in the criteria range to enter the criteria you want database records to match. The criteria can be simple, such as matching a name, or the criteria can be based on a calculation. Once you have entered criteria into the blank cells in the criteria range, you can begin to search the database to find records that match the criteria.

Suppose, for example, that you want to search an invoice database for records with a balance due amount of $2,000 or greater. To find the database records that match the criteria, follow these steps:

1. Enter the criteria > = 2000 in the cell directly below the criteria field name AMOUNT.

11

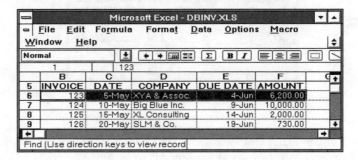

The criteria is defined in the criteria range.

2. Choose the Data menu and select the Find command. If the active cell was outside the database before the command was selected, the search begins at the top of the database. If the active cell was inside the database, the search begins at the active cell and moves forward.

The first record in the database matching the criteria is selected. The area to the left of the formula bar displays the number of the database record.

The scroll bars appear with diagonal stripes indicating that the worksheet is in database Find mode.

3. Press ← or → if you want to move the active cell within the selected record.

The selected record in the database matches the criteria.

4. Click the up or down arrow in the scroll bar area, or press ⬆ or ⬇ to move forward or backward to the next matching record.

   If there are no more records that match the criteria, you hear a beep.

5. Choose the Data menu and select the Exit Find command to return to the normal worksheet mode, or click anywhere outside the database area.

Extracting Records from a Database

The procedures described in the preceding section enable you to view records that match a specified criteria. In many cases, you will want not only to view the matching records, but also to work with the matching records as a group. Excel enables you to copy records that match the criteria defined in the criteria range to a selected range, or a range defined as the extract range.

In Excel, you have the option of defining an extract range. If you do not define an extract range, you must select the extract field names and at least one blank row below the field names. You can extract data into the selected area even if the extract range has not been set. If you use the Data Set Extract command to define an area of the worksheet as the extract range, you do not have to select the area prior to choosing the Data Extract command. The extract range must contain the field names of the data you want to extract. You can use some of the field names or all of the field names when extracting records from a database. Like the criteria range, the field names in the extract range must match the field names in the database.

11

To set up an extract range, follow these steps:

1. Copy the field names from the database field names to the area you want to use as the extract range.

Copying the field names reduces the possibility of error.

```
Microsoft Excel - DBINV.XLS
 File  Edit  Formula  Format  Data  Options  Macro
 Window  Help
 Normal            ± ◄ ► ▦ ▦  Σ  B I  ≣ ≣ ≣  ▢ ◁
      B12          INVOICE
        B        C        D          E          F        ◀
  3
  4
  5  INVOICE  DATE     COMPANY    DUE DATE  AMOUNT
  6     123   5-May  XYA & Assoc.    4-Jun   6,200.00
  7     124  10-May  Big Blue Inc.   9-Jun  10,000.00
  8     125  15-May  XL Consulting  14-Jun   2,000.00
  9     126  20-May  SLM & Co.      19-Jun     730.00
 10
 11
 12  INVOICE  DATE     COMPANY    DUE DATE  AMOUNT
 13
 14
 Ready
```

2. Select the extract field names and the range below the field names that will contain the copied data.

Records will be extracted into the selected area.

```
Microsoft Excel - DBINV.XLS
 File  Edit  Formula  Format  Data  Options  Macro
 Window  Help
 Normal            ± ◄ ► ▦ ▦  Σ  B I  ≣ ≣ ≣  ▢ ◁
      B12          INVOICE
        B        C        D          E          F        ◀
  5  INVOICE  DATE     COMPANY    DUE DATE  AMOUNT
  6     123   5-May  XYA & Assoc.    4-Jun   6,200.00
  7     124  10-May  Big Blue Inc.   9-Jun  10,000.00
  8     125  15-May  XL Consulting  14-Jun   2,000.00
  9     126  20-May  SLM & Co.      19-Jun     730.00
 10
 11
 12  INVOICE  DATE     COMPANY    DUE DATE  AMOUNT
 13
 14
 15
 16
 17
 Ready
```

3. Choose the Data menu and select the Set Extract command.

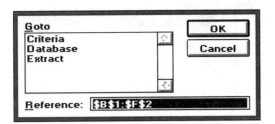

Excel names the
selected range
Extract.

The named range can be referenced with the GoTo command or used
with Excel's database functions.

Once the database, criteria, and extract ranges have been set, you can extract
data from a database. To extract records, follow these steps:

1. Choose the Data menu and select the Extract command.

The Extract dialog
box appears.

2. If you do not want to extract duplicate records, select the Unique
    Records Only check box.

3. Choose OK or press ⏎Enter to accept the settings and clear the dialog
    box.

    All records in the database that match the criteria are copied to the
    selected extract range.

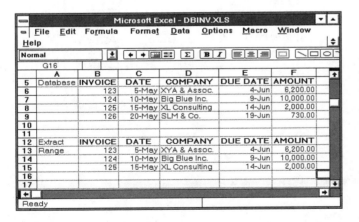

Records matching
the defined
criteria are copied
to the extract
range.

289

11

If the selected range is not large enough to accommodate all matching records, a dialog box appears.

You have the option of creating an unlimited extract range that will extract all matching records. To define an unlimited extract range, select only the cells containing the extract field names. Choose the **D**ata Set Extract command if you want to name this range Extract. When you use an unlimited extract range, all cells below the field names are cleared when you choose the **D**ata Extract command. The cells are cleared even if data copied from the database does not fill the cells. If you are using an unlimited extract range, make sure that all cells below the extract field names are clear of data. You do not receive any warning that data has been wiped out as a result of the data extraction.

In the previous database example, the criteria was defined to find or extract all records in the database that have an invoice amount greater than $2000. You also can define multiple criteria in the criteria range on the worksheet or using the data form. The following example shows the criteria defined to extract all records that are due after June 5, and have an invoice amount equal to or greater than $2000.

The data form lists multiple criteria.

DBINV.XLS	
INVOICE:	**Criteria**
D**A**TE:	New
C**O**MPANY:	**C**lear
D**U**E DATE: >6-5	**R**estore
A**M**OUNT: >=2000	Find **P**rev
	Find **N**ext
	Form
	C**l**ose

290

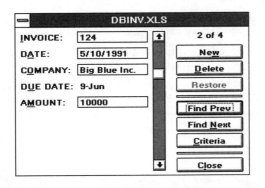

11

The first record
that matches the
criteria appears.

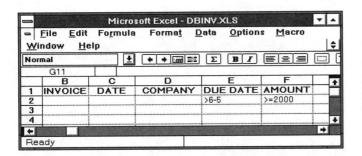

The multiple
criteria is entered
in the criteria
range on the
worksheet.

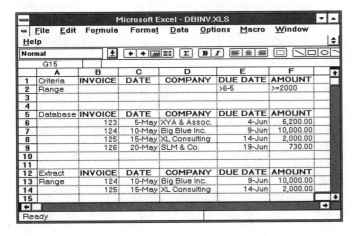

The Extract
command copied
records meeting
the multiple
criteria.

11

In addition to defining multiple criteria, you can define multiple criteria and find or extract records that match one criteria OR another criteria. To find or extract records where one criteria OR the other is met, you must use the criteria range on the worksheet. You cannot use the data form if you are looking for records that match one criteria or the other. To define multiple criteria in the criteria range of the worksheet, you may need to redefine the criteria range. To find or extract records from a database where one criteria OR the other is met, each criteria must be entered in a separate row below the criteria range field names.

Each criteria is defined in a separate row in the criteria range of the worksheet.

	Microsoft Excel - DBINV.XLS					

File Edit Formula Format Data Options Macro Window Help

Normal

B1   INVOICE

	A	B	C	D	E	F
1	Criteria	INVOICE	DATE	COMPANY	DUE DATE	AMOUNT
2	Range					>=2000
3					>6-5	
4						
5	Database	INVOICE	DATE	COMPANY	DUE DATE	AMOUNT
6		123	5-May	XYA & Assoc.	4-Jun	6,200.00
7		124	10-May	Big Blue Inc.	9-Jun	10,000.00
8		125	15-May	XL Consulting	14-Jun	2,000.00
9		126	20-May	SLM & Co.	19-Jun	730.00
10						
11						
12	Extract	INVOICE	DATE	COMPANY	DUE DATE	AMOUNT
13	Range	124	10-May	Big Blue Inc.	9-Jun	10,000.00
14		125	15-May	XL Consulting	14-Jun	2,000.00
15						

Ready

The defined criteria looks for records that are due after June 5, OR records that have an invoice amount equal to or greater than $2000.

Records that match one criteria OR the other are extracted.

	Microsoft Excel - DBINV.XLS					

File Edit Formula Format Data Options Macro Window Help

Normal

G17

	A	B	C	D	E	F
1	Criteria	INVOICE	DATE	COMPANY	DUE DATE	AMOUNT
2	Range					>=2000
3					>6-5	
4						
5	Database	INVOICE	DATE	COMPANY	DUE DATE	AMOUNT
6		123	5-May	XYA & Assoc.	4-Jun	6,200.00
7		124	10-May	Big Blue Inc.	9-Jun	10,000.00
8		125	15-May	XL Consulting	14-Jun	2,000.00
9		126	20-May	SLM & Co.	19-Jun	730.00
10						
11						
12	Extract	INVOICE	DATE	COMPANY	DUE DATE	AMOUNT
13	Range	123	5-May	XYA & Assoc.	4-Jun	6,200.00
14		124	10-May	Big Blue Inc.	9-Jun	10,000.00
15		125	15-May	XL Consulting	14-Jun	2,000.00
16		126	20-May	SLM & Co.	19-Jun	730.00
17						

Ready

Summary

This chapter introduced you to fundamental database concepts. You learned what a database is and how to create a database on an Excel worksheet. Other topics in the chapter included entering data in a database and using the database form to add and delete records. You learned how to set the database range, the criteria range, and the extract range. Additionally, you learned how to define criteria and find records that match the criteria, and you learned how to copy data to an extract range.

If you want to explore databases in more depth and experiment with some of Excel's advanced database features, you may want to read Que's book *Using Excel 3 for Windows*. It includes instructions on how to use Excel's Q+E add-in feature, which enables you to access external databases and bring the data into an Excel worksheet.

In this chapter, you were introduced to the following key information about Excel:

- A database is a range of cells on a worksheet composed of field names in the first row followed by records in subsequent rows.

- A field name must be text, and each field name must be unique.

- The **Data Set Database** command defines the selected field names and records as the database. The selected range is named Database.

- You can use the database form to add new records to the end of the database. You also can use the form to delete records and find records that match a specified criteria.

- Inserting cells through the database area expands the database downward. Records added at the end of the database worksheet are not included as part of the database.

- Use the **Data Sort** command to sort selected data in ascending or descending order.

- A criteria range must include field names that match the field names in the database. The **Data Set Criteria** command defines the selected field names and the row containing the criteria as the criteria range.

- The **Data Find** command locates records in the database that match the criteria defined in the criteria range.

- The **Data Extract** command copies records that match the criteria in the criteria range to a selected or defined range.

- The Extract range must include field names that match the field names in the database.

11

■ Setting the Extract range is an optional command. If you choose the **Data Set Extract** command, the selected range is named Extract and can be used with the **GoTo** command or other Excel database functions.

■ An unlimited extract range is defined when only the extract field names are selected. An unlimited extract range clears all cells below when you choose the **Data Extract** command.

Chapter 12, the next chapter, introduces you to macros. In the chapter, you will learn what a macro is and how to create a macro on an Excel macro sheet. You will learn to use Excel's macro recorder, and you will learn how to assign a macro to an object.

Using Macros

In addition to the many other powerful features, Excel includes the capability to automate repetitive tasks. Using Excel's macro capability, you can assign to a speed key a series of keystrokes or commands you select on a repetitive basis, and you can name the key. Instead of completing a task that may ordinarily require 15 keystrokes, you press the key assigned to the task, and Excel executes the keystrokes or commands for you.

Excel has extensive macro capabilities. This chapter is intended to provide you with a basic understanding of what a macro is and how to plan and record a macro. You are introduced to macro sheets and Excel's macro commands. This chapter also provides an overview of how to run a macro, debug a macro, and assign a macro to an object. If you want to explore Excel's macro features in greater detail, consult Que's book *Using Excel 3 for Windows*.

Command macros

Function macros

Macro names

Macro recordings

Macros and objects

12

Key Terms in This Chapter

Macro	A recording of keystrokes and commands.
Macro sheet	A worksheet used to record macro functions.
Command macro	Actions recorded on a macro sheet that you can play back.
Function macro	Macro functions entered on a macro sheet to create a custom formula or function.

What Is a Macro?

A *macro* is a recording of keystrokes. Just as you might use a tape recorder to record music, you can use Excel's macro recorder to record keystrokes. Once you turn the macro recorder on, it begins recording every key you press or every command you select. When you have recorded all the keystrokes or commands you want to record, you choose a command to stop the recorder. You can play back a macro by pressing its assigned keystroke or by selecting the macro name.

Most of the work you do in Excel is on a worksheet. When you start recording a macro, the keystrokes are recorded on a macro sheet. A macro sheet looks very similar to a worksheet, except that a macro sheet has much wider columns. The title bar of the macro sheet indicates that the document is a macro sheet. While you are recording a macro, the macro sheet is in the background entering the keystrokes on the macro sheet, using function names. The macro function names are very similar to the actual commands you select. For example, the macro function name for changing column width is COLUMN.WIDTH. If you need to edit a macro sheet, you easily can follow the macro recording on the macro sheet.

Types of Macros

You can create two types of macros in Excel: command macros and function macros. This chapter primarily deals with command macros. A command macro records actions, such as keystrokes and selected commands. A function macro enables you to build a custom formula, such as the functions listed in the dialog box when you select the Formula Paste Function command.

Command Macros

Command macros are easy to create and edit. You can create a command macro by starting the macro recorder. You can assign a name and a keystroke to a command macro before the macro recorder actually begins recording. The macro recorder records all selected commands and keystrokes on a macro sheet. When the recorder is stopped, it no longer records actions.

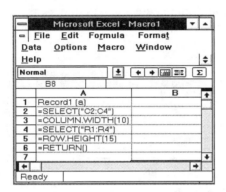

This macro sheet contains a command macro that changes column width and row height.

The first cell of the macro recording shows the name of the macro, `Record1`, and the key assigned to the macro, (a). The first recorded command selects the second column on the worksheet through the fourth column, (`"C2:C4"`), which is column B through column D. The second command, `=COLUMN.WIDTH(10)`, chooses the Forma**t** Column Width command and enters the number 10. This command is followed by commands that select rows 1 through 4, choose Forma**t** **R**ow Height, and enter the number 15. The last cell in the macro displays `=RETURN()`, the macro function that ends the recording of keystrokes and commands.

To play back a command macro, you can press the key assigned to the macro or choose the macro name from a dialog box. When a macro is played back, it executes all actions that were recorded. The specific details for recording and executing a command macro are covered in the rest of this chapter.

Function Macros

Excel has more than 140 built-in functions to perform mathematical, statistical, financial, and other types of calculations. The functions appear in a dialog box list when you choose the Fo**r**mula Pa**s**te Function command. Sometimes

12

you may need a formula that is not one of the predefined functions. A function macro enables you to build a custom function that is added to the list of Excel functions.

Creating a function macro requires a bit more structure than creating a command macro. The macro functions cannot be recorded; you must enter or paste each function with the Formula Paste Functions command. A macro sheet records functions down a column. The first cell at the top of the column contains the name of the function as the name appears in the Paste Function dialog box list. The Paste Function dialog box displays different functions when a macro sheet is active.

This simple function macro creates a custom function for calculating profit.

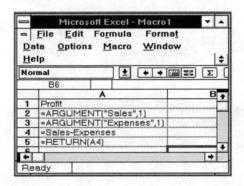

The name of the function macro is entered in the first cell. The ARGUMENT functions in cells A2 and A3 identify the arguments that will appear in parentheses when the function is pasted into the worksheet, using the Formula Paste command. The number 1 following each argument name defines the type of data that must be entered in the referenced cell. The number 1 means the referenced cells Sales and Expenses must contain a value. The formula is entered in cell A4 of the macro sheet. The formula takes the value in the cell referenced by Sales and subtracts from that number the value in the cell address referenced by Expenses. The last cell in the function macro is the =RETURN function. The cell address A4 is displayed in parentheses. The result of the formula in cell A4 on the macro sheet is returned on the worksheet where the function is pasted or entered.

Planning a Macro

As with most tasks, the time you spend preparing a macro usually pays off later. Spend some time organizing your macro before you actually build it.

You should have a complete understanding of exactly what you want the macro to accomplish. Planning is especially important if you are working on long macros that involve subroutines and other more complex macro functions.

Perform the macro on a test basis before you record the macro. Remember, Excel is recording every command or keystroke you use once the recorder is turned on. If you press the wrong key or select the wrong action, the mistake is recorded.

As you practice recording the macro on a test basis, try to identify any problems that may occur. If you are creating a long macro, break the macro into smaller tasks, and then test each task to make sure it works properly. If each task performs correctly, the entire macro should work when the tasks are all linked together.

You can edit a macro to correct most problems, but you save time if you avoid problems from the start.

Creating a Command Macro

Creating a command macro is a fairly simple procedure. The steps for starting the recorder, assigning a macro name, and assigning a key are described in the section that follows. You also learn how to stop the recorder and how to document a macro.

Recording the Macro Commands

To record a command macro, follow these steps:

1. Choose the Macro menu and select the Record command.

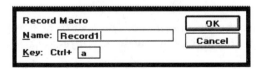

The Record Macro dialog box appears.

2. Enter a name for the macro to replace the default name in the text box.

3. Select the Key text box and enter the key you want to use with the Ctrl key to execute the macro.

299

12

The macro is
named Border
and is assigned to
Ctrl+B.

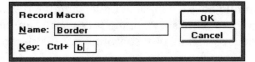

4. Choose **OK** or press ⏎Enter. Continue choosing the commands and
   entering the data you want to record. The recorder records all keystrokes and selections. The status bar displays the message Recording
   as long as the recorder is turned on.

If you want to create a macro that applies a thick border to the bottom of
selected cells, you can follow these steps:

1. Choose the Forma**t** menu and select the **B**order command.
2. Click on **B**ottom or press Alt B.
3. Choose the style of line you want from the lower section of the dialog
   box.
4. Choose **OK** or press ⏎Enter.

To stop the macro recorder, choose the **M**acro **S**top Re**c**order command.

The macro sheet
displays the
recorded
commands.

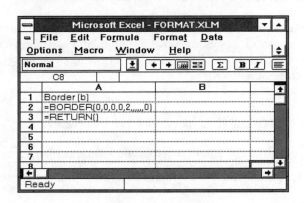

To view the macro sheet, choose the **W**indow menu. The macro sheet appears
in the list. Select the macro sheet from the Window menu, or press Ctrl+F6
until the macro sheet is in view.

Stopping the Recorder

One of the most common steps overlooked in the process of creating a macro
is turning the macro recorder off. Although this step is not difficult, you may

forget it. The status bar at the bottom of the screen is the only reminder that the macro recorder is on.

After you have recorded a command macro, turn the macro recorder off by choosing the **Macro** menu and selecting the **Stop Recorder** command.

You also can use the **Macro Stop Recorder** command to stop the recorder temporarily. You may want to complete some actions that you do not want to record as part of the macro. If so, stop the recorder, complete the actions you do not want recorded, and resume the macro recording by choosing the **Macro Start Recorder** command. The macro recorder resumes where you stopped it.

Understanding the Macro Sheet

When you record a macro, Excel lists the actions on a macro sheet. Macro functions are used to identify each action. The macro sheet opens automatically when you choose the **Macro Record** command.

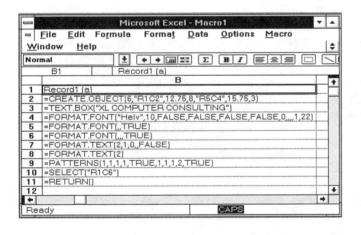

The command macro recorded in this macro sheet creates a text box; enters text; formats the text to be centered, bold, and italicized; and formats the text box to have rounded corners and a shadow.

The first cell of the macro sheet records the macro name and the assigned key in parentheses. The functions are listed down the column. Each macro function is entered into a cell. The RETURN( ) function is entered on the macro sheet when the recorder stops.

A macro sheet can store multiple macros. Related macros should be stored on a single macro sheet. When the macro sheet is open, you have access to all macros on the sheet. You can avoid opening several macro sheets by

12

recording multiple macros on a single macro sheet. A macro cannot be executed unless you have opened the macro sheet on which the macro is stored. The procedure for opening a macro sheet is the same as the procedure for opening all Excel documents. Choose the **File Open** command and select the macro file name from the dialog box. All macro sheets end with the extension XLM.

Saving a macro sheet is the same as saving any other Excel document. Choose the **File Save** command; the dialog box prompts you to enter a name for the macro sheet. Excel assigns the extension XLM to the file name to identify it as a macro sheet.

Documenting a Macro

Most of the functions on the macro sheet can be interpreted to some degree. Not all macro results, however, are recognized by looking at a macro sheet. Many macro functions identify dialog box settings by numbers. In most cases, you will not know for certain what the number represents. For this reason, document the steps of a macro. If a macro sheet is documented, you know what it is intended to accomplish. Later, if you or someone else has to edit the macro, the process is much easier to understand. Macro documentation is especially necessary when you are working with long, complex macros.

You can use the column to the right of the macro functions to document each step of the macro. You can use formatting commands and cell borders to define sections of the macro.

This macro sheet has been formatted with documentation in column C.

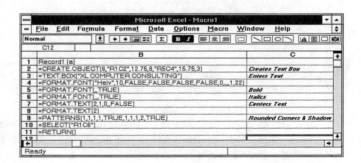

Creating a Function Macro

In Chapter 7, you were introduced to Excel functions. A function is a pre-defined formula. Excel includes over 130 built-in functions that enable you to perform various types of calculations, including mathematical and statistical calculations. You can use the Formula Paste Function command to enter an Excel function in a worksheet. A function macro enables you to create a custom formula that Excel adds to the list of built-in functions. These functions are displayed when you choose the Formula Paste Function command. You enter macro functions on a macro sheet to set up a predefined formula that you can use as a built-in function.

Entering the Macro Commands

To create the simple function macro that creates a custom function for calculating profit (shown earlier in the chapter), follow these procedures:

To open a new macro sheet, follow these steps:

1. Choose the **File New** command.

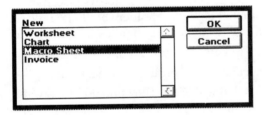

The File New dialog box appears.

2. In the File New dialog box, choose Macro Sheet and choose **OK** or press ⏎Enter.

To open an existing macro sheet, follow these steps:

1. Choose the **File Open** command.

2. From the File Open dialog box, choose the macro sheet to which you want to add a macro.

3. When the macro sheet opens, scroll to a blank column. You will record your macro in this column, starting at the top cell.

Once you have a macro sheet open and active, follow these steps to create a function macro:

12

1. Enter into the first cell of the first blank column the name you want to give the function.

2. Choose the Formula Paste Function command.

The Formula
Paste Function
dialog box
appears.

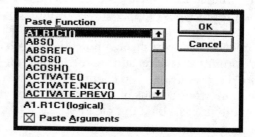

3. Choose the ARGUMENT( ) function from the list in the dialog box. The Paste Arguments check box should be turned on if you want argument placeholders displayed.

4. Choose **OK** or press ↵Enter. The selected function appears in the formula bar of the macro sheet.

5. Select each argument placeholder in the formula bar, and replace each placeholder with the actual argument. (Text is always placed in quotation marks. The number type placeholder should be replaced by the number **1** for a numeric result and a **2** for a text result.)

6. Repeat steps 3 through **5** to enter the next argument function.

7. Enter the formula for calculating the profit in the next cell.

8. The function macro must end with a RETURN function followed by the cell address on the macro sheet that contains the formula producing the result.

Defining the Function Name

To name the function macro so that it appears in the Formula Paste Function list box, follow these steps:

1. Select the first cell on the macro sheet containing the function name.

2. Choose the Formula Define Name command.

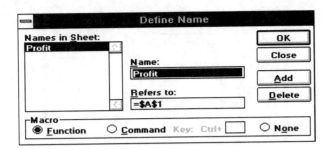

The Define Name
dialog box
appears.

12

The name in the selected cell on the macro sheet appears in the Name
text box.

3. Select the Function option button to define the name as a function
   name.

4. Select the Keys option if you want to assign the macro to a key combined with the Ctrl key.

5. Choose OK or press ⏎Enter.

The defined name appears at the end of the list of functions in the Formula
Paste Function dialog box.

The preceding steps explained how to create a function macro on a macro
sheet and how to define the macro so that the custom function appears in the
Formula Paste Function list box. After you create and define the function
macro as a function, you can use it in a worksheet as long as the macro sheet
containing the function is open.

The Profit
function will
be entered in
this worksheet.

12

When the macro
sheet is open, the
Formula Paste
Function com-
mand displays the
custom function
at the end of the
list box.

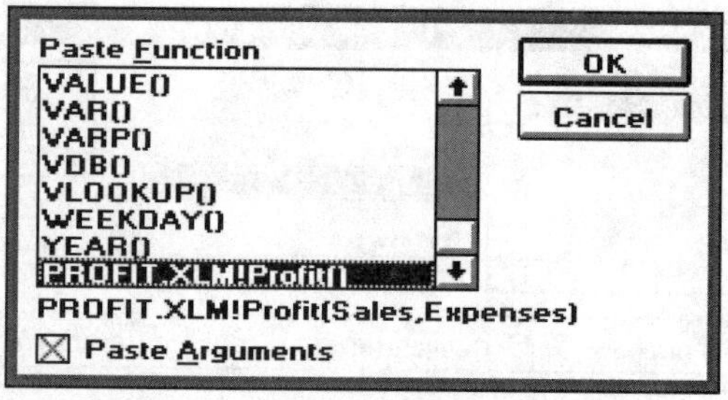

The Profit func-
tion appears in
the formula bar.

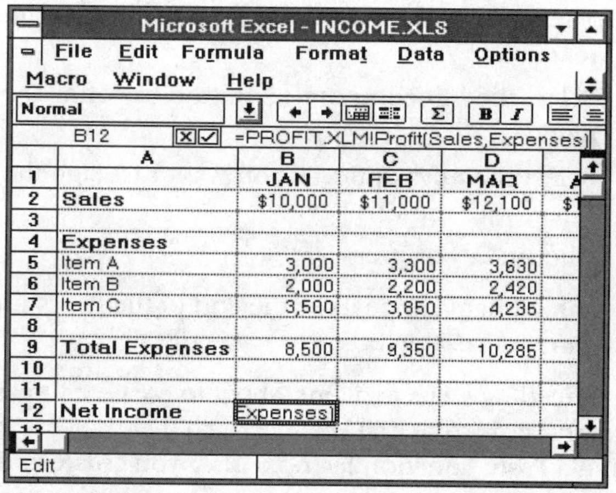

The argument
placeholders
must be replaced
with the cell
addresses con-
taining the data to
be calculated.

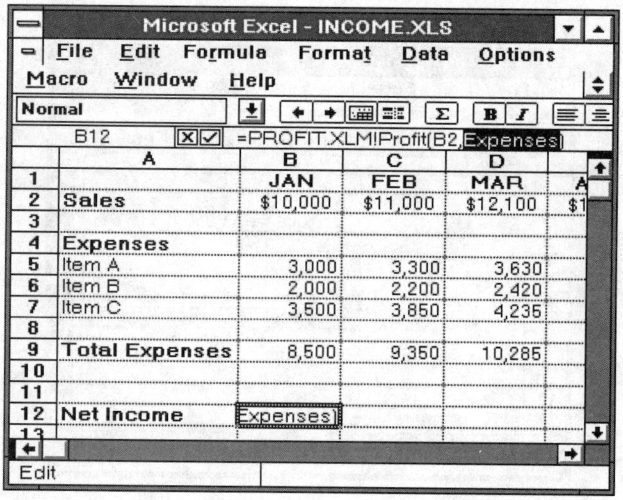

306

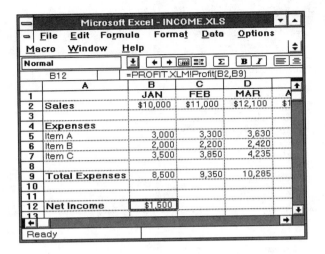

The result of the profit function appears in the active cell.

Editing a Macro

If you need to make changes to a macro, you can edit the macro on the macro sheet. Suppose that you want to edit the formatted text box macro by changing the text that is entered in the text box. The steps for editing a macro are the same as the steps for editing on a worksheet. If you want to edit a portion of the cell, edit the active cell in the formula bar.

Removing a Macro Function

If you want to remove a macro step, select the cell and choose the **Edit Delete** command.

12

The cell that contained the command for italics has been edited; the italics command in the FORMAT.FONT macro function has been removed.

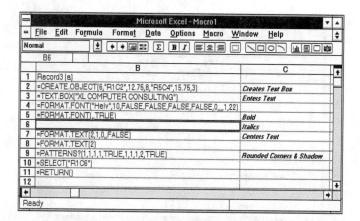

Pausing a Macro

You can edit a macro function to pause at a particular point. In the text box macro example, suppose that you want to make other choices in the Patterns dialog box. In this case, you want to pause the dialog box so that you can make the selections you want.

For a dialog box to pause for input, the function must be followed by a question mark (?) in front of the parentheses.

The Patterns function has been edited to include a pause.

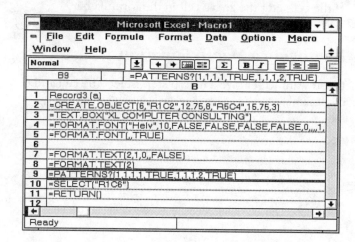

When the macro reaches the Patterns dialog box, the macro pauses until the OK command button is selected or the Enter key is pressed. The function then resumes and completes the rest of the macro.

Setting and Starting the Recorder

You may want to record additional commands to add to an existing macro, or you may want to record another macro on an open macro sheet. Before you begin recording, you must set the recorder to define the recording area on the macro sheet.

The **Macro Set** Recorder command determines where the macro will start recording when you choose the **Macro Start** Recorder command. To access these macro commands, you must be in Full Menus mode. If you are not in Full Menus mode, the commands are not displayed on the Macro menu. Choose the **Options** menu and select the Full **Menus** command to display all menu commands.

If a single cell is selected on the macro sheet and set with the recorder, all the cells below in the same column are used for storing the macro functions. All cells must be blank. If you select a range of cells on a macro sheet and set the cells as the recording range, the macro functions are recorded until the selected range is full.

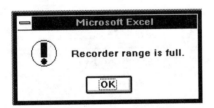

A dialog box displays a message telling you that the recorder range is full.

If you are starting a new macro and you want to record it on an existing macro sheet, follow these steps:

1. Select the cell at the beginning of the next available column. All columns below the selected cell are used for the recording.

2. After the **Macro Set** Recorder command has been selected, choose the **Macro Start** Recorder command.

3. Activate the worksheet where you will carry out the recorded commands. Select the worksheet from the Window menu, or press [Ctrl] [F6] until the document is displayed as the active document.

Defining a Macro Name

When you start a macro recording with the **Macro Rec**ord command, Excel prompts you with a dialog box to name the macro and assign a key for the macro. If you start the macro recorder with the **Macro S**tart Recorder command, you are not given an opportunity to name the macro or assign a macro key. To name a macro and assign a macro key, follow these steps:

1. Activate the macro sheet that contains the macro you want to name. Choose the macro sheet from the Window menu, or press `Ctrl` `F6` until the macro sheet is displayed.
2. Select the first cell of the macro.
3. Choose the Formula menu and select the **D**efine Name command.

The Define Name
dialog box
appears.

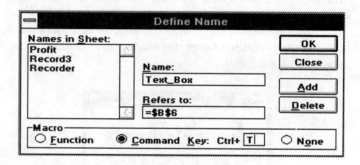

4. Enter the macro name in the **N**ame text box.
5. Select the **C**ommand **K**ey option and enter the Ctrl+key character you want to assign to the macro.
6. Choose **OK** or press `↵Enter`.

Running a Macro

You can only run a command macro when the macro sheet it is written on is open. After the macro sheet is open, you can access the macro by holding down the Ctrl key and pressing the assigned key. You also can execute a macro by using the **Macro R**un command.

310

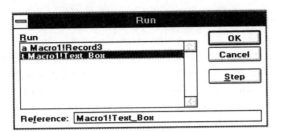

If you choose to run a macro using the Macro **Run** command, this dialog box appears.

12

The dialog box lists all macros on any open macro sheets. Select the macro you want to run. All worksheets have access to all macros on an open macro sheet.

Debugging a Macro

If you are having problems executing a macro properly, you can execute the macro one step at a time and evaluate where the error might be. The Macro Step feature helps you spot problems in your macro. If you need to edit the macro, you must do so on the macro sheet. You cannot edit the macro in Step mode.

To execute a macro one step at a time, follow these steps:

1. Choose the Macro menu and select the Run command. The Run dialog box appears.

2. Select the macro you want to test from the list in the dialog box.

3. Choose the Step button. The Step dialog box appears.

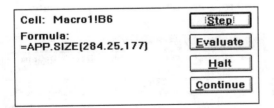

The Step dialog box.

The Step button moves you to the next step in the macro. The Halt button stops the macro and clears the dialog box. The Continue button resumes the macro. The Evaluate button calculates formulas in segments.

311

Assigning a Macro to an Object

Excel's tool bar includes a Button tool that enables you to create a button on a worksheet. These buttons resemble the buttons you see in Excel dialog boxes. Once you draw a button on a worksheet, you can assign a macro to the button. You also can assign a macro to any graphic object or picture on a worksheet. Assigning a macro to a button or object makes the macro more visible and easier to access for users who may not be familiar with accessing macros.

To assign a macro to a button or object, follow these steps:

1. Select the button or object you want to link to a macro.

2. Choose the Macro menu and select the Assign To Object command.

The Assign Macro dialog box appears.

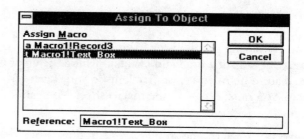

3. Select the macro you want to assign to the selected button or object.

4. Choose OK or press ⏎Enter.

When a macro has been assigned to an object on a worksheet, the mouse pointer changes to a pointing hand when positioned on the object. Click on the object with the pointing hand to execute the macro automatically.

This is an example of a button created with the Button tool.

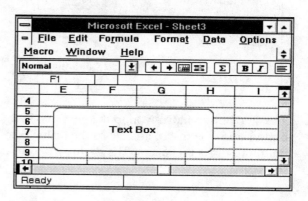

You easily can record repetitive keystrokes with the macro recorder. When you find yourself accessing the same series of commands over and over, consider recording a macro that will play the commands and keystrokes back for you in a single keystroke.

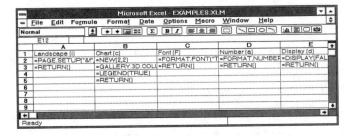

Five command macros have been created on a macro sheet saved as Examples.

The first macro is named Landscape; this macro changes the page orientation to landscape. The second macro is named Chart; this macro creates a 3-D column chart of selected data. The third macro is named Font; this macro changes the font type and font size. The fourth macro is named Number; this macro changes the number format to display currency with two decimal places. The last macro is named Display; this macro turns worksheet gridlines off.

To create the Setup macro, follow these steps:

1. Choose the Macro menu and select the Record command.
2. Choose the File menu and select the Page Setup command.
3. Choose the Landscape option.
4. Choose OK or press ↵Enter.
5. Choose the Macro menu and select the Stop Recorder command.

To run the macro, press Ctrl+S or choose the Macro Run command and select the Landscape macro from the list box.

To create the Chart macro, follow these steps:

1. Select the data on the worksheet that you want to chart.
2. Choose the Macro menu and select the Record command.
3. Press F11 or Alt F1.

313

4. Choose the Gallery menu and select the 3-D Column command.
5. Choose the 3-D Column chart format you want and choose OK or press [⏎Enter].
6. Choose the Chart menu and select the Add Legend command.
7. Choose OK or press [⏎Enter].
8. Choose the Macro menu and select the Stop Recorder command.

To run the macro, press Ctrl+C or choose the **Macro Run** command and select the Chart macro from the list box.

To create the Font macro, follow these steps:

1. Choose the Macro menu and select the Record command.
2. Choose the Format menu and select the Font command.
3. Select the font type you want from the Font list.
4. Select the font point size you want from the Size list.
5. Choose OK or press [⏎Enter].
6. Choose the Macro menu and select the Stop Recorder command.

To run the macro, press Ctrl+F or choose the **Macro Run** command and select the Font macro from the list box.

To create the Number macro, follow these steps:

1. Choose the Macro menu and select the Record command.
2. Choose the Format menu and select the Number command.
3. Select the number format you want from the list box.
4. Choose OK or press [⏎Enter].
5. Choose the Macro menu and select the Stop Recorder command.

To run the macro, press Ctrl+N or choose the **Macro Run** command and select the Number macro from the list box.

To create the Display macro, follow these steps:

1. Choose the Macro menu and select the Record command.
2. Choose the Options menu and select the Display command.
3. Select the Gridlines check box.
4. Choose OK or press [⏎Enter].
5. Choose the Macro menu and select the Stop Recorder command.

To run the macro, press Ctrl+D or choose the **Macro Run** command and select the Display macro from the list box.

Summary

12

In this chapter, you were introduced to macros. You learned what a macro is and how to record a macro using Excel's macro recorder. This chapter also explained the difference between a command macro and a function macro. Specific macro topics included the macro sheet, how to edit macros, setting the macro recorder, starting the recorder, and stopping the recorder. Additionally, you learned how to assign a key to a macro, and name, run, and debug a macro. The chapter concluded with a section on assigning a macro to a button or object and executing a macro with a single click on the object.

In this chapter, you were introduced to the following key information about Excel:

- A macro recorder is used to record keystrokes and commands.
- A macro is recorded on a macro sheet using function names.
- Excel has two types of macros: command macros and function macros. A command macro is a recorded series of actions. A function macro cannot be recorded.
- A function macro is created on a macro sheet by entering functions or pasting functions with the Formula Paste Function command.
- If a function macro has a defined name, the function appears at the end of the list of functions in the Paste Function dialog box.
- You can record several macros on a single macro sheet. A macro sheet is saved with the extension XLM.
- You can execute a macro only when the macro sheet on which the macro is stored is open.
- The RETURN( ) function is entered when a macro is completed.
- You can edit a macro sheet with the same editing procedures you use on a worksheet.
- If the macro function name has a question mark next to it, you can pause a dialog box for input.
- Choosing the Formula Define Name command when a macro sheet is active enables you to name a macro and assign a key that you can use with the Ctrl key.
- You can execute a macro, using an assigned keystroke, or with the Macro Run command.
- You can step through a macro one step at a time and evaluate where a problem may occur. Choose the Macro Run command and select the Step button to execute a macro in Step mode.

315

12

■ The Macro Assign To Object command lets you assign a macro to a selected object or button. A pointing hand appears when the mouse pointer is positioned on an object that is linked to a macro.

Installing Excel 3.0 for Windows

A

Because Excel runs in the Windows environment, Windows must be installed on your computer before you can install Excel. Consult your Windows manual for instructions on installing Windows.

Other system requirements for installing Excel include:

1. Excel program disks
2. An Industry Standard Architecture (ISA) or Micro Channel Architecture (MCA) computer with a 80286 or higher processor
3. A hard disk with at least 2.5 megabytes of free disk space
4. 1M RAM (Random-Access Memory)
5. EGA, VGA, Hercules, or other graphics card compatible with Windows 3.0

At the beginning of the installation process, Excel might display a message stating that Standard or Enhanced Mode Windows is required. If so, you may need to add additional memory to your computer to install Excel. Consult your Windows manual for details on Windows operating modes.

A

To install Excel 3.0, follow these steps:

1. Insert the Setup disk in drive A.

2. Type **win** at the DOS prompt and press ⏎Enter. The Windows Program Manager appears on the screen when Windows is loaded. (Your computer will take a few seconds to load Windows.)

3. Choose the File Manager in the Main program group and double-click on the icon or press ⏎Enter. From the File Manager window, choose the File menu and select the Run command. A dialog box appears. (You also can choose the Run command from the File menu in the Windows Program Manager.)

4. Type **a:setup** in the text box of the dialog box.

5. Choose OK or press ⏎Enter.

6. Follow the instructions on the screen to enter your name and organization.

7. Choose the Continue button.

   A dialog box tells you where the Excel files will be installed. (The dialog box states the drive and directory).

8. You can edit the line in the dialog box if you want the files to be installed in another directory.

9. Choose the Continue button to proceed with the installation. If the directory does not exist, Excel prompts you with a dialog box to create the directory. Choose OK or press ⏎Enter, and the directory is created.

   A dialog box appears with several check boxes. All the check boxes display an X. An X indicates that the option will be installed during the installation.

10. If you do not want to install an option, turn off the option by selecting the check box. The X in the box disappears.

    The lower left corner of the dialog box informs you how much disk space is required and how much disk space is available on your hard drive. If more space is required for installation than is available, you cannot install Excel until some of the options are turned off.

11. If you are ready to begin installing the checked options, choose the Install button. A dialog box lets you know the percentage of completion for the installation. (The installation takes a few minutes.)

12. Continue to follow the instructions on the screen.

    When the installation of Excel is complete, you return to the Windows File Manger.

318

After Excel is installed, the Program Manager displays an additional program group. The Excel program group contains icons for four programs: Excel, Q+E, Dialog Editor, and Macro Translator. Q+E is an add-in program that comes with Excel and helps you access external database programs. Dialog Editor enables you to create custom dialog boxes. Macro Translator helps you convert macros from other spreadsheet programs. The Excel icon starts Excel. You can access Q+E, Dialog Editor, and Macro Translator within the Excel program, using the **Run** command in the application Control menu.

To start the Excel program, double-click on the Excel icon, or select the icon and press Enter. The first time Excel starts, the screen displays an Excel preview that highlights the features in Excel. The preview is actually a macro that takes about three minutes to view. If you want to exit the preview, use the buttons displayed on the screen. If you want to view the preview at a later time, you can access the preview macro by activating the PREVIEW.XLM file.

The procedures for starting Windows are covered in greater depth in Chapter 2, "Getting Started."

A

Summary of Excel 3.0 for Windows Commands

B

Controlling Windows

Task	Keyboard	Mouse
Start Windows application	Select application icon; press `↵Enter`	Double-click on application icon
Exit an application	`Alt`, space bar, Close	Double-click on program Control menu icon
Move an application window	`Alt`, space bar, Move	Drag application window title bar
Move a document window	`Alt`, `-` (hyphen), Move	Drag document window title bar

Task	Keyboard	Mouse
Resize an application window	Alt, **space bar**, Size	Drag application window border
Resize a document window	Alt, - (hyphen), Size	Drag document window border
Restore an application window	Alt, **space bar**, Restore	Click on Restore icon (upper right)
Restore a document window	Alt, - (hyphen), **Restore**	Click on Restore icon (upper right)
Maximize an application window	Alt, **space bar**, Maximize	Click on Maximize icon (upper right)
Maximize a document window	Alt, - (hyphen), Maximize	Click on Maximize icon (upper right)
Minimize an application window	Alt, **space bar**, Minimize	Click on Minimize icon (upper right)
Select a menu command	Alt, **underlined menu letter, underlined command letter**	Click on menu, click on command
Switch between open documents	Ctrl F6	Click on Window menu and select file name

Using Dialog Boxes

Task	Keyboard	Mouse
Select text box	Tab or Alt + **underlined letter**	Click on text box
Select option button	Tab, **arrow key**	Click on button
Select (deselect) check box	Tab, **space bar**	Click on check box
Choose command button	Alt+**underlined letter**	Click on command
Choose OK button	Enter	Click on OK button
Choose Cancel	Esc	Click on Cancel button

B

322

Moving the Active Cell

Task	Keyboard	Mouse
Move one cell left	←	Click on cell with cell pointer
Move one cell right	→	Click on cell with cell pointer
Move one cell up	↑	Click on cell with cell pointer
Move one cell down	↓	Click on cell with cell pointer
Move to next block of data separated by a blank cell	Ctrl + arrow key	Click on cell with cell pointer
Move to column A of active row	Home	Click on cell with cell pointer
Move to cell A1	Ctrl Home	Click on cell with cell pointer
Move to rightmost column containing data	End	Click on cell with cell pointer
Move to last cell used in worksheet	Ctrl End	Click on cell with cell pointer
Move up one full window	PgUp	Click in vertical scroll bar above scroll box
Move down one full window	PgDn	Click in vertical scroll bar below scroll box
Move one screen left	Ctrl PgUp	Click in horizontal scroll bar left of scroll box
Move one screen right	Ctrl PgDn	Click in horizontal scroll bar right of scroll box
Move to specified cell	F5	Choose Edit GoTo and enter cell address

B

323

Editing in the Formula Bar

Task	Keyboard	Mouse
Activate formula bar	F2	Click in formula bar
Move cursor	← →	Click at desired location in formula bar
Move cursor to end of line	End	Click at end of formula bar
Move cursor to beginning of line	Home	Click at beginning of line
Delete character to left of cursor	← Backspace	Select character and press Del
Delete character to right of cursor	Del	Select character and press Del
Accept formula bar entry	↵ Enter	Click on check mark box
Cancel formula bar entry	Esc	Click on X box

Saving, Opening, Closing, and Deleting Files

Task	Keyboard	Mouse
Save a file	Alt, F, S, or ⇧ Shift F12	Click on File menu and select Save
Save a copy of a named file	Alt, F, A, or F12	Click on File menu and select Save As
Save a workspace	Alt, F, W	Click on File menu and select Save Workspace
Save a file to another file format	Alt, F, A, Alt O	Click on File menu, select Save As, and choose Options button
Close a file	Alt, F, C	Click on File menu and select Close

324

Task	Keyboard	Mouse
Close all open files	Hold down `⇧Shift`, press `Alt`, `F`, `C`	Hold down `⇧Shift`, click on File menu, and select Close All
Delete a file from disk	`Alt`, `F`, `D`	Click on File menu and select Delete

Working with Ranges

Task	Keyboard	Mouse
Select a range of cells	Hold down `⇧Shift`, or press `F8` to use Extend mode; press **arrow keys** to select range of cells	Drag over range of cells you want to select
Define a range name	`Alt`, `R`, `D`, or press `Ctrl` `F3`	Click on Formula menu and select Define Name
Create range names from selection	`Alt`, `R`, `C`, or press `Ctrl` `⇧Shift` `F3`	Click on Formula menu and select Create Names
Apply range names to a selection	`Alt`, `R`, `A`	Click on Formula menu and select Apply Names
Select a defined range	`F5`	Click on Edit menu and select GoTo; double-click on range you want to select
Delete a range name	`Alt`, `R`, `D`, or press `Ctrl` `F3`; select name you want to delete and press `Alt` `D`	Click on Formula menu and select Define Name; select name you want to delete and choose Delete button

Modifying a Worksheet

Task	Keyboard	Mouse
Insert blank cells	Select number of cells you want to insert; press `Alt`, `E`, `I`	Select number of cells you want to insert; click on Edit menu and select Insert

325

Task	*Keyboard*	*Mouse*
Delete cells	Select cells you want to delete; press [Alt], [E], [D]	Select cells you want to delete; click on Edit menu and select Delete
Insert a blank column	[Ctrl]+space bar to select active column; press [Alt], [E], [I]	Click on column heading; click on Edit menu and select Insert
Delete a column	[Ctrl]+space bar to select active column; press [Alt], [E], [D]	Click on column heading; click on Edit menu and select Delete
Insert a row	[Shift]+space bar to select active row; press [Alt], [E], [I]	Click on row heading; click on Edit menu and select Insert
Delete a row	[Shift]+space bar to select active row; press [Alt], [E], [D]	Click on row heading; click on Edit menu and select Delete
Erase cell contents	[Del] or press [Alt], [E], [L]	Click on Edit menu and select Clear
Copy cell contents to clipboard	Select cells to be copied; press [Alt], [E], [C], or press [Ctrl][Ins]	Select cells to be copied; click on Edit menu and select Copy
Paste copied cells	[Alt], [E], [P], or press [Shift][Ins]	Click on Edit menu and select Paste
Copy cell contents to adjacent cells to the right	[Alt], [E], [H]	Click on Edit menu and select Fill Right
Copy cell contents to adjacent cells below	[Alt], [E], [W]	Click on Edit menu and select Fill Down
Copy cell contents to adjacent cells above	Hold down [Shift]; press [Alt], [E], [W]	Click on Edit menu and select Fill Up (w)
Copy cell contents to adjacent cells to the left	Hold down [Shift]; press [Alt], [E], [H]	Click on Edit menu and select Fill Left (h)

Task	*Keyboard*	*Mouse*
Move cell contents	Select cells you want to move; press `Alt`, `E`, `T`, or press `⇧Shift` `Del`; select cell marking new location; press `Alt`, `E`, `P`, or press `↵Enter` to move selected data from old location to new location	Select cells you want to move; click on Edit menu and select Cut; select cell marking new location; click on Edit menu and select Paste
Change column width	`Alt`, `T`, `C`	Drag right border of column heading until desired column width is reached
Adjust column width to widest cell in the column	`Alt`, `T`, `C`, `Alt` `B`	Double-click on right border of column heading
Hide a column	`Alt`, `T`, `C`, `Alt` `H`	Drag right border of column heading until column is no longer visible, or click on Format menu and select Column Width; choose the Hide button
Unhide a column	Select columns bordering on both sides of hidden column; press `Alt`, `T`, `C`, `Alt` `U`	Select columns bordering on both sides of hidden columns; click on Format menu and select Column Width; choose the Unhide button
Change row height	`Alt`, `T`, `R`,	Drag bottom border of row heading until desired row height is reached
Hide a row	`Alt`, `T`, `R`, `Alt` `H`	Drag bottom border of row heading until row is no longer visible, or click on Format menu and select Row Height; choose the Hide button

B

327

B

Task	Keyboard	Mouse
Unhide a row	Select rows bordering on both sides of hidden row; press `Alt`, `T`, `R`, `Alt``U`	Select rows bordering on both sides oh hidden columns; click on Format menu and select Row Height; choose Unhide button
Find specific cell contents	`Alt`, `R`, `F`, or press `⇧Shift``F5` (`F7` to find next occurrence, `⇧Shift``F7` to find previous occurrence)	Click on Formula menu and select Find
Replace cell contents	`Alt`, `R`, `E`	Click on Formula menu and select Replace
Reverse last action	`Alt`, `E`, `U`	Click on Edit menu and select Undo

Formatting A Worksheet

Task	Keyboard	Mouse
Format a number	`Alt`, `T`, `N`	Click on Format menu and select Number
Format a date or time	`Alt`, `T`, `N`	Click on Format menu and select Number
Change cell alignment	`Alt`, `T`, `A`	Choose Left, Right, or Center icon on tool bar, or click on Format menu and select Alignment
Make selection bold or italic	`Alt`, `T`, `F`	Choose Bold or Italic icon on tool bar, or click on Format menu and select Font
Change a font	`Alt`, `T`, `F`	Click on Format menu and select Font
Justify cells to align within a selected range	`Alt`, `T`, `J`	Click on Format menu and select Justify

328

Task	Keyboard	Mouse
Add borders to selected cells	Alt, T, B	Click on Format menu and select Border
Add patterns to selected cells	Alt, T, P	Click on Format menu and select Patterns
Add borders patterns to selected object	Alt, T, P	Click on Format menu and select Patterns
Create a style based on selected formatting	Alt, T, S, Alt D	Click on Format menu and select Style; choose Define button

B

Entering Functions

Task	Keyboard	Mouse
Enter a predefined function into cell or formula	Alt, R, T, or press ⇧Shift F3	Click on Formula menu and select Paste Function

Printing

Task	Keyboard	Mouse
Select a range to be printed	Hold down ⇧Shift and press arrow keys to select range	Drag over area you want to select
Select nonadjacent ranges	Select first area, press ⇧Shift F8 for Add mode, move to next area using arrow keys; hold down ⇧Shift and press arrow keys to add range to selection	Drag over first area you want to select; hold down t l and drag over next area
Define selected area to be printed	Alt, O, A	Click on Options menu and select Set Print Area
Add titles to print on every page	Alt, O, T	Click on Options menu and select Set Print Titles
Enter a page break	Alt, O, B	Click on Options menu and select Set Page Break

Task	Keyboard	Mouse
View document before it prints	Alt, F, V	Click on File menu and select Print Preview
Add headers and footers to document	Alt, F, T	Click on File menu and select Page Setup
Change page orientation	Alt, F, T	Click on File menu and select Page Setup
Adjust margins	Alt, F, T	Click on File menu and select Page Setup
Switch to another printer or change the default settings on the current printer	Alt, F, R	Click on File menu and select Printer Setup
Print the defined print area	Alt, F, P	Click on File menu and select Print

Working with Multiple Documents

Task	Keyboard	Mouse
Display all open files on the screen	Alt, W, A	Click on Window menu and select Arrange All
Activate another open document	Alt, W, and window number, or press Ctrl F6 until document is displayed	Click on Window menu and select file name from list
Save open files on screen as a workspace	Alt, F, W	Click on File menu and select Save Workspace
Change, update, or open a linked document	Alt, F, L	Click on File menu and select Links
Consolidate data from several worksheets into a single worksheet	Alt, D, N	Click on Data menu and select Consolidate

Charting

Task	Keyboard	Mouse
Create a chart from selected data	F11 or Alt F1	Click on File menu and select New; select Chart from dialog box and choose OK
Change the chart type	Alt, G (select chart type from the gallery menu); select a predefined chart format displayed in dialog box by entering number of chart format	Click on Gallery menu on chart menu bar and select a chart type from list; double-click on predefined chart format displayed in dialog box
Change the preferred chart type	Alt, G, T	Click on Gallery menu and select Set Preferred
Add a chart title	Alt, C, T	Click on Chart menu and select Attach Text
Add a chart legend	Alt, C, L	Click on Chart menu and select Attach Legend
Add an arrow	Alt, C, A	Click on Chart menu and select Add Arrow
Format a selected chart object with border and patterns	Alt, T, P	Double-click on chart object you want to format
Change the chart axes	Alt, C, X	Click on Chart menu and select Axes
Change the appearance of selected axis	Alt, T, S	Click on Format menu and select Scale
Add a chart overlay	Alt, C, O	Click on Chart menu and select Add Overlay
Add gridlines to chart	Alt, C, G	Click on Chart menu and select Add Gridlines
Edit or add a new data series	Alt, C, S	Click on Chart menu and select Edit Series

B

331

Task	Keyboard	Mouse
Modify view of a 3-D chart	Alt, T, 3	Click on Format menu and select 3-D View
Change chart type without losing custom formatting	Alt, T, M	Click on Format menu and select Main Chart
Change font	Alt, T, F	Click on Format menu and select Font
Change text orientation or alignment	Alt, T, T	Click on Format menu and select Text

B

Database

Task	Keyboard	Mouse
Define a database	Select field names and records; press Alt, D, B	Click on Data menu and select Database
View a database by form	Alt, D, O	Click on Data menu and select Form
Add a record to a database form	Alt, D, O, Alt A	Click on Data menu and select Form. Choose Add button
Delete a record from a database form	Alt, D, O, Alt D	Click on Data menu and select Form; choose Delete button
Sort selected records	Alt, D, S	Click on Data menu and select Sort
Define range for criteria	Alt, D, C	Click on Data menu and select Set Criteria
Find records that match criteria	Alt, D, F	Click on Data menu and select Find
Define range for extracting records from a database	Alt, D, X	Click on Data menu and select Set Extract

Task	Keyboard	Mouse
Extract records that match the defined criteria from database	Alt, D, E	Click on Data menu and select Extract

Macros

Task	Keyboard	Mouse
Start the macro recorder	Alt, M, C	Click on Macro menu and select Record
Stop the macro recorder	Alt, M, C	Click on Macro menu and select Stop Recorder
Change recording from absolute to relative references	Alt, M, A	Click on Macro menu and select Relative Record
Set the recorder to record in an existing macro or on an existing macro sheet	Alt, M, T	Click on Macro menu and select Set Recorder
Resume macro recorder after it has been stopped	Alt, M, S	Click on Macro menu and select Start Recorder
Run a macro	Alt, M, R	Click on Macro menu and select Run
Step through a macro one step at a time	Alt, M, R, Alt S	Click on Macro menu and select Run; choose the Step button
Assign a macro to a selected object	Alt, M, O	Click on Macro menu and select Assign to Object

B

Splitting a Document Window
Freezing Window Panes
Creating a New Window of a Document
Protecting A Document

B

Task	Keyboard	Mouse
Split a document window into panes	`Alt` `-` (hyphen), `S`; press **arrow key** to split screen into panes; press `↵Enter`	Drag black bar above vertical scroll bar and to left of horizontal scroll bar to split screen into panes
Freeze a window pane from scrolling	`Alt`, `O`, `F`	Click the Options menu and select Freeze
Unfreeze a frozen pane	`Alt`, `O`, `F`	Click on Options menu and select Unfreeze
View a single document in two separate windows	`Alt`, `W`, `N`	Click on Window menu and select New Window
Protect a document from unwanted changes	`Alt`, `O`, `P`	Click on Options window and select Protect Document
Assign a password to protect a document	`Alt`, `O`, `P`	Click on Options menu and select Protect document
Remove document protection	`Alt`, `O`, `P`	Click on Options menu and select Unprotect Document

Using On-Line Help

Task	Keyboard	Mouse
Access the Help index	`F1`	Click on Help menu and select Index

334

Index

creating cell names from text, 94-95
criteria, 332
deleting names, 95-96, 325
editing names, 95-96
extract, 332
justifying cells within, 328
moving within, 90
names, 90-93, 325
selecting, 73-75, 93, 325, 329
RATE financial function, 166
Record Macro
  command, 299-301
recording
    changing from absolute to
      relative references, 332
    command macros, 299-301
    existing macros, 333
records, 266, 270
    adding, 272-274
      with data form, 272, 332
    deleting, 275-276
      with data form, 274-275, 332
    extracting, 287-292, 332
    finding, 283-287, 332
      with data form, 281-283
    numbering, 279-281
    sorting, 332
relative cell addresses, 108, 115-116
    changing from absolute, 332
removing
    document protection, 334
    manual page breaks, 189-190
Replace dialog box, 126-127
REPLACE text function, 175
replacing cell contents, 327
REPT text function, 175
resizing
    graphic objects, 146
    windows, 44, 322
restoring windows, 43-44, 322

RIGHT text function, 175
ROUND mathematical function, 172
Row Height dialog box, 123
ROW information function, 169
rows
    adjusting height, 123
    deleting, 121, 326
    hiding, 123-124
    inserting, 121, 326
    unhiding, 123-124
ROWS information function, 169
running macros, 310-311, 333

S

Save Workspace dialog box, 202
saving
    files, 80-81, 324
    worksheets in other file
      formats, 210-212
    workspaces, 102, 324, 330
Scale dialog box, 242-244
scaling axes in charts, 242-244
screens, 39-40
    application window, 41, 43
    displaying multiple files, 330
    document window, 41-43
    formula bar, 46
    scroll bars, 46
    tool bar, 44-45
scroll bars, 46
scrolling worksheets, 59-60
SEARCH text function, 175
searching for help topics, 48-49
SECOND date function, 164
selecting
    cells, 73-75
    chart types, 225-226
      preferred chart type, 226-227
    commands, 12-13, 75-76, 322
    dialog box elements, 322
    fonts, 138-139

351

W

Teach Yourself
With QuickStarts From Que!

The ideal tutorials for beginners, Que's QuickStart books use graphic illustrations and step-by-step instructions to get you up and running fast. Packed with examples, QuickStarts are the perfect beginner's guides to your favorite software applications.

1-2-3 Release 2.2 QuickStart, 2nd Edition
Releases 2.01 & 2.2

Order #1207	$19.95 USA
0-88022-612-9, 400 pp., 7 3/8 x 9 1/4	

1-2-3 Release 3.1 QuickStart, 2nd Edition
Releases 3 & 3.1

Order #1208	$19.95 USA
0-88022-613-7, 400 pp., 7 3/8 x 9 1/4	

dBASE IV QuickStart
dBASE IV

Order #873	$19.95 USA
0-88022-389-8, 384 pp., 7 3/8 x 9 1/4	

dBASE IV QuickStart, 2nd Edition
Through Version 1.1

Order #1209	$19.95 USA
0-88022-614-5, 400 pp., 7 3/8 x 9 1/4	

Excel QuickStart
IBM Version 1 & Macintosh Version 2.2

Order #957	$19.95 USA
0-88022-423-1, 334 pp., 7 3/8 x 9 1/4	

MS-DOS QuickStart, 2nd Edition
Version 3.X & 4.X

Order #1206	$19.95 USA
0-88022-611-0, 400 pp., 7 3/8 x 9 1/4	

Q&A QuickStart
Versions 3 & 4

Order #1264	$19.95 USA
0-88022-653-6, 400 pp., 7 3/8 x 9 1/4	

Quattro Pro QuickStart
Through Version 2.0

Order #1305	$19.95 USA
0-88022-693-5, 450 pp., 7 3/8 x 9 1/4	

WordPerfect QuickStart
WordPerfect 5

Order #871	$19.95 USA
0-88022-387-1, 457 pp., 7 3/8 x 9 1/4	

WordPerfect 5.1 QuickStart
WordPerfect 5.1

Order #1104	$19.95 USA
0-88022-558-0, 427 pp., 7 3/8 x 9 1/4	

Windows 3 QuickStart
Ron Person & Karen Rose

This graphics-based text teaches Windows beginners how to use the feature-packed Windows environment. Emphasizes such software applications as Excel, Word, and PageMaker and shows how to master Windows' mouse, menus, and screen elements.

Version 3

Order #1205	$19.95 USA
0-88022-610-2, 400 pp., 7 3/8 x 9 1/4	

MS-DOS 5 QuickStart
Que Development Group

This is the easy-to-use graphic approach to learning MS-DOS 5. The combination of step-by-step instruction, examples, and graphics make this book ideal for all DOS beginners.

DOS 5

Order #1293	$19.95 USA
0-88022-681-1, 400 pp., 7 3/8 x 9 1/4	

To Order, Call:
(800) 428-5331 OR (317) 573-2510

Find It Fast With Que's Quick References!

Que's Quick References are the compact, easy-to-use guides to essential application information. Written for all users, Quick References include vital command information under easy-to-find alphabetical listings. Quick References are a must for anyone who needs command information fast!

Que—The Leader In Spreadsheet Information!

Using Quattro Pro 3, Special Edition

Patrick Burns

This complete, easy-to-follow introduction to Quattro Pro includes in-depth tutorials, tips, and a tear-out Menu Map.

Through Version 3

Order #1348   **$27.95 USA**

0-88022-721-4, 750 pp., 7 3/8 x 9 1/4

Using Excel 3 for Windows

Ron Person

This introduction to Excel includes **Quick Start** tutorials plus tips and tricks to help improve efficiency and trouble-shoot problems. It also provides advanced techniques for using Windows 3.

Version 3

Order #1297   **$29.95 USA**

0-88022-685-4, 984 pp., 7 3/8 x 9 1/4

More Spreadsheet Titles From Que

Excel Quick Reference
Version 2.1

Order #1023   **$8.95 USA**

0-88022-473-8, 160 pp., 4 3/4 x 8

Excel QuickStart
IBM Version 1 & Macintosh Version 2.2

Order #957   **$19.95 USA**

0-88022-423-1, 334 pp., 7 3/8 x 9 1/4

Using Lotus Spreadsheet for DeskMate
Version 1.0

Order #1150   **$22.95 USA**

0-88022-575-0, 500 pp., 7 3/8 x 9 1/4

Using Excel: IBM Version
IBM Version 2 & 2.2

Order #87   **$29.95 USA**

0-88022-284-0, 804 pp., 7 3/8 x 9 1/4

Using Quattro Pro
Version 2.0

Order #1114   **$24.95 USA**

0-88022-562-9, 500 pp., 7 3/8 x 9 1/4

Using SuperCalc5, 2nd Edition
SuperCalc4 & SuperCalc5

Order #938   **$29.95 USA**

0-88022-404-5, 575 pp., 7 3/8 x 9 1/4

To Order, Call:
(800) 428-5331 OR (317) 573-2510

Complete Coverage From A To Z!

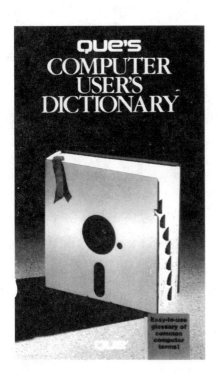

Que's Computer User's Dictionary
Que Development Group

This compact, practical reference contains hundreds of definitions, explanations, examples, and illustrations on topics from programming to desktop publishing. You can master the "language" of computers and learn how to make your personal computers more efficient and more powerful. Filled with tips and cautions, *Que's Computer User's Dictionary* is the perfect resource for anyone who uses a computer.

IBM, Macintosh, Apple, & Programming

Order #1086   **$10.95 USA**

0-88022-540-8, 500 pp., 4 3/4 x 8

The Ultimate Glossary Of Computer Terms— Over 200,000 In Print!

"Dictionary indeed. This whammer is a mini-encyclopedia...an absolute joy to use...a must for your computer library...."

Southwest Computer & Business Equipment Review

To Order, Call:
(800) 428-5331 OR (317) 573-2510

Free Catalog!

Mail us this registration form today, and we'll send you a free catalog featuring Que's complete line of best-selling books.

Name of Book _____

Name _____

Title _____

Phone ( ) _____

Company _____

Address _____

City _____

State _____ ZIP _____

Please check the appropriate answers:

1. Where did you buy your Que book?
   - ☐ Bookstore (name: _____)
   - ☐ Computer store (name: _____)
   - ☐ Catalog (name: _____)
   - ☐ Direct from Que
   - ☐ Other: _____

2. How many computer books do you buy a year?
   - ☐ 1 or less
   - ☐ 2-5
   - ☐ 6-10
   - ☐ More than 10

3. How many Que books do you own?
   - ☐ 1
   - ☐ 2-5
   - ☐ 6-10
   - ☐ More than 10

4. How long have you been using this software?
   - ☐ Less than 6 months
   - ☐ 6 months to 1 year
   - ☐ 1-3 years
   - ☐ More than 3 years

5. What influenced your purchase of this Que book?
   - ☐ Personal recommendation
   - ☐ Advertisement
   - ☐ In-store display
   - ☐ Price
   - ☐ Que catalog
   - ☐ Que mailing
   - ☐ Que's reputation
   - ☐ Other: _____

6. How would you rate the overall content of the book?
   - ☐ Very good
   - ☐ Good
   - ☐ Satisfactory
   - ☐ Poor

7. What do you like *best* about this Que book?
   _____
   _____

8. What do you like *least* about this Que book?
   _____
   _____

9. Did you buy this book with your personal funds?
   - ☐ Yes   ☐ No

10. Please feel free to list any other comments you may have about this Que book.
   _____
   _____
   _____

que

Order Your Que Books Today!

Name _____

Title _____

Company _____

City _____

State _____ ZIP _____

Phone No. ( ) _____

Method of Payment:

Check ☐   (Please enclose in envelope.)

Charge My: VISA ☐   MasterCard ☐

American Express ☐

Charge # _____

Expiration Date _____

Order No.	Title	Qty.	Price	Total

You can **FAX** your order to **1-317-573-2583**. Or call **1-800-428-5331, ext. ORDR** to order direct.

Please add $2.50 per title for shipping and handling.

Subtotal _____

Shipping & Handling _____

Total _____

que

BUSINESS REPLY MAIL
First Class Permit No. 9918   Indianapolis, IN

Postage will be paid by addressee

11711 N. College
Carmel, IN 46032

BUSINESS REPLY MAIL
First Class Permit No. 9918   Indianapolis, IN

Postage will be paid by addressee

11711 N. College
Carmel, IN 46032